D0471753

# PALEO DESSERTS

# PALEO DESSERTS

## 125 Delicious Everyday Favorites, Gluten- and Grain-Free

### Jane Barthelemy

**Da Capo**

**LIFE LONG**

A Member of the Perseus Books Group

Copyright © 2012 by Jane Barthelemy
Photos by Lloyd Lemmermann

All rights reserved. No part of this publication may be reproduced, stored in a retrieval system, or transmitted, in any form or by any means, electronic, mechanical, photocopying, recording, or otherwise, without the prior written permission of the publisher. Printed in the United States of America. For information, address Da Capo Press, 44 Farnsworth Street, 3rd Floor, Boston, Massachusetts 02210.

Designed by Pauline Brown
Set in 11 point Warnock Pro Light by the Perseus Books Group

Cataloging-in-Publication data for this book is available from the Library of Congress.

First Da Capo Press edition 2012
ISBN 978-0-7382-1643-0 (paperback)
ISBN 978-0-7382-1644-7 (e-book)

Published by Da Capo Press
A Member of the Perseus Books Group
www.dacapopress.com

Note: The information in this book is true and complete to the best of our knowledge. This book is intended only as an informative guide for those wishing to know more about health issues. In no way is this book intended to replace, countermand, or conflict with the advice given to you by your own physician. The ultimate decision concerning care should be made between you and your doctor. We strongly recommend you follow his or her advice. Information in this book is general and is offered with no guarantees on the part of the author or Da Capo Press. The author and publisher disclaim all liability in connection with the use of this book. The names and identifying details of people associated with events described in this book have been changed. Any similarity to actual persons is coincidental.

Da Capo Press books are available at special discounts for bulk purchases in the U.S. by corporations, institutions, and other organizations. For more information, please contact the Special Markets Department at the Perseus Books Group, 2300 Chestnut Street, Suite 200, Philadelphia, PA, 19103, or call (800) 810-4145, ext. 5000, or e-mail special.markets@perseusbooks.com.

10 9 8 7 6 5 4 3 2

*This book is dedicated to my parents, Dick and Margaret, and to the great chain of ancestors, the men and women that we stem from, to the wise ones who show the way in every age, and to all people of the future, that they may enjoy health and sweetness in their lives.*

# CONTENTS

# INTRODUCTION

*Eat food. Not too much.*
*Mostly plants.*

—MICHAEL POLLAN, AUTHOR OF
*IN DEFENSE OF FOOD: AN EATER'S MANIFESTO*

I have a confession to make. The book you're holding in your hands is here for one reason and one reason only—my *enormous* passion for sweets. A passion so strong, I had to find a way to create sweets that are also good for my body. As a chef, health practitioner, and ex-sugar-holic, I discovered that I had just the right combination of excitement, knowledge, and tools to invent a collection of original Paleo recipes for my favorite desserts. I hope they'll soon be yours, too.

Sneaking sweets is not an option for me. For my body, refined foods and sugars are toxic. In many people, the reaction to poor-quality food is delayed. They feel crummy after a few months, and a true disease or metabolic dysfunction doesn't appear until months or years later. However, in my body, the response is immediate. My eyes glaze over; I become lethargic, moody, and experience a brain fog. I can't remember what I was doing last and I can't focus my mind. I must then drink copious amounts of pure water and exercise, until eventually the haze passes. Although my condition has no name, I'd like to think my body recognizes what is real food and what is not.

After twenty years of a low-carb diet—all the while still craving sweets—I decided to do something about it. Instead of running away or avoiding my desires, I decided to turn and face them. I dove into them with a passion, and this book is the result. Imagine my surprise when I had *no* reaction to these sweets. What a discovery! After eating them I felt balanced and happy. I had been so deprived of simple sweets, I wanted to celebrate! This journey is part of my healing process and I'm so thrilled to be able to share it with you.

The Paleo diet was first brought into the spotlight by Loren Cordain, PhD, considered the world's leading expert on the Paleolithic diet, and author of the best-selling *The Paleo Diet: Lose Weight and Get Healthy by Eating the Food You Were Designed to Eat*. Dr. Cordain's extensive research focused on the evolutionary and anthropological basis for dietary health and the links between modern diets and disease.

What did our ancestors really eat? Dr. Cordain studied human diets during the Paleolithic period spanning 2.5 million years, gleaning evidence from microscopic scratches and wear patterns on teeth. According to Dr. Cordain, our ancestors were omnivores, eating a hunt-and-gather diet of fresh wild fruits, vegetables, and animals, depending upon the climate in which they lived. The major difference between their diet and our modern diet is the development of agriculture about ten thousand years ago, which brought us grains and legumes (beans). More recent changes to grain cultivation and refining methods came about around 1890 with the advent of refined flour. In the last sixty years, the introduction of industrial farming methods, preservatives, chemicals, and longer shelf lives has brought major changes to our tables. With a global food industry narrowly focused on volume at the expense of nutritional value and environmental balance, it is no surprise that chronic health problems are increasing worldwide.

Our ancestors were physically strong, fit, and active. They had to walk miles to gather food, migrate to distant areas, and outrun wild animals. Just two hundred years ago, Lewis and Clark crossed the American Pacific Northwest wilderness on foot with a company of soldiers, walking as far as 50 to 75 miles per day. Do you know anyone who could do that today?

Dr. Cordain's view that our modern diet is inadequate to sustain good health is supported by Dr. Weston Price, a renowned nutritionist and dentist. He traveled the world, studying indigenous peoples, and his findings clearly demonstrate the strong connection between diet and health. Wherever he went, he found that native people living on a traditional diet had very low rates of dental decay and sickness, whereas the same genetic groups eating a modern Western diet had higher rates of tooth decay and disease. His fascinating accounts are documented in the book *Nutrition and Physical Degeneration* (see Resources).

Recently, the Paleo diet has surged in popularity. Also known as the primal diet, caveman diet, Stone Age diet, or hunter-gatherer diet, it consists of fresh vegetables, fruits, roots, nuts, wild fish, free-range poultry, and grass-fed meat. It excludes all grains, legumes, dairy products, refined sugars, and processed oils. The modern Paleo diet is a whole lifestyle of particular foods and exercise, and it has many interpretations.

If you're intolerant to gluten and enjoy delicious sweets, this book can be your best friend. The Paleo diet is the ultimate gluten-free solution, because it uses no grains. Gluten intolerance is the inability to digest gluten, the sticky protein found primarily in wheat. Millions of people worldwide suffer from gluten intolerance and celiac disease.

Gluten intolerance is the proverbial tip of an iceberg. We're often told that whole grains are healthier than refined grains. And that is mostly true. However, increasing scientific evidence shows that all seeds, nuts, grains, and beans contain antinutrients that actually block their digestion. Mother Nature has done her job well, ensuring that seeds pass straight though the body undigested, in order to be planted in the ground.

What are antinutrients? They are natural chemicals in seeds, and include lectins, enzyme blockers, trypsin, and phytic acid. They may taste slightly bitter and can cause intestinal permeability or poor absorption of foods. Most grains, nuts, and seeds—including wheat, corn, and rice, the world's primary foods—contain these natural antinutrients. Even gluten-free flours, made from almond, sorghum, amaranth, quinoa, fava, tapioca, chickpea, or teff, have antinutrients that can impede digestion.

When these flours are refined, they become less nutritious and are no longer a whole food. Now add preservatives and industrial farming chemicals, which must also be processed by the digestive system, and then top it off with refined sugar, which causes an imbalance in blood glucose levels, and you have an open invitation to many of our modern digestive diseases—gluten intolerance, celiac disease, metabolic syndrome, obesity, diabetes, and so on. In simple words, it is my observation that poorly cultivated and prepared grains, plus sugar and chemicals, are a toxic combination in my gut and that of many people. Soaking is the best way to dissolve antinutrients and make whole grains digestible. Evidence shows that our Biblical ancestors soaked grains, and our great-grandmothers as well. Somewhere along the line this practice was forgotten, and we are left with indigestible grains. That's why I adopted the Paleo diet. And I'm so glad I did.

Instead of grains, these recipes use coconut. Pure unrefined coconut is delicious, nutritious, and easy to digest. It is free of chemicals and antinutrients. That's why many people find the Paleo diet a perfect solution to living gluten-free. We can enjoy our favorite foods with no deprivation. We can have chocolate cupcakes and ice-cream sandwiches without guilt or discomfort.

The recipes in this book follow the strict guidelines developed by Dr. Cordain. They use no refined foods or high-carb sweeteners—no grains, coconut flour, coconut sugar, stevia, agave nectar, or even honey—with a zero or low impact on your blood sugar.

If you're on a special diet and feel deprived, this book can be a true companion. Paleo Desserts are compatible with many alternative diets. Besides being Paleo and gluten-free/celiac-friendly, all these recipes are vegetarian, meaning they contain no meat. All recipes in this book are free of the common allergens: dairy, corn, potatoes, peanuts, and soy. They are also diabetic-friendly. In this book you will find 73 vegan recipes, such as Key Lime Pie. There are 67 tree nut-free recipes, and 35 desserts that are raw, such as Easy Chocolate Mousse. And the good news is they're all made with fresh, whole-food ingredients, which I find even more delicious than their refined counterparts.

If you thought you had to give up sweets on the Paleo Diet, think again. In this book I offer you a full collection of favorite traditional desserts that conform 100 percent to the Paleo diet, with a zero or low impact on your blood sugar. Rather than thinking about what you're eliminating, just take a look at the tremendous assortment of nutritious fruits, vegetables, roots, nuts, and seeds that are available for you. These are all the best ingredients—straight from Nature. And you'll see—it is truly amazing, the huge variety of easy, luscious desserts you can enjoy using just these ingredients. In fact, my guests can't tell the difference. Whether it's pumpkin pie or chocolate cake, people love Paleo desserts and come back for more.

Paleo desserts are for everyone. When we remove refined and inflammatory foods from our diet, we reduce the risk of chronic diseases such as diabetes, arthritis, obesity, heart disease, and cancer. Most people on the Paleo diet report that they lose weight and experience higher energy levels. They feel younger and enjoy life more fully. If you're in good health and want to keep it that way,

Paleo desserts can allow you to enjoy sweets that are both delicious and nourishing. The high quality, nutrient-dense foods in these recipes—plus no refined ingredients—will help maintain and increase your vitality. For more information on the Paleo diet, see Resources (page 219).

Every recipe in this book has been carefully tested by my own sensitive palate, and against my body's resistance to refined foods. Anything that didn't pass my stringent test was not included in the book. You can have the utmost confidence in knowing that each recipe went through a rigorous (well, if you call eating tasty treats for months on end rigorous) testing process.

Now, I have to warn you. You will find many new techniques in this book. The basis of most of my recipes is to use coconut to emulate our favorite desserts. For example, I found a way to grind shredded coconut by mixing it with a granulated sweetener. All you need is a food processor. I call it sweet coconut powder and use it instead of flour. This sweet coconut powder is an extremely flexible food that lends itself to delicious, low-carb desserts at a very moderate cost.

Many of my testers failed in their attempts to make these recipes. I was confused, because these were experienced cooks. Then I noticed they were substituting other sweeteners, flours, and oils than were specified in the recipes. Another common mistake was to disregard the temperature instructions, and subsequently, the dessert failed completely. Even if you are an experienced cook, please follow the recipes *exactly* until you develop experience with these new methods. After that, I hope you'll be creative and teach me a few new tricks.

For some of you, this may be a completely new way of preparing food. These new methods may totally transform your relationship to desserts and your health. And don't worry—I've methodically mapped it all out for you. You only need to take it one step at a time. You can then imagine yourself as your own ancestor ten thousand years ago, preparing food for your family from what you could gather in the wild (pretty neat, right?).

## CRAVING SWEETS AND LOWERING CARBS

Many of us crave sweets. This has a direct impact on our eating habits and our health. What do the ancient medical systems in the world say about food cravings? Chinese medicine, one of the oldest known systems, recognizes five flavors that the body needs to be in balance: sweet, spicy, salty, sour, and bitter. Our ancestors understood that it's important to have a bit of each flavor at every meal.

Which of these five flavors do you crave most? Craving signals a need or an imbalance in the body. If you've cut out all the sweet tastes from your diet, such as dairy, grains, and legumes, then it's understandable you

*There are no requirements in human nutrition for carbohydrates. Grains are totally unnecessary.*

—MARK SISSON, CHAMPION IRON MAN AND AUTHOR OF THE BEST-SELLING *PRIMAL BLUEPRINT*

might feel a desire for sweets. Chinese medicine also observes that a diet high in refined sugar accelerates aging in the body. The role of this book is to help you to feel young and achieve a balance of flavors by enjoying natural sweets that do not raise blood sugar levels or cause an insulin response. In the recipes that follow, you'll find a host of delicious recipes aimed at stabilizing your metabolism for optimum health.

When we eat—what happens? We first sense the texture—is it crunchy or smooth? Then the taste informs our mouth and sense of smell, telling us if what we're eating is sweet, or bitter, or chocolate. Then we swallow, and this is the real litmus test for me. How does it feel in my body? Is it a *yes*? A *maybe*? Or a definite *no*? What I call real food—food made with pure, natural ingredients—is delicious all the way down into the body. And these desserts are real food. After all, the underlying reason to eat good food is to enjoy health. Knowing that you *can* have sweets on the Paleo diet is great news. Real food promotes health on all levels—body, mind, and spirit. Eating real food shows respect for your body, and allows you to live in harmony with planet Earth. And who doesn't want that?

In our modern society, refined carbs are cheap and readily available. In fact, many people have become dependent on them instead of on real foods, at the expense of our health.

We love sweets. We sneak them, we break our diets for them, and we feel guilty about it. Whenever we even think about desserts, we feel a combination of joy and shame. Many of us simply cut them completely from our diet. Others overindulge. What if delicious desserts were low carb and made of nourishing, healthy food? That's what you get here with these Paleo desserts.

Let's look at the following numbers. Conventional desserts are made of high-carb flours and high-carb sweeteners. White flour is the most common, with 73 percent carbs. Whole wheat, rice, and coconut flour are not much better . . . they're all very high in carbs. By contrast, these delicious Paleo desserts are made with low-carb shredded coconut, with only 27 percent carbs. Shredded coconut has about one-third the carbs of white flour. This huge difference in Paleo desserts can impact your health in a positive way.

The sweeteners that I use are an even bigger surprise. Compare the common sweeteners in the following chart. Most conventional sweeteners are high in carbs. However, the natural Paleo sweeteners used in these recipes have zero carbs.

| Sweeteners Carbohydrate Comparison | carbs net impact |
| --- | --- |
| Just Like Sugar Table Top | 0% |
| Organic Zero Erythritol | 0% |
| Raw yacón syrup | 55% |
| High-fructose corn syrup | 79% |
| Agave nectar | 79–95% |
| Honey, raw, unprocessed | 82% |
| Maple syrup | 85–93% |
| Coconut sugar/nectar | 92% |
| Cane sugar | 100% |

| Coconut Is Low in Carbohydrates | % carbs |
| --- | --- |
| Shredded unsweetened coconut | 27 |
| Whole wheat flour | 67 |
| Coconut flour | 71 |
| White flour | 73 |
| Brown rice flour | 78 |

**The top three sweeteners** on the chart are the ones I use in my recipes. In addition to having *zero* carbs and *zero* calories, these all-natural sweeteners are delicious. They blend and enhance the authentic flavors in every recipe from chocolate brownies to pumpkin pie. After testing hundreds of sweeteners, these top three are the only ones I can wholeheartedly recommend. They offer delicious, sweet results, excellent texture, convenient measuring, and minimum blood sugar or insulin response in the body.

So go on, forget the guilt of desserts. Instead, delight in the flavors, textures, and colors of these beautiful low-carb Paleo sweets. Are you ready to get started?

# INGREDIENTS

*Perhaps the most important lifestyle change we can make to improve our health and well-being is to put our 21st-century diet in sync with the Stone Age by mimicking our ancestors in the food groups they ate.*
—DR. LOREN CORDAIN, AUTHOR OF *THE PALEO DIET: LOSE WEIGHT AND GET HEALTHY BY EATING THE FOODS YOU WERE DESIGNED TO EAT*

**T**here are just a few must-have ingredients to stock in your pantry.

- Medium-shredded unsweetened coconut flakes (not coconut flour)
- Just Like Sugar Table Top sweetener in the 1-pound green bag (not Baking) (see page 23)
- Thick unsweetened coconut milk, such as canned Thai Kitchen brand
- Raw, unrefined coconut oil
- Arrowroot powder
- Pure cacao powder
- Agar flakes

Here's a complete list of everything used in these recipes:

**Chocolate:** These recipes use pure cacao powder or pure baking chocolate, both unsweetened. I suggest always buying 100% cacao, which is unsweetened. Anything less than 100% has sugar added, and sugar is not Paleo. I prefer to buy unsweetened chocolate so that I can choose to add my own Paleo sweetener.

You can buy chocolate in two forms: bars and powder. A bar of pure unsweetened baking chocolate contains 100% cacao and full fat. Most chocolate bars vary from 35 to 80% cacao content. Unsweetened baking chocolate can be used the same as chocolate paste or cacao paste. The cacao powder used in these recipes is 100 percent pure, having been defatted and dried; it may also be labeled "pure cocoa." You can convert any recipe from 100% baking chocolate or bar to cacao powder: For every ounce of unsweetened baking chocolate, use 3 tablespoons of pure cacao powder plus 1 tablespoon of coconut oil.

True Paleo chocolate is 100% cacao. When you buy any type of chocolate, check the label to make sure it contains 100% cacao and no added ingredients. The bitterness of pure chocolate may vary, depending on the type of tree and cultivation. As for 100% cacao chocolate that can be used for eating or baking, Dagoba Prima Materia is pure and widely available, although bitter. Unsweetened cacao nibs qualify as Paleo. The sweetest pure chocolate bar I've found is Le 100% Criollo Dark Chocolate Bar by Pralus, made from the finest criollo cacao beans, with no sweetener. It tastes divine.

You can substitute carob in any of these recipes for a milder, zero-caffeine alternative.

**Coconut:** Coconut is the fundamental ingredient in most of these recipes. I'll talk about it more on page 17. All forms should be unsweetened and unrefined: I use coconut milk, medium-shredded unsweetened coconut flakes, coconut butter (also called creamed coconut), and large coconut flakes.

**Oils:** Coconut oil—raw, first press, unrefined is best.

**As for essential oils:** Use 100 percent pure oil, undiluted, food-grade lavender oil or rose oil.

**Sweeteners:** Just Like Sugar Table Top chicory root sweetener (not Baking) (see page 23) and Organic Zero Erythritol by Wholesome Sweeteners (see page 24) are key ingredients.

**Raw yacón syrup:** Use small amounts for optional caramel flavor. Buy it at a good whole foods market, at www.navitasnaturals.com, or at other whole foods Web sites. See page 24 for more about *raw* yacón syrup.

**Tart fruits:** These include tart apples (such as Granny Smith, Fuji, and Pink Lady), blueberries, cranberries, açaí berries, sour cherries, avocados, limes, and lemons—especially Meyer lemons. (**Tip**: Meyer lemons are not always available; however, they freeze beautifully. You can even zest a frozen Meyer lemon, and juice it later.)

**Sweet fruits:** These include oranges, pears, kumquats, raspberries, strawberries, goji berries, açaí berry puree, elderberries, black currants, and chokeberries, all unsweetened. I use these only occasionally because of their higher sugar content.

**Leafy green vegetables:** These are kale, chard, spinach, and so on.

**Squash:** Summer and winter varieties include zucchini, butternut squash, and pumpkin.

**Root vegetables:** Root vegetables and their derivatives include carrots, beets, sweet potatoes, fresh ginger, carob (powdered), maca root (powdered), chicory root (roasted granules), and dandelion root (roasted granules). Since coffee is not permitted on the Paleo diet, I use this last as a coffee substitute. If you can't find dandelion root granules already roasted, roast them yourself. Bake the raw granules on a baking sheet at 300°F, stirring every 5 minutes, for 20 minutes, or until they turn a slightly golden color.

**Seaweed/sea vegetables:** These include hijiki, wakame, and chlorella powder,

**Thickeners:** These include eggs, agar flakes, arrowroot powder, and flaxseeds—both dark and golden (the only difference is that dark flaxseeds make your baked goods a dark color). Grind flaxseeds easily in a home coffee grinder and refrigerate.

**Salt, herbs, and spices:** All should be 100 percent pure and unrefined. Use unprocessed salt, such as Himalayan salt, Celtic salt, or unprocessed sea salt. Unprocessed sea salt is more flavorful than processed table salt. It contains trace minerals that are essential for health, and is free of chemical additives and anticaking agents. It is never perfectly white, and may have colored specs of minerals in it. I use finely ground Himalayan salt as it dissolves more easily. Or you can grind it finely yourself. Herbs include mint and parsley. Spices include cinnamon, cloves, fresh or ground ginger, and nutmeg.

**Other ingredients and flavorings:** Use pure vanilla extract, almond extract, maple flavoring, and Bragg's Raw Organic Apple Cider Vinegar or any live vinegar. Nutritional yeast adds a buttery flavor to baked goods; however, you may omit it and the recipe will be fine.

**Tea and coffee:** I use Tulsi tea, also called Holy Basil tea, and instant decaffeinated coffee powder or crystals. Some people don't like decaf powder because of the chemicals used in the decaffeinating process. Look for naturally decaffeinated coffee. Mount Hagen sells coffee made by a 100 percent natural $CO_2$ decaffeination process that I consider safe. I buy Mount Hagen coffee crystals and grind the whole contents of the jar so they dissolve easily.

**Seeds and nuts:** Buy them whole, fresh, and raw: almonds, Brazil nuts, cashews, hazelnuts, macadamia nuts, pecans, pistachios, sesame seeds, sunflower seeds, pumpkin seeds, walnuts, hemp seeds, poppy seeds, or buckwheat pure, unsweetened nut butters, such as almond butter and hazelnut butter.

## ABOUT NUTS

Nuts are a true Paleo food, rich in proteins, healthy fats, and enzymes. However, they are also high in enzyme inhibitors, making them difficult to digest. Soaking nuts in lukewarm salted water neutralizes the enzyme inhibitors. Native peoples in Central America soak their nuts and seeds in seawater and then dry them. Even squirrels know how to sprout nuts by burying them in the ground! Soaking nuts is optional in these recipes. However, when you taste the difference after soaking and drying them, you'll find they are even more delicious. There's no bitterness and they are easier to digest. Just try it and notice the difference.

Nuts are delicate. It is important to find a reliable source for fresh nuts that are cultivated with care. Because nuts are high in natural oils, they can easily become rancid. Many groceries stock nuts for years without rotating or refrigerating them. Buy nuts from a store with a rapid turnover. Look for nuts in a food co-op where they are rotated and refrigerated, or find a reliable source online, such as www.sunorganicfarm.com.

### How to Soak Nuts

For almonds, pecans, pumpkin seeds, sesame, sunflower seeds, or walnuts: Soak 4 cups of shelled nuts in filtered water warmed in a pan on the stove with 2 teaspoons of unprocessed salt for 7 hours or longer (up to 24 hours). For cashews, soak no more than 6 hours, as they have been partially soaked and heated, so that more than 6 hours of soaking may make them bitter. There is no need to soak Brazil nuts, hemp seeds, pine nuts, or pistachios. Store soaked nuts in the refrigerator for 2 to 5 days.

### How to Make Crispy Nuts for Storing

Crispy nuts will store for months in an airtight container. For all nuts: Soak, rinse well, drain, and spread them on a stainless-steel or glass baking pan. Heat them in a low oven, no more than 150°F. with the door cracked open, turning them from time to time. If you have a dehydrator, dehydrate for 12 hours, or until dry and crispy. The drying time will vary from 10 to 24 hours, depending on the size of your nuts, their moisture content, and the temperature of your oven or dehydrator. Check them every few hours. I find it easiest to buy nuts, soak them all immediately, and then crisp them, so they're always ready for snacking and using in recipes.

### How to Toast Nuts

Toasted nuts are super delicious! Some of these recipes call for toasted nuts. Heating them adds depth and richness to the flavors.

Toast them on a baking sheet at 350°F for 9 to 12 minutes, depending on the size of the nut, stirring occasionally. Set a timer and take care not to overbake them.

## WHAT'S *NOT* IN THESE RECIPES?

Well, frankly, a lot:

- These recipes do not use grains (wheat, spelt, barley, rye, oats, rice, etc.), corn (cornstarch, corn syrup, etc.), beans or legumes (fava beans, chickpeas, etc.), soy (tofu, soy milk), dairy (milk, cream, yogurt, cheese, butter), peanuts (or peanut butter), or potatoes (potato starch/flour).
- They contain no processed or prepared foods, and no sugars or artificial sweeteners.

- There are no refined or extracted sweeteners, such as agave nectar, maple syrup, coconut palm sugar, brown rice syrup, stevia, or stevioside.
- There are no high-carb Paleo sweeteners such as honey. And no dried fruits, such as raisins, dates, and so on.
- These recipes do not use commercial coconut flour, which has been defatted and processed, except as an optional grain-free flour to dust baking pans.

With our food basics in place, let's take a look at the baking tools that will make your life so much easier.

# PALEO DESSERT TOOLS

*Everything should be made*
*as simple as possible, but not simpler.*
—Albert Einstein

I love simplicity. And because my kitchen is small, I try to keep only the most basic tools on hand. My favorites are my high-speed blender and rubber spatula. I feel quite fortunate to have these tools, considering my (and yours, too!) Paleolithic ancestors were limited to scraping tools, hand grinders, and flint stones for cutting. They would have had great difficulty making a creamy pudding or a fluffy cake. Aren't we lucky to be living in the twenty-first century? Here's a list of my favorite Paleolithic tools.

## EQUIPMENT

- A good food processor is a must for many of these recipes. It can be either large or small. More important than the size is the power. It needs a strong motor and a fast-processing "S" blade to grind shredded coconut. There are many good food processors. I use a 12-cup KitchenAid KFPW760 that's eight years old and still going strong.
- Any good-quality blender. The type that can grind ice well is recommended.
- A digital kitchen scale to measure ounces and grams.
- An electric handheld mixer for beating egg whites, or a standing mixer.
- A high-speed blender—this is my favorite kitchen tool. Although it is not required for these recipes, it will give you superior, smooth results. I recommend either the Blendtec or the Vitamix. If you buy the Blendtec, ask for the additional Twister container, which is invaluable for blending small quantities. Likewise for the

Vitamix; the small 32-ounce container will make your work easy. These high-speed blenders are pricey, but my Blendtec is still going strong after ten years. You will quickly recover your investment in time saved, increased nutrition, flexibility, and better-tasting food.

- A small blender is very useful for blending 2 cups or less. Although it is not absolutely necessary for these desserts, you'll find it saves you time. I like the Tribest Personal Blender. If you already own a high-speed blender, consider getting the Blendtec Twister or the Vitamix 32-ounce container, as these do the same thing.
- A home coffee grinder is useful to grind flaxseeds, instant coffee crystals, and for making finely ground sweetener.
- A waffle iron is a must for Belgian waffles.
- An ice-cream machine is helpful but not required for ice cream.

## BAKING PANS

- A 9-inch square cake pan
- Three 8- or 9-inch round cake pans, for layer cakes
- Four mini loaf pans, about 5.75 by 3.25 inches
- A 9 by 5-inch loaf pan
- Round springform pans: 6-inch, 8-inch, and 9- or 10-inch

- A twelve-compartment cupcake pan
- A twenty-four-compartment mini cupcake pan
    - A 9-inch pie pan
    - A 9 by 13-inch rectangular sheet pan, preferably glass
    - A shallow, nonstick skillet for cooking agar and crepes (I use an 8-inch titanium pan.)
    - Two 8 by 11-inch rectangular tart pans for tiramisu and sponge cakes

## HAND TOOLS

- A good oven thermometer—it needn't be fancy. Because most ovens are inaccurate, baked goods can come out over- or underbaked. Your best insurance is to check the thermometer and adjust your dial manually until it reaches your desired temperature.
- A few good rubber spatulas (both large and small), with a corner on them. They're essential for stirring the bottom of the food processor, for folding batter, for cooking agar, and for absolutely everything else. Trust me on this one.
- A pastry brush is useful for brushing a thin layer of oil onto pans or dough.
- Three mixing bowls: small, medium, and large. If they have a pour spout, it's great for pouring batter into cupcake tins.

- A rack will help your baked goods cool evenly.
- A set of nested stainless-steel measuring cups
- A set of stainless-steel measuring spoons, including ⅛ teaspoon
- Glass measuring cups for liquids, with 1- and 2-cup capacity
- A small metal spatula (a flat palette knife) is an invaluable tool for frosting cupcakes.
- Three wire whisks: very small, medium, and large. These are great for mixing sauces and beating the lumps out of cake batter.
- Cookie cutters: 2-inch and 3-inch, for ice-cream sandwiches and Finger Tarts
- A pastry wheel cutter for making Finger Tarts, with a zigzag crimp blade if possible
- A fine-gauge mesh tea strainer—I use this for making Paleo Caffè, sifting lumps out of cacao powder, dusting baking pans, and sprinkling finely ground sweetener on finished desserts.
- A medium-gauge strainer is useful for draining soaked nuts or steamed vegetables and for straining seeds out of raspberries.
- Any lemon juicer—I use an old-fashioned wooden citrus reamer.
- A Microplane grater is ideal for zesting oranges, lemons, and nutmeg.
- A rolling pin for piecrust
- A nylon nut milk bag. I like it better than cheesecloth for straining solids out of nut milks. Ask for it in any natural grocery store.
- Cake decorating tools: A simple solution is to frost cakes with a knife or palette. It's also fun to buy a few decorating tools, such as a 12-inch pastry bag and a few tips. The decorating tips I use most are #21, #809, and #827.

So, that's it! Now that you've got your tools, let's learn more about those essential ingredients you just can't live without.

# PALEO DESSERT ESSENTIALS

*If we change our interaction with our environment,*
*we change our genetic potential. . . . There is nothing*
*fixed in our biology. It's always changeable.*
—Dr. Bruce Lipton

There are two essential ingredients that you'll find in nearly every recipe. In fact, without them, the delicious desserts on these pages would be impossible. That's pretty essential, no? So, drum roll please . . .

The first one is coconut. A truly amazing natural wonder, coconut has been widely consumed in Asia for centuries. Its flexibility and many uses are just now coming to light worldwide. The second essential ingredient is a natural, low-carb sweetener.

## ESSENTIAL #1: COCONUT, THE TREE OF LIFE

*Let your food be your medicine and your medicine be your food.*

—Hippocrates, Greek physician

Hippocrates was often called the father of modern medicine, and he taught that the body must be treated as a whole rather than separate parts. Turns out, he was right!

In parts of Asia, coconut is called the tree of life because it is the "the tree of a thousand uses." It has been used since ancient times for its pulp, meat, oil, and leaves. When you buy a coconut in an Asian market, the vendor will grate the fresh white meat for you. Or you can pick up a coconut and grate it yourself. Coconut forms the basis of many of these recipes. This simple ingredient can be used to make delicious cakes, cookies, mousses, ice creams, and more.

In these recipes, coconut is used in five ways:

1. Coconut milk is made from shredded coconut pulp blended with water or coconut water.

2. Shredded coconut flakes are made by grating and drying mature coconut pulp.
3. Coconut butter, or creamed coconut, comes from blending the entire dry pulp, much like a nut butter.
4. Coconut oil is made by pressing or heating coconut meat.
5. Sweet coconut powder is finely granulated sweetener mixed with shredded coconut flakes, ground into a fine powder. This is very easy to make in a food processor.

## Coconut Milk

Coconut milk is a delicious creamy blend of coconut meat and water. There are many types of coconut milk; in fact, there's no industry standard for it. You'll find a variety of qualities in stores: Some coconut milk is thick like pudding, while other brands are thin like cow's milk. Some are pure and some are mixed with other ingredients. You can also make coconut milk yourself. The good news is, you've got choices.

In a nutshell, there are three choices: You can buy it in a can, buy it in a carton, or make it at home. It is very important to look for unsweetened coconut milk with no preservatives and the fewest number of ingredients. When buying coconut milk in a can, I look for the thickest quality. I shake the can and listen for the one that has no liquid sloshing around, and I buy that one. So far, the thickest brand I've come across is Organic Thai Kitchen Coconut Milk. In addition, I buy the full-fat coconut milk, because so-called lite coconut milk just has more water added to it. I prefer full-nutrition products, and I can choose to add my own water for a fraction of the cost. When I open the can, I stir the contents to combine the thick cream on the top with the thinner liquid on the bottom, and then I use the entire contents. I hope someday we'll be able to buy coconut milk without guar gum, and canned coconut milk that says "BPA free" on the label.

There are three ways to make homemade coconut milk.
1. From shredded coconut flakes
2. From a mature coconut
3. From a young coconut

### How to Make Coconut Milk from Shredded Coconut Flakes

You will need a high-speed blender such as a Blendtec or Vitamix (a regular blender or food processor won't be able to grind the coconut finely enough); a 4-cup jar, or two 2-cup jars; a nut milk bag or a fine-mesh paint strainer bag; and the following ingredients, depending on whether you desire a thin or thick milk.
1. First, choose the kind of coconut milk you want to create. Do you want thin coconut milk, which is similar in consistency to cow's milk? Or thick coconut milk, which is more like heavy cream? Choose your column and follow the quantities.

| Homemade Coconut Milk | Thin Milk | Thick Milk |
|---|---|---|
| Medium-shredded unsweetened coconut flakes (not coconut flour) | 1 cup | 4 cups |
| Very hot filtered water | 4 cups | 4 cups |
| Unprocessed salt | Pinch | Pinch |
| Pure vanilla extract | ½ teaspoon | ½ teaspoon |
| Yield | 4 cups | 6 cups |

Homemade coconut milk is fresher and you save a lot of money making it yourself. And your homemade milk is also pure and free of additional ingredients, such as guar gum.

### How to Make Coconut Milk from a Mature Coconut

You will need an ice pick, hammer and nail, or corkscrew; a coconut knife and a grater, or an oven; a high-speed blender; a nut milk bag or cheesecloth; and a mature coconut.

1. Use a sharp, pointed tool such as an ice pick, a hammer and nail, or a corkscrew to poke through the two softest of the three "eyes" on the coconut. Drain the juice into a glass or cup. Open the coconut with a hammer.

2. Use a coconut knife and grater to remove the meat. If you don't have a coconut knife and grater, you can bake the open coconut at 325°F for 30 minutes, and the meat will come out easily.

3. Place the coconut meat in a high-speed blender. Heat 2 cups of filtered water on the stove to almost boiling and pour it into the blender to barely cover the coconut. or heat pure coconut water. Blend well into a fine puree.

4. Strain the solids with a nut milk bag or cheesecloth into a jar. If you use a minimum amount of water, your coconut milk will be thicker. Refrigerate the coconut milk and consume it

2. Place the shredded coconut flakes in the high-speed blender and grind briefly, no more than 10 seconds. Be mindful not to grind them longer, or they'll soften and turn into butter. You just want to grind them for a bit so they're in smaller pieces.

3. Heat filtered water on the stove almost to a boil. Add to the blender and blend for about a minute. Stop and allow the blender to rest. Then blend again, and repeat until you have blended three times.

4. Now you're ready to strain out the solids. Strain them by pouring some of the warm milk into a nut milk bag inside a jar. Squeeze the milk out of the bag into the jar. Here's your beautiful coconut milk. Refrigerate and use it within a few days. The leftover pulp is still nutritious, although to a lesser extent. It's great for Coconut Macaroons (page 67), and my birds love it.

within 3 days. Discard the remaining coconut meat or use it in your favorite desserts, such as Coconut Macaroons (page 67) or Coconut Pecan Frosting (page 183).

### How to Make Coconut Milk from a Young Coconut

Young coconuts are unripe coconuts found in whole foods markets and Asian markets. They are white in color as they are only partially pared, and are sold covered in plastic. They contain coconut water and soft, gelatinous white meat, both very delicious and nutritious. The meat can be scooped out and blended into wonderful desserts. There are two steps to this. First, open the coconut. That's the challenging part. Then, blend the milk.

To open the coconut, you will need a large cleaver or knife.

1. Hold the coconut on its side on a large counter. Whack the knife against the tip of the coconut at an outward angle. Be careful! Rotate the coconut so that in three or four whacks, you have removed the entire top of the coconut. Using the heel of the knife, pry open the round top of the coconut, to reveal water and pulp inside. I suggest you search online for a video showing how to "open a young coconut" before you try this.
2. Pour the coconut water out into a glass jar. Using a large spoon, remove the soft meat from inside the coconut.

To make the milk, you will need a high-speed blender, 2 cups of coconut water or filtered water, and 1 cup of young coconut pulp.

1. Place the water and pulp in a high-speed blender.
2. Blend until smooth and creamy. You can adjust the thickness of your milk by varying the amount of water.

### Homemade Coffee Creamer Cubes

You can make your own nondairy creamer with coconut milk. It's easy!

1. Just fill an ice cube tray with any coconut milk.
2. Freeze it.
3. Store the frozen cubes in a resealable plastic bag and use in any beverage. It's great for iced lattes.

## Coconut Butter

This is one of my favorites. Often called creamed coconut, or coconut cream, this is pure coconut meat, ground into nut butter. It is not to be confused with coconut oil. Coconut butter is a wonderful ingredient used in many of these recipes. My favorite brand is Artisana Coconut Butter. There are other good brands available in any whole foods grocery or online. Coconut butter is easy to measure if you first soften it by putting the jar in a bowl of lukewarm water. Coconut butter can be expensive. You can save a lot of money by making it yourself.

### How to Make Homemade Coconut Butter

You will need a high-speed blender and 2 to 7 cups of medium-shredded unsweetened coconut flakes (not coconut flour).

1. Fill your blender at least halfway with flakes (that's a lot!) so it can stir properly. If your blender is small, start with 2 cups. If it is large, you can use up to 7 cups. It should be quite full. If your high-speed blender has a tamper tool, this may be useful.

2. Blend the coconut meat on high speed. The coconut will begin to break up, and after 30 seconds it will begin to liquefy. Slowly it will turn to butter. Blend until smooth and fine, at least a minute. Then pour the butter into a jar. This butter is highly condensed coconut meat. Just to give you an idea: 5 cups of shredded coconut will yield 2 cups coconut butter. It's really delicious.

## Coconut Oil

Coconut oil comes from pressing or heating coconut meat. Unrefined coconut oil is a healthy oil, smooth and creamy. It can withstand high oven temperatures without smoking or burning, which is wonderful in baking. It's important to know how coconut is unique from other oils, so you can be successful in using it in my recipes.

Coconut oil is highly temperature sensitive. It is rock hard in the refrigerator, and solid yet soft at room temperature. However, it melts quickly at 78°F. The melting point is very different from butter, which melts at 90°F. Coconut oil is delicate. It can make your dessert magical, or it can ruin it, and we don't want that. It is important to be gentle with coconut oil, and to not subject it to radical temperature changes. Many of these recipes call for melted coconut oil. The best way to melt it is to set the whole jar or container of oil in a bowl of lukewarm tap water for a few minutes. This is easy and gentle. *Do not microwave the oil or heat it on the stove.* If your oil gets too warm, your dessert may separate or get lumpy. Temperature is a critical factor in using coconut oil. Some recipes just won't work on a warm summer day when your kitchen is 85°F. Once you understand the delicate temperature sensitivity of coconut oil, you can use it to make a variety of wonderful desserts.

## Sweet Coconut Powder

Sweet coconut powder has been used for centuries in Asian desserts. This is shredded, dried coconut flakes that have been ground into a fine powder with a granulated sweetener. If you try to grind coconut meat alone, it may get stuck or turn into thick coconut butter. However, when you mix shredded coconut with a sweetener, the lighter-weight crystals aerate the coconut. Sweet coconut powder is a whole nutritious food, 100 percent Paleo, and very delicious.

This simple discovery of first grinding a granulated sweetener, and then adding shredded coconut, has changed my entire way of creating desserts. It makes an ideal flour that is nutritious, rich, naturally sweet, gluten-free, and grain-free. It's a lovely low-carb flour that's perfect for making luscious cakes, cookies, and anything you want. To make it, all you need is a food processor. A regular blender will not work at all. I do not recommend a high-speed blender, either, as it tends to get stuck and stress the motor (I almost ruined my Blendtec trying!).

### How to Make Sweet Coconut Powder

You will need: a food processor, granulated Paleo sweetener (such as 1 cup of Just Like Sugar Table Top natural chicory root sweetener (not Baking) A second choice is 1⅓ cups of Organic Zero Erythritol, and 1 cup of medium-shredded unsweetened coconut flakes (not coconut flour).

1. In a dry food processor fitted with the "S" blade, grind the sweetener to a very fine powder.
2. Add the shredded coconut to the sweetener in the food processor. Spin it for a minute to become a very fine powder. Open the lid, stir the bottom, replace the lid, and grind again until the powder is uniformly fine. That's it!

**Here's a tip for more experienced Paleo chefs:** Now that you can grind your coconut powder, you may wish to make it in advance to keep it on hand. Just remember that 1 cup of Just Like Sugar Table Top sweetener plus 1 cup of shredded unsweetened coconut flakes prepared as described will yield 1⅔ cups (not 2 cups) of sweet coconut powder.

Once you learn to grind your own sweet coconut powder in a food processor, you can make every recipe in this book.

The recipes in this book use pure, unsweetened shredded coconut flakes. Commercially sold coconut flour is a refined food made by pressing unpared coconuts, including the hull, into milk or oil. Once pressed, the remaining meat and hulls are dried and ground into powder. The resulting coconut flour is very high in fiber, with reduced flavor and nutrition. In parts of Asia, this pressed pulp is thrown away or fed to the pigs. (I use it to flour baking pans.) Commercial coconut flour is not used in these desserts. Instead, these recipes use the full-bodied flavor and high-nutrition pure coconut meat, and I am so excited for you to taste the difference.

## ESSENTIAL #2: SWEETENERS

*As the consumption of sugar has increased, so have all the "civilized" diseases.*
—SALLY FALLON, FOUNDER OF WESTON PRICE FOUNDATION, AUTHOR OF THE BEST-SELLING COOKBOOK *NOURISHING TRADITIONS*

Only three natural sweeteners are used in this book. After testing hundreds of sweeteners, the following are the only ones I can wholeheartedly recommend.

- Just Like Sugar Table Top natural chicory root sweetener (not Baking)

- Organic Zero Erythritol
- *Raw* yacón syrup

## Just Like Sugar
## Table Top Sweetener

Just Like Sugar Table Top is my favorite sweetener by far. I use this in most recipes because it dissolves easily, it tastes like table sugar, and is easy to measure cup for cup—like table sugar. It also happens to be a zero-calorie, zero-carb granulated sweetener that can be used very much like sugar. It gently sweetens everything, and I get no sugar rush or aftertaste from it. The Table Top version gives me the best sweet flavor and texture in desserts. It is also delicious in coffee and tea. Let me say right away that I am not paid or endorsed in any way by Just Like Sugar, Inc.—I just love this product.

Just Like Sugar Table Top is a blend of crystalline chicory root that is 96 percent dietary fiber, with calcium and vitamin C. Its added sweetness comes from orange peel. Chicory root is high in sweet carbohydrate dietary fiber called inulin (IN-you-lin), not to be confused with insulin. Because of the structure of the inulin molecule, it is not digested in the human body and does not metabolize as a carbohydrate. This means effectively that although it tastes sweet, it does not affect blood sugar levels, and it does not cause weight gain.

The health benefits of Just Like Sugar are unique among sweeteners:

- Just Like Sugar is high in chicory root dietary fiber. Clinical research shows that a diet high in dietary fiber greatly benefits digestive functions.
- This is the nutritional makeup per the manufacturer's labeling: A 100-gram serving contains 0 calories, 0 sugar, 0 fat, 0 cholesterol, 0 sodium, 0 net impact carbohydrates, and 0 protein.
- Just Like Sugar is not fermentable and will not promote tooth decay.
- Just Like Sugar acts as a prebiotic in the body, meaning it helps to stimulate the growth and activity of healthy digestive bacteria.
- Chicory root is often used to control blood sugar levels. It can be used to help stabilize the body blood sugar levels for diabetics and nondiabetics alike.
- It is gluten-free, wheat-free, dairy-free, kosher, and vegan-safe. It does not contain soy, yeast, animal derivatives, or preservatives.

Bottom line: I love Just Like Sugar and I know you will, too.

You can find it in some good whole foods markets. If they are out of stock, you can ask them to order it for you. Or buy it online from www.justlikesugarinc.com, www.vitacost.com, www.netrition.com, www.amazon.com, and so on. Make sure you ask for the Table Top version in the 1-pound green bag, to use for my recipes, and not the Baking variety in the blue bag, because it is measured differently.

## Organic Zero Erythritol

Erythritol (Ah-REETH-ra-tall) looks and tastes like table sugar. Don't be fooled by its name; erythritol is a natural sweetener. It is made by fermenting whole plant pulp into a zero-carb, granulated sweetener that can be used like sugar. In fact, if you have the starter yeast *Moniliella pollinis*, you can make this in your own kitchen, sort of like *kombucha*. And it's easy to do. For this reason I consider erythritol a 100 percent Paleo sweetener.

Erythritol is 70 percent as sweet as sugar, so it is measured differently: 1 cup of table sugar equals 1⅓ cups of erythritol. Erythritol has a cooling flavor, which is lovely in Blueberry Lemon Cheesecake Bars (page 83), but not as desirable in pumpkin pie. Erythritol does not cause gastric distress as do other fermented sweeteners, and it helps prevent tooth cavities. A great bonus!

One caveat—erythritol does not dissolve easily unless it is heated. Even after heating, it often re-forms crystals when chilled or frozen. You can sense a crunchy crystalline texture between your teeth, and many people do not like this. Therefore erythritol isn't the best choice for chilled desserts and ice creams. It is best in warm or baked fruity desserts, such as the Fluffy Lemon Cupcakes (page 51). I find that Organic Zero dissolves more easily than other erythritol brands, as the granules are small. Therefore I do not recommend other brands, or erythritol blends with other sweeteners. In general, I find erythritol challenging to work with, and I prefer Just Like Sugar Table Top sweetener for best results.

You can buy Wholesome Sweeteners brand Organic Zero at whole foods markets, at www.wholesomesweeteners.com, or www.amazon.com.

## *Raw* Yacón Syrup

This delicious syrup comes from a South American root. Yacón syrup has a natural flavor something like caramel or molasses. It contains fructo-oligosaccharides, which have a sweet taste but are low in calories and carbs. There is little standardization in the industry, and so I suggest care in buying it, especially if you are sensitive to sugars. Always look for *raw* yacón, which is lower in carbs and sugars. Yacón is optional in these recipes and you should use it at your own discretion. While it is expensive, just one tablespoon adds a distinctive flavor, and a small jar lasts me several months. I love yacón syrup in chocolate chip cookies, pumpkin bread, and fudge. If you try it I think you will enjoy the rich caramel taste.

You can find it at whole foods markets, www.navitasnaturals.com, or www.amazon.com.

**Note:** The sweeteners I recommend are suitable for the vast majority of people, including those with gluten intolerance, celiac disease, and diabetes. However, every person's digestion is unique, therefore these products may not be suitable for everyone; for example, a few people suffering from IBS may not tolerate chicory root fiber. Before starting any new diet, please check with your medical practitioner.

# PALEO DESSERT RECIPES

**I**'m so excited to share these delicious recipes with you. However I must begin with a warning. Many of the desserts use new techniques, and some of the ingredients are brand-specific.

You will be tempted to use other ingredients and methods. But if you do not follow the recipe exactly as written, it is very likely you will be disappointed with the results.

Even if you are an experienced cook, you must follow the recipe. *All* of my testers failed in their attempts to make these desserts when they substituted other sweeteners or flours, or if they disregarded the temperature indications. None of them used the Just Like Sugar Table Top sweetener indicated. Instead they bought Just Like Sugar Baking, which is measured differently and does not work here.

After you gain experience with these ingredients and techniques, you'll better know how to make subtle modifications. That's when you'll really have fun making your own creations. Until then, please follow the recipes. I am suggesting this because I wish you the utmost success and sweet pleasure enjoying these desserts.

*I love vegetables. Especially carrot cake, pumpkin bread, and zucchini cupcakes.*

—JANE BARTHELEMY (THAT'S ME!)

# CAKES AND CUPCAKES

I f you're 100 percent Paleo, you may have thought that you'd have to give up cupcakes. Not so! With a few new methods, you can enjoy traditional cakes such as Red Velvet Cake (page 39), Fluffy Lemon Cupcakes (page 51), and Strawberry Shortcake (page 42). Some of my testers say they're even more delicious than the originals. To make these magical creations, you'll need a food processor. Pure, natural ingredients will do the rest.

So, may the cakes and cupcakes rise to the occasion!

The trick is, Paleo batters are gluten-free, so they don't rise as much as wheat flour. What to do? Well, over the years I've figured out a few tricks to make this happen. The best way to make your cakes and cupcakes rise more and dome in the middle is to start the oven temperature high and lower it slowly.

Here's how: Preheat the oven to 375°F. Place the cake or cupcakes in the oven and set the timer for 5 minutes. After 5 minutes, lower the heat to 350°F and set the timer for

10 minutes. When it goes off, lower the oven temperature to 325°F. You'll need another 5 to 8 minutes, so I set the timer for 5 minutes and bake until a toothpick inserted into the center comes out clean. The higher temperature causes cake to rise quicker, and forces the center of the cake up. The dome holds better while the cake finishes baking at a lower temperature. It won't rise quite as much as a conventional cake, but will rise more than if baked at one temperature throughout. This system works for any cake or cupcake. If you want your cake or cupcakes flat, then bake at 350°F the whole time.

Also, cupcakes dome a little better with liners. Just sayin' . . .

**Amazing tip:** If you add 2 teaspoons of guar gum to your wet ingredients for 12 cupcakes, they will dome in the center and hold their height better. This *really* works (as I was thrilled to discover). However, the cupcakes containing guar gum will start rising right in the mixing bowl, so get them over to the oven quickly. Guar gum comes from the outer hull of guar seeds and is considered a legume. Therefore it may not be acceptable for Paleo purists. This works for cakes, as well; however I prefer my cakes flat for easy frosting. I leave it for you to test as an option, if you feel so inclined.

## THINK OUTSIDE THE CAKE BOX

Even though a recipe may say it's for cupcakes, you have the option to make any cake in another form whether it's as cupcakes, a layer cake, a loaf, or a sheet cake. For example, a banana bread recipe can become a delicious layer cake or muffins. The only caution is that smaller sizes, such as cupcakes, will rise more quickly and look better. Larger cakes such as big loaves may fall because there's no gluten in the batter.

Here's a rough guide, so you can have some fun and be creative with all of this Paleo baking:

- If the recipe is for twenty-four mini cupcakes, you could also make ten regular cupcakes; a one-layer 8-inch round cake; or a mini loaf.
- If the recipe is for twelve regular cupcakes, you can also make a double-layer 8- or 9-inch round cake; or three mini loaves.
- If the recipe is for four mini loaves, you could also make a triple-layer 8- or 9-inch cake; or a 9 by 13-inch sheet cake.

Here are baking times for different size pans:

- mini cupcakes: 14 to 18 minutes
- regular cupcakes or muffins: 18 to 23 minutes
- mini loaf: 20 to 23 minutes
- 9 by 5 loaf: 45 to 55 minutes
- 8- or 9-inch round cake: 35 to 40 minutes
- 9 by 13-inch cake: 30 to 35 minutes
- 10- to 12-cup Bundt cake: 35 to 60 minutes

## TO GREASE OR NOT GREASE?

I prefer to line cake pans with parchment paper whenever possible, as gluten-free batter is delicate and I don't like broken cakes when removing them from the pan. I cut circles for the round pans, and make strips for the square ones so the paper hangs over the edge for easy removal. I usually grease cupcake pans with coconut oil and dust them with whatever flour I have on hand, such as commercial coconut flour, arrowroot powder, or cacao powder, depending on the color of the cake. Cupcake liners are optional.

## GO AHEAD AND OVERBEAT!

You can't overbeat Paleo cake batter. Overbeating wheat batter develops the gluten and the cake becomes tough. But these batters have no gluten, so don't worry about overbeating eggs, sweetener, oil, coconut, or any gluten-free flour.

## ALL ABOUT EGGS

The temperature of the dough really makes a difference, and cold eggs can ruin a cupcake. If you're like me and forget to take your eggs out of the refrigerator an hour beforehand, just immerse them in a cup of lukewarm water for 20 minutes to bring them to room temperature. Be mindful not to use hot water, as this may cause other ingredients to melt.

Most of us are used to buying eggs and throwing them into any recipe. I buy eggs from a local farm and they vary in size. Some of my so-called large eggs are enormous, and some of them are tiny. For cakes and cookies, the egg volume makes a big difference in the result. Because they are radically different, I found it helpful to weigh the eggs before putting them in. You'll need a digital scale for this. An average large egg out of the shell weighs 55 grams. Two large eggs are 110 grams, three large eggs are 165 grams, four large eggs are 220 grams. Leftover eggs don't have to go to waste—partial eggs can be used later in omelets or smoothies!

## HOW TO MEASURE DRY INGREDIENTS

I use the dip-and-sweep method to measure dry ingredients (also called scoop and level).

First, loosen the ingredient in the bag or canister it's in, as powder tends to settle when left sitting. You can stir it a bit with a whisk or a spoon. Then dip the measuring cup or spoon into the bag without shaking or tapping and sweep off the excess with a spatula or knife.

## HOW TO ASSEMBLE A LAYER CAKE

1. Using a thin knife, release the edges from each pan, and gently allow the cake layer to pull away. I find it is easy to flip it onto the small, flat disk from a springform pan about 8 inches in diameter, and then it's even easier to center on the serving plate (and we like easy). Tuck a few strips of parchment paper under the edges of the cake to keep the plate clean while you frost it.
2. Place the first cake layer on a large serving plate. Spread it with frosting or filling. Place the second cake layer on top. Spread it with more frosting. If you have three layers, repeat this for the third layer. Then, frost the sides. Serve and enjoy!

Now, let's get to the most exciting part—the recipes.

# Yellow Birthday Cake

*This is a great basic recipe for yellow cake. My favorite birthday cake has layers of Whipped Crème and Raspberry "Jam." If you prefer, this basic yellow cake also pairs well with Coconut Crème Cheese Frosting (page 180), or Chocolate Buttercream Frosting (page 177) instead. Eat the cake plain, add a sauce, frost it, fill it with pastry cream, use it for Strawberry Shortcake (page 42) or Tiramisu (page 43) . . . the possibilities are endless!*

**[ YIELD: One double-layer 8-inch round cake or two 8 by 11-inch sheet cakes • EQUIPMENT NEEDED: Any style blender and a food processor ]**

3 cups 5-Minute Whipped Crème Topping (page 174) or Vanilla Pastry Cream with Coconut (page 186)

1 recipe Raspberry "Jam" (page 192)

1¼ cups Just Like Sugar Table Top natural chicory root sweetener (not Baking). A second choice is 1²/₃ cups Organic Zero Erythritol.

1¼ cups medium-shredded unsweetened coconut flakes (not coconut flour)

¼ cup arrowroot powder

1 teaspoon baking soda

1 teaspoon baking powder

¼ teaspoon unprocessed salt

1 teaspoon nutritional yeast (optional)

6 large eggs, at room temperature, separated

1 tablespoon pure vanilla extract

¼ teaspoon almond extract

½ cup thick unsweetened coconut milk, or ¼ cup thin

Unsweetened coconut or raspberries, for garnish (optional)

1. Prepare the 5-Minute Whipped Crème Topping or Vanilla Pastry Cream and chill well.
2. Prepare the Raspberry "Jam."
3. Preheat the oven to 350°F. Cut parchment paper into circles to line either two 8-inch round cake pans or two 8 by 11-inch tart pans.
4. In a dry food processor fitted with the "S" blade, grind the sweetener to a very fine powder.
5. Add the shredded coconut to the sweetener in the food processor. Spin it for a minute to become a very fine powder. Open the lid, stir the bottom, replace the lid, and grind again until the powder is uniformly fine.
6. To the ingredients in the food processor, add the arrowroot, baking soda, baking powder, salt, and nutritional yeast (if using). Mix well, pour into a large mixing bowl, and set aside.
7. Place in the empty food processor the egg yolks, vanilla, almond extract, and coconut milk. Mix well and then let the mixture sit while you beat the egg whites.
8. With an electric mixer in a medium-size mixing bowl, beat the egg whites at medium speed until foamy. Gradually increase the mixer speed to high until soft peaks form. Do not beat until dry.
9. Pour the wet ingredients from the food processor into the dry mixture. Stir the batter briefly and thoroughly.
10. With a rubber spatula, gently fold the beaten egg whites into the batter in three parts.

**continues . . .**

11. Pour the batter into the prepared cake pans and spread it out flat. Bake for 23 to 28 minutes, or until a toothpick inserted into the middle of the cake comes out clean. Don't peek or the cake may fall. Check on it after 20 minutes, as the cake can easily dry out. Let cool for about 30 minutes in the pan on a rack.

12. Place one cake layer on a serving plate. Tuck a few strips of parchment paper under the edges to keep the plate clean while you frost it. Spread it generously with half of the Whipped Crème, and then cover it with all of the Raspberry "Jam." Place the second cake layer on top. Spread with the remaining Whipped Crème, and leave the sides unfrosted so the "Jam" is visible. Garnish with sprinkles of shredded coconut and/or a few raspberries, if you desire. Serve and enjoy.

# Chocolate Cake with Raspberry Filling

*This cake is moist, flavorful, and a very dark chocolate color. Rich with cacao, it uses blueberries and apple for flavor and to help bind the cake. This is super luscious with Raspberry "Jam" (page 192) and Instant Mocha Buttercream Frosting (page 184). For the most delightful flavor and texture, follow this recipe exactly.*

[ YIELD: One triple-layer 8-inch round cake • EQUIPMENT NEEDED: A food processor; any style blender; and a digital scale, as apples vary in size ]

2 recipes Raspberry "Jam" (page 192)

2¼ cups Just Like Sugar Table Top natural chicory root sweetener (not Baking). A second choice is 3 cups Organic Zero Erythritol.

1¾ cups medium-shredded unsweetened coconut flakes (not coconut flour)

1 cup pure cacao powder

1 teaspoon baking soda

1 teaspoon baking powder

½ teaspoon unprocessed salt

¼ cup arrowroot powder

3 large eggs, at room temperature

1 cup fresh or frozen blueberries, well drained, at room temperature

1½ tart apples, unpeeled, cored, and cut into chunks (275 grams)

1½ tablespoons pure vanilla extract

1 teaspoon instant decaffeinated coffee powder or crystals

1 recipe Instant Mocha Buttercream Frosting (page 184)

1. Make the Raspberry "Jam" and chill.
2. Preheat the oven to 350°F. Line three 8-inch round cake pans with parchment paper.
3. In a dry food processor fitted with the "S" blade, grind the sweetener to a fine powder.
4. Add the shredded coconut to the sweetener in the food processor. Spin it for a minute until a very fine powder. Open the lid, stir the bottom, replace the lid, and grind again until the powder is uniformly fine.
5. To the ingredients in the food processor, add the cacao powder, baking soda, baking powder, salt, and arrowroot. Mix well and pour into a large mixing bowl.
6. Place in any style blender the eggs, blueberries, apples, vanilla, and coffee crystals. Blend well until liquefied.
7. Pour the wet ingredients into the dry mixture. Mix briefly to remove any lumps. Pour the batter evenly into the three prepared cake pans, and smooth flat. Bake for 30 to 35 minutes.
8. Prepare the Instant Mocha Buttercream Frosting.
9. Remove the cake from the oven. Let cool for about 1 hour in the pan. Using a thin knife, release around the edges of each cake pan, and gently allow the cake to pull away.
10. To assemble the cake: Place one cake layer on a large serving platter. Spread it with half of the Raspberry "Jam." Place the second layer on top and repeat with the remaining "Jam." Place the third cake layer on top. Frost the top and sides with Instant Mocha Buttercream Frosting.

# Honey Cake

*Honey cake may be the oldest dessert known to man. It is said that in prehistoric times, honey was revered as a treat for special times of year. This recipe is adapted from a traditional Jewish honey cake, similar to an ancient Egyptian honey cake. I love the rich taste of honey; however, it is extremely high in carbs. So to keep your blood sugar levels balanced, there's no honey in this cake at all. Instead it uses yacón syrup, fresh orange, and cardamom. Follow this recipe to a T and you'll be pleased with the results. The cake is yummy plain, with Espresso Latte Buttercream Frosting (page 176), or with Vanilla Crème Cheese Frosting (page 180).*

**[ YIELD: One single-layer 9-inch round cake • EQUIPMENT NEEDED: A food processor ]**

1¼ cups Just Like Sugar Table Top natural chicory root sweetener (not Baking). A second choice is 1⅔ cups Organic Zero Erythritol.

1 cup medium-shredded unsweetened coconut flakes (not coconut flour)

1 teaspoon baking powder

½ teaspoon baking soda

½ teaspoon unprocessed salt

1 teaspoon ground cinnamon

1 teaspoon ground cardamom

¼ teaspoon ground cloves

¼ teaspoon ground allspice

1 teaspoon instant decaffeinated coffee powder or crystals, ground finely (optional)

3 large eggs, at room temperature

2 tablespoons *raw* yacón syrup

2 teaspoons pure vanilla extract

Zest of 1 orange

Pulp of ½ orange, pith removed, sliced, and seeded

½ teaspoon maple flavoring (optional)

1 cup very coarsely chopped nuts, soaked if possible (see page 10)

1. Preheat the oven to 350°F. Prepare a 9-inch round cake pan or springform pan: Cut parchment paper into a circle to line the bottom of the pan and grease the paper.

2. In a dry food processor fitted with the "S" blade, grind the sweetener to a very fine powder.

3. Add the shredded coconut to the sweetener in the food processor. Spin it for a minute to become a very fine powder. Open the lid, stir the bottom, replace the lid, and grind again until the powder is uniformly fine.

4. To the ingredients in the food processor, add the baking powder, baking soda, salt, cinnamon, cardamom, cloves, allspice, and coffee powder. Mix well.

5. To the dry ingredients in the food processor, add the eggs, yacón syrup, vanilla, orange zest, orange pulp, and maple flavoring (if using). Process briefly to mix well; do not overmix.

6. Pulse in the chopped nuts very briefly so they remain intact.

7. Pour the batter into the prepared pan. Bake for 45 to 55 minutes, or until a toothpick inserted into the center comes out clean. Let cool for 2 hours in the pan on a rack. Cut and serve.

# Luscious Lemon Layer Cake

*Lemon is a refreshing treat any time of year, and great for special occasions. This spectacular dessert consists of three layers of lemon cake, tangy lemon filling, and a voluptuous lemon frosting. Make this recipe in three steps: Start with the frosting, followed by the lemon filling, and make the cake last. For best results, follow this recipe exactly.*

**[ YIELD: One triple-layer 8-inch cake • EQUIPMENT NEEDED: Any style blender and a food processor ]**

3 cups Lemon Crème Cheese Frosting (page 180) or Lemon Buttercream Frosting (page 176)

**LEMON FILLING**
2 lemons
Zest of 1 orange
¼ cup thick unsweetened coconut milk
1¼ cups Just Like Sugar Table Top natural chicory root sweetener (not Baking). I do not recommend erythritol for this recipe, as you may taste the crystals.
3 tablespoons melted coconut oil (place jar in lukewarm water to melt oil)
1 tablespoon agar flakes
¼ cup any unsweetened coconut milk, to cook agar

**CAKE**
2 cups plus 1 tablespoon Just Like Sugar Table Top natural chicory root sweetener (not Baking). A second choice is 2⅔ cups Organic Zero Erythritol.
2 cups plus 1 tablespoon medium-shredded unsweetened coconut flakes (not coconut flour)
¼ cup arrowroot powder
½ teaspoon baking powder
½ teaspoon baking soda
¼ teaspoon unprocessed salt
Zest of 2½ to 3 lemons
⅓ cup freshly squeezed lemon juice
5 large eggs, at room temperature
2 teaspoons pure vanilla extract

1. Make the lemon frosting.
2. For the filling: Zest both lemons into a small bowl. Place half of the zest in a blender, and set aside the rest for a final garnish. Cut away the remaining outer peel and pith from both lemons with a knife. Slice both lemons and remove any seeds with the tip of a knife. Place the lemon slices into any style blender.
3. Add to the blender the orange zest, coconut milk, and sweetener. Blend well until completely liquefied. Add the coconut oil slowly and blend until smooth.
4. In a shallow nonstick pan over medium heat, stir the agar into the ¼ cup of coconut milk. Cook and stir gently for 2 to 3 minutes, until it is bubbling and gummy, and the flakes begin to dissolve. Add the agar mixture to the blender immediately and blend well to remove any lumps. Pour the filling into a bowl and refrigerate for 1 to 2 hours to thicken.
5. For the cake: Preheat the oven to 350°F. Cut parchment paper circles to fit three 8-inch round cake pans, grease the paper, and dust with coconut flour or arrowroot powder.

**continues . . .**

6. In a dry food processor fitted with the "S" blade, grind the sweetener to a very fine powder.

7. Add the shredded coconut to the sweetener in the food processor. Spin it for a minute until a very fine powder. Open the lid, stir the bottom, replace the lid, and grind again until the powder is uniformly fine.

8. To the ingredients in the food processor, add the arrowroot, baking powder, baking soda, and salt. Mix well and pour into a large mixing bowl.

9. Place in the empty food processor the lemon zest, lemon juice, eggs, and vanilla. Mix well.

10. Pour the wet ingredients into the dry mixture. Stir briefly with a spoon or large whisk.

11. Pour the batter into the three prepared baking pans. Bake at 350°F for 30 to 35 minutes, or until a toothpick inserted into the center comes out clean. Let cool for 1 hour in the pan on a rack, then chill the cake layers in the pans for 30 minutes. This is a delicate cake and frosts more easily when chilled.

12. To assemble: Place one cake layer on a serving platter. Tuck a few parchment paper strips under the edges to keep the platter clean. Spread it with half of the lemon filling. Repeat with the second cake layer, spreading it with the remaining filling. Place the third cake layer on top. Smooth the edges of the filling on the sides and remove any leakage so the sides are smooth. Spread the lemon frosting on the top and sides of the cake. Garnish with the reserved lemon zest. Serve chilled.

# Poppy-Seed Hot Fudge Sundae Cake

*I have a weakness for Poppy-Seed Hot Fudge Sundae Cake. Never heard of it? Well, it's a traditional old-world poppy-seed cake adapted from my friend Merle's grandmother—all the way from Eastern Europe via Rudi's Bakery. It's easy to make, not to mention rich and moist. Serve it with 1-Minute Whipped Crème Topping (page 173), Chocolate Sauce (page 189), or Chocolate Crème Cheese Frosting (page 181) and a few slices of banana. For the most delicious flavor and texture, please follow this recipe exactly.*

**[ YIELD: One 9- or 10-inch Bundt cake or two 9 by 5-inch loaves • EQUIPMENT NEEDED: A food processor ]**

1¾ cups Just Like Sugar Table Top natural chicory root sweetener (not Baking). A second choice is 2⅓ cups Organic Zero Erythritol.
2½ cups medium-shredded unsweetened coconut flakes (not coconut flour)
½ cup arrowroot powder
1½ teaspoons baking soda
¼ teaspoon unprocessed salt
1 teaspoon nutritional yeast (optional)
5 large eggs, at room temperature, separated
1 teaspoon pure vanilla extract
¾ cup unsweetened medium to thick coconut milk
Zest of 1 lemon
2 tablespoons freshly squeezed lemon juice
1 teaspoon apple cider vinegar
½ cup poppy seeds

1. Preheat the oven to 350°F. Grease and dust with coconut flour or arrowroot powder a 9- or 10-inch Bundt pan or line two 9 by 5-inch loaf pans with parchment paper so it hangs over the sides for easy removal. In a dry food processor fitted with the "S" blade, grind the sweetener to a very fine powder.
2. Add the shredded coconut to the sweetener in the food processor. Spin it for a minute until a very fine powder. Open the lid, stir the bottom, replace the lid, and grind again until the powder is uniformly fine.
3. To the ingredients in the food processor, add the arrowroot, baking soda, salt, and nutritional yeast (if using). Mix well, pour into a large mixing bowl, and set aside.
4. Place in the empty food processor the egg yolks, vanilla, coconut milk, lemon zest, lemon juice, vinegar, and poppy seeds. Mix well and then let the mixture sit while you beat the egg whites.
5. In a medium-size mixing bowl, beat the egg whites until stiff but not dry.
6. Pour the wet mixture from the food processor into the dry mixture. Stir briefly to form a smooth batter.
7. Fold the beaten egg whites gently into the batter in three parts. Fold; do not stir.

**continues . . .**

8. Pour the batter into the baking pan(s). Bake for 40 to 50 minutes, or until a toothpick inserted into the center comes out clean. Don't peek! Let cool for 10 minutes in the pan. For a Bundt pan, pick up the cake pan with hot pads, and gently move the pan from side to side to see whether the cake is loose. If it is sticking, carefully insert a plastic knife to loosen the cake around the center tube and sides. Then gently invert the cake onto a serving plate or rack and continue to let cool 30 minutes. For loaf pans, let cool 10 minutes and transfer the cake from the pans to a rack to cool for an additional 30 minutes.

# Red Velvet Cake or Cupcakes

*This cake is a luscious deep red color because it includes beets. I think it's even yummier than my mom's. It is moist and very tasty with either basic Crème Cheese Frosting (page 179) or Raspberry Crème Cheese Frosting (page 180). It took twelve trials for me to finally get this recipe's rich burgundy color and velvety texture. And let me tell you, that's a lot of beets! So, in any event, I hope you truly enjoy it. For best results, follow this recipe exactly.*

**[ YIELD: One double-layer 8-inch round cake or 12 regular cupcakes • EQUIPMENT NEEDED: A food processor; any style blender; and a digital scale, as apples and beets vary in size ]**

1¼ cups Just Like Sugar Table Top natural chicory root sweetener (not Baking). A second choice is 1⅔ cups Organic Zero Erythritol.

1¼ cups medium-shredded unsweetened coconut flakes (not coconut flour)

¼ cup arrowroot powder

½ teaspoon baking powder

¼ teaspoon unprocessed salt

1 teaspoon nutritional yeast (optional)

1 tablespoon pure cacao powder

1 large beet, cubed and lightly steamed (170 grams)

4 large eggs, at room temperature

¼ tart apple, unpeeled, cored, and cut into chunks (50 grams)

1 tablespoon pure vanilla extract

½ teaspoon almond extract

1 tablespoon *raw* yacón syrup (optional, for a caramel flavor)

1. Preheat the oven to 350°F (if you want your cake or cupcakes to dome, follow the instructions on page 27). Grease and lightly dust with coconut flour or arrowroot powder two 8-inch round cake pans or a 12-cupcake pan.

2. In a dry food processor fitted with the "S" blade, grind the sweetener to a very fine powder.

3. Add the shredded coconut to the sweetener in the food processor. Spin it for a minute until a very fine powder. Open the lid, stir the bottom, replace the lid, and grind again until the powder is uniformly fine.

4. To the ingredients in the food processor, add the arrowroot, baking powder, salt, nutritional yeast, and cacao powder. Mix well and pour into a large mixing bowl.

5. For the wet ingredients, it is better to use a blender for a smooth red color. Place in the blender the beet, eggs, apple, vanilla, almond extract, and yacón syrup (if using). Blend very well until the beet and apple are liquefied and smooth.

6. Pour the wet ingredients into the dry ingredients. Stir briefly until smooth.

7. Pour the batter into the prepared baking pan(s). Bake cupcakes for 20 to 25 minutes, or 8-inch layers for 25 to 35 minutes, until a toothpick inserted into the center comes out clean. Let cool completely in the pan(s) on a rack.

**variation Red Velvet Mini-Cupcakes:** Follow the recipe above, using a 24-compartment mini muffin tin. Bake the mini cupcakes for 14 to 18 minutes. Let cool for 15 minutes in the pan, and then transfer to a rack or serving plate.

# Spicy Carrot Ginger Cake

*This Carrot Ginger Cake is moist and alive with flavor. Fresh carrot, apple, and nuts add whole-food nutrition and keep the cake moist. It goes perfectly with basic Crème Cheese Frosting (page 179) or Orange Buttercream Frosting (page 176). For the most delicious flavor and texture, follow this recipe exactly.*

**[ YIELD: One 9 by 13-inch sheet cake or one double-layer 8-inch round cake • EQUIPMENT NEEDED: A food processor and a digital scale, as carrots and apples vary in size ]**

1⅓ cups Just Like Sugar Table Top natural chicory root sweetener (not Baking). A second choice is 1¾ cups Organic Zero Erythritol.

1⅓ cups medium-shredded unsweetened coconut flakes (not coconut flour)

¼ cup arrowroot powder

1 teaspoon baking soda

1 teaspoon baking powder

½ teaspoon unprocessed salt

1 teaspoon nutritional yeast (optional)

2 teaspoons ground cinnamon

¼ teaspoon grated nutmeg

¼ teaspoon ground cloves

¼ teaspoon ground allspice

½ cup chopped nuts, soaked if possible (see page 10)

½ cup raisins (optional; these are high in sugars)

2½ carrots, cut into 1-inch pieces (250 grams)

4 large eggs, at room temperature

½ tart apple, unpeeled, cored, and cut into chunks (100 grams)

Zest of 1 orange

2 inches fresh ginger, chopped or grated (about 20 grams)

1 tablespoon pure vanilla extract

½ teaspoon maple flavoring (optional)

1 tablespoon *raw* yacón syrup (optional, for a caramel flavor)

1. Preheat the oven to 350°F. Grease and lightly dust with coconut flour or arrowroot powder one 9 by 13-inch pan or two 8-inch round cake pans.

2. In a dry food processor fitted with the "S" blade, grind the sweetener to a very fine powder.

3. Add the shredded coconut to the sweetener in the food processor. Spin it for a minute until a very fine powder. Open the lid, stir the bottom, replace the lid, and grind again until the powder is uniformly fine.

4. To the ingredients in the food processor, add the arrowroot, baking soda, baking powder, salt, nutritional yeast, cinnamon, nutmeg, cloves, and allspice. Mix well and pour into a large mixing bowl. Add the nuts and raisins (if using) to the bowl, and stir.

**continues . . .**

## Spicy Carrot Ginger Cake (continued)

5. Place in the empty food processor the carrots, eggs, apple, orange zest, ginger, vanilla, maple flavoring (if using), and yacón syrup (if using). Mix well, until the carrot and apple are well liquefied.

6. Pour the wet ingredients into the dry mixture. Stir briefly to incorporate.

7. Pour the batter into the prepared baking pan(s). Bake for 35 to 40 minutes, or until a toothpick inserted into the center comes out clean. Let cool for 2 hours in the pan(s) or on a rack.

> **variation Spicy Carrot Ginger Mini Cupcakes:** Follow the recipe above, using a 24-compartment mini muffin tin. Bake the mini cupcakes for 14 to 18 minutes. Let cool for 15 minutes in the pan, and then transfer to a rack or serving plate.

# Strawberry Shortcake

*A luscious treat in the summer or any time of year, this is a triple-layer Strawberry Shortcake you won't forget. The Paleo version uses coconut sponge cake, which is light, easy, and absorbs the strawberry juices perfectly. Make it in three steps: First blend the Whipped Crème Topping, then bake the cake, and last, prepare the strawberries. For best results, follow this recipe exactly.*

**[ YIELD: One triple-layer 8-inch round shortcake with all the trimmings • EQUIPMENT NEEDED: Any style blender, a food processor, and either a standing or handheld mixer ]**

3 cups 5-Minute Whipped Crème Topping (page 174)
1 recipe White Coconut Sponge Cake (page 47)
2 pounds fresh strawberries
¼ cup Just Like Sugar Table Top natural chicory root sweetener (not Baking). A second choice is ⅓ cup Organic Zero Erythritol.
2 tablespoons filtered water

1. Prepare the 5-Minute Whipped Crème Topping.
2. Prepare the White Coconut Sponge Cake batter and bake in three 8-inch round cake pans.
3. Let the cake cool in the pan for 15 minutes, cover with a towel, and refrigerate to keep the layers firm.
4. Wash and drain the strawberries. Take about six of the prettiest strawberries, cut them in half, and reserve for the top of the cake. In a medium-size mixing bowl, dice or crush one-quarter of the remaining strawberries (it's easy with a pastry cutter). Slice the rest of the strawberries very thinly and place them in the mixing bowl. Sprinkle with the sweetener and water, and stir to macerate. Chill until ready to assemble the shortcake.
5. To assemble: Place one cake layer on a large serving plate. Spread it with one-third of the macerated strawberries and juices. Make sure the berries lie flat, so the next layer of cake will be stable. Spread one-third of the Whipped Crème on top. Place the second cake layer on top and press flat. Repeat the above process. Place the third cake layer on top. Spread it with the last third of the Whipped Crème and spoon the rest of the macerated strawberries on top. Garnish the top with the reserved halved strawberries. Chill the cake until serving. It is best to enjoy immediately, as shortcakes are delicate.

# Tiramisu

Tiramisù *means "pick-me-up" in Italian. A favorite dessert worldwide, it definitely does that, with layers of luscious pastry cream, espresso syrup, and chocolate. This Paleo version is every bit as delicious as the cake you'll taste in Rome or Florence. As tiramisu is traditionally served in squares, I use two 8 by 11-inch tart pans with removable bottoms for the cake, and serve it on a rectangular platter. It's worth the investment in pans and platter, as everyone goes crazy for this dessert and I make it a lot. However, if you don't have the rectangular setup, it comes out just as good with two 8- or 9-inch square cake pans. For the best flavor and texture, follow this recipe exactly.*

**[ YIELD: 12 to 16 servings • EQUIPMENT NEEDED: A food processor and any style blender ]**

1 recipe Vanilla Pastry Cream with Coconut (page 186), Vanilla Pastry Cream with Cashews (page 185), or Chocolate Bavarian Cream Filling (page 100)

1 recipe Yellow Birthday Cake (page 31)

1 tablespoon pure cacao powder

**ESPRESSO SYRUP**

½ cup Just Like Sugar Table Top natural chicory root sweetener (not Baking). A second choice is ⅔ cup Organic Zero Erythritol.

1 cup warm filtered water

2 teaspoons instant decaffeinated coffee powder or crystals

1 teaspoon maple flavoring (optional)

1. Make the pastry cream, pour it into a bowl, and chill well.

2. Make the Yellow Birthday Cake, baking it in two 8 by 11-inch tart pans with removable bottoms, or two 8- or 9-inch round cake pans. Let cool completely in the pans.

3. For the espresso syrup: In a 1-cup glass measuring cup or a small dish, stir together the sweetener, warm water, coffee powder, and maple flavoring (if using). Stir until the crystals dissolve. (Do *not* add the traditional 1 tablespoon of Sambuca [anise liqueur] that is part of the traditional recipe—it is not Paleo.)

4. To assemble: Remove one cake layer from its baking pan and flip it onto a serving dish. This is easier with a removable-bottom pan. Brush it with half of the espresso syrup. With a fork, poke holes in the cake so it can soak up lots of syrup like a sponge. Spread evenly with half of the chilled pastry cream (smooth out so it is flat).

5. Place the second layer of cake on top of this, soak it with the rest of the espresso syrup, and spread evenly with the rest of the pastry cream.

6. Garnish the top with a dusting of cacao powder. (It's easy to dust with a fine-mesh tea strainer.) *Mamma mia!* I'm in Italy!

# Tres Leches Cake

*The original Latino Tres Leches Cake is a buttery cake soaked in evaporated milk and condensed milk, and covered with whipped cream. I think this dairy-free Paleo version is incredible—even better than the original (shh... don't tell anyone!). And while it looks complicated, it's really easy— I promise. Just soak a double-layer cake in sweet coconut milk and top with 5-Minute Whipped Crème Topping. Follow this recipe exactly and you'll be pleased with the results.*

[ YIELD: One double-layer 8-inch round or one 8 by 11-inch rectangular cake • EQUIPMENT NEEDED: A food processor, any style blender, and a large serving platter with edges that curve upward a bit, to hold juices ]

3 cups 5-Minute Whipped
Crème Topping(page 174)
1 recipe Yellow Birthday Cake
(page 31)

**SWEET COCONUT MILK**
1½ cups unsweetened
coconut milk (thinner will
absorb better into the cake)
1 teaspoon pure vanilla extract
¾ cup Just Like Sugar Table
Top natural chicory root
sweetener (not Baking). I do
not recommend erythritol,
as you may taste the crystals.
2 to 3 tablespoons coconut oil
Pinch of unprocessed salt
2 tablespoons *raw* yacón syrup
(optional, for drizzling as
you serve)

1. Make the 5-Minute Whipped Crème Topping. Set aside at room temperature.
2. Prepare the Yellow Birthday Cake, baking in two 8-inch round cake pans or two 8 by 11-inch rectangular sheet pans. Let cool for 1 hour in the pan, then chill until ready to assemble.
3. For the sweet coconut milk: Place the coconut milk, vanilla, sweetener, coconut oil, and salt in any style blender. Blend until smooth.
4. To assemble the Tres Leches cake: With a thin knife, release one cake layer from its pan and place it on a large serving platter. Pierce it all over with the tines of a fork, and slowly pour half of the Sweet Coconut Milk over the cake, allowing it to soak in for 30 minutes to 8 hours or overnight. Spread one-third of the Whipped Crème over this layer. Keep the cake chilled, if possible, so it will stay firm.
5. Repeat with the second layer: Place it on top, poke holes gently with tines of a fork, and slowly pour the remaining Sweet Coconut Milk over it, allowing it to soak in for several hours or overnight. Frost the top and sides of the cake with the remaining Whipped Crème. Serve cold with a drizzle of *raw* yacón syrup (if using), for a flavor of *dulce de leche*. *Muy delicioso!*

# Whole Apple Spice Cake with Orange Maple Glaze

*This is a rich cake made with whole apple, spices, and nuts. Easy to make in the food processor, it is a dense and satisfying breakfast, lunchbox treat, snack, or dessert. The soft texture and sweet apple flavor made this cake a favorite with my tasters. The easy Orange Maple Glaze is optional and adds a luscious sheen on top of the cake. You can also skip the glaze and serve with Orange Crème Cheese Frosting (page 180) or Orange Buttercream Frosting (page 176). For the most outstanding flavor and texture, please follow this recipe exactly.*

[ YIELD: One 9 by 13-inch sheet cake or one double-layer 8-inch round cake • EQUIPMENT NEEDED: A food processor and a digital scale, as apples vary in size ]

**CAKE**

1⅔ cups Just Like Sugar Table Top natural chicory root sweetener (not Baking). A second choice is 2¼ cups Organic Zero Erythritol.

1⅔ cups medium-shredded unsweetened coconut flakes (not coconut flour)

¼ cup arrowroot powder

½ teaspoon unprocessed salt

2 teaspoons ground cinnamon

½ teaspoon ground cloves

½ teaspoon grated nutmeg

½ teaspoon ground allspice

2 teaspoons baking soda

1 teaspoon baking powder

4 large eggs, at room temperature

2 large tart apples, unpeeled, cored, and cut into large pieces (400 grams)

1 teaspoon pure vanilla extract

Zest of 1 orange

2 inches fresh ginger, chopped or grated (about 20 grams)

2 tablespoons *raw* yacón syrup (optional)

1 teaspoon maple flavoring (optional)

1½ cups coarsely chopped nuts, soaked if possible (see page 10)

½ cup raisins (optional; these are high in sugar)

**ORANGE MAPLE GLAZE**

2 tablespoons boiling filtered water

3 tablespoons Just Like Sugar Table Top natural chicory root sweetener (not Baking)

Zest of ½ orange

1 tablespoon *raw* yacón syrup

¼ teaspoon maple flavoring

1. Preheat the oven to 350°F. Grease a 9 by 13-inch pan or two 8-inch round cake pans. Dust with coconut flour or arrowroot powder.

2. In a dry food processor fitted with the "S" blade, grind the sweetener to a very fine powder.

3. Add the shredded coconut to the sweetener in the food processor. Spin it for a minute until a very fine powder. Open the lid, stir the bottom, replace the lid, and grind again until the powder is uniformly fine.

4. To the ingredients in the food processor, add the arrowroot, salt, cinnamon, cloves, nutmeg, allspice, baking soda, and baking powder. Mix well.

5. To the dry ingredients in the food processor, add the eggs, apple, vanilla, orange zest, ginger, yacón syrup, and maple flavoring (if using). Mix well but briefly until the apple is

**continues . . .**

mostly liquefied. A few apple chunks are yummy. Then pulse in the nuts and raisins (if using) so they remain in large pieces.

6. Pour the batter into the prepared baking pan(s). Bake for 45 to 50 minutes.

7. While the cake bakes, prepare the Orange Maple Glaze (if using): In a 1-cup glass measure or a small heatproof cup, place the boiling water followed by the sweetener. Stir with a small whisk or spoon until the sweetener dissolves. Then add the orange zest, yacón syrup, and maple flavoring. Stir well.

8. After the cake has been baking for 35 minutes, open the oven door and pour the glaze on top of the cake. You should hear it sizzle—that's a good sign. Then finish baking for the full 45 to 50 minutes. The glaze will bake into a sweet crust. Test for doneness; a toothpick inserted into the center should come out clean. Let cool for 2 hours in the pan on a rack before cutting.

# White Coconut Sponge Cake

*This white sponge cake is so moist and flavorful, no one will ever guess it's completely grain-free and Paleo (in fact, I recommend not telling people until they gush over how amazing it is). This is the perfect cake for birthdays, weddings, or other special occasions. It is very flavorful with Chocolate Crème Cheese Frosting (page 181) or Raspberry Buttercream Frosting (page 176) but, of course, feel free to play by pairing it with any of the fillings and frostings in this book. For best results, follow the recipe exactly.*

**[ YIELD: One triple-layer 8-inch cake • EQUIPMENT NEEDED: A food processor ]**

Frosting of your choice
2 cups Just Like Sugar Table Top natural chicory root sweetener (not Baking). A second choice is 2⅔ cups Organic Zero Erythritol.
2 cups medium-shredded unsweetened coconut flakes (not coconut flour)
6 tablespoons arrowroot powder
1 teaspoon baking soda
1 teaspoon baking powder
½ teaspoon unprocessed salt
1 cup thick unsweetened coconut milk, or ½ cup thin
1 teaspoon pure vanilla extract
½ teaspoon almond extract
10 large egg whites

1. Prepare the frosting of your choice.
2. Preheat the oven to 350°F. Cut parchment paper circles to line three 8-inch round cake pans.
3. In a dry food processor fitted with the "S" blade, grind the sweetener to a very fine powder.
4. Add the shredded coconut to the sweetener in the food processor. Spin it for a minute until a very fine powder. Open the lid, stir the bottom, replace the lid, and grind again until the powder is uniformly fine.
5. To the ingredients in the food processor, add the arrowroot, baking soda, baking powder, and salt. Mix well, pour into a large mixing bowl, and set aside.
6. Place in the empty food processor the coconut milk, vanilla, and almond extract. Mix well and then let the mixture sit while you beat the egg whites.
7. With an electric mixer in a medium-size mixing bowl, beat the egg whites at medium speed until foamy. Gradually increase to high speed until the peaks are soft but not dry.
8. Pour the wet ingredients from the food processor into the dry mixture. Mix the batter briefly and thoroughly.
9. With a rubber spatula, gently fold the beaten egg whites into the batter in three parts.
10. Pour the batter into the prepared cake pans and spread it out flat. Bake for 23 to 28 minutes, or until a toothpick inserted into the middle of the cake comes out clean. Don't peek or the cake may fall. Check on it after 20 minutes, as the cake can easily dry out. Let cool for about 30 minutes in the pan on a rack.

# Applesauce Cupcakes

*These Applesauce Cupcakes come alive with flavor from the fresh apple and ginger. Instead of cooking the applesauce, you'll grind whole raw apples in a food processor. Apples are high in pectin, so the result is fluffy, moist cupcakes that hold together with a delicious flavor. I suggest trying these with Crème Cheese Frosting (page 179) or Orange Buttercream Frosting (page 176). For the best texture and flavor, follow the recipe exactly.*

**[ YIELD: 24 mini cupcakes or 10 regular cupcakes • EQUIPMENT NEEDED: A food processor and a digital scale, as apples vary in size ]**

1 tablespoon finely ground golden flaxseeds

3 large eggs, at room temperature

⅔ cup Just Like Sugar Table Top natural chicory root sweetener (not Baking). A second choice is ⅞ cup Organic Zero Erythritol.

⅔ cup medium-shredded unsweetened coconut flakes (not coconut flour)

2 tablespoons arrowroot powder

½ teaspoon baking soda

⅛ teaspoon unprocessed salt

1 tablespoon ground cinnamon

¼ teaspoon grated nutmeg

¾ tart apple, unpeeled, cored, and cut into ½-inch pieces (130 grams)

Zest of 1 orange

1 inch fresh ginger, chopped or grated, or ¼ teaspoon ground ginger

½ tablespoon pure vanilla extract

½ cup chopped nuts, soaked if possible (see page 10)

1. Preheat the oven to 350°F. Grease and flour or line with cupcake liners twenty-four compartments of a mini cupcake pan or ten compartments of a regular cupcake pan. See cupcake rising tips page 27.

2. In a bowl, stir the ground flaxseeds with the eggs and let them soak for 10 minutes.

3. In a dry food processor fitted with the "S" blade, grind the sweetener to a very fine powder.

4. Add the shredded coconut to the sweetener in the food processor. Spin it for a minute until a very fine powder. Open the lid, stir the bottom, replace the lid, and grind again until the powder is uniformly fine.

5. To the ingredients in the food processor, add the arrowroot, baking soda, salt, cinnamon, and nutmeg. Mix well.

6. To the dry ingredients in the food processor, add the flaxseed mixture, apple, orange zest, ginger, and vanilla. Mix briefly and thoroughly until the apple is liquefied.

7. Add the nuts and pulse briefly so they remain in large pieces.

8. Pour the batter into the prepared baking pan. Bake mini cupcakes for 14 to 18 minutes, regular cupcakes for 18 to 20 minutes. Don't peek!

9. Let cool for 1 hour in the pan, then frost and serve.

# Carrot Mini Cupcakes

*These carrot cupcakes are fluffy, sweet, and spicy, just like my mother's. Pure shredded coconut gives them a moist texture that's low in carbs, grain-free, and—dare I say—mightily divine. They pair well with Cinnamon Crème Cheese Frosting (page 180) or basic Crème Cheese Frosting (page 179). For best results, follow this recipe exactly.*

**[ YIELD: 24 mini cupcakes or 10 regular cupcakes • EQUIPMENT NEEDED: A food processor and a digital scale, as carrots and apples vary in size ]**

1 tablespoon finely ground golden flaxseeds

3 large eggs, at room temperature

¾ cup Just Like Sugar Table Top natural chicory root sweetener (not Baking). A second choice is 1 cup Organic Zero Erythritol.

¾ cup medium-shredded unsweetened coconut flakes (not coconut flour)

1 tablespoon arrowroot powder

½ teaspoon baking soda

⅛ teaspoon unprocessed salt

2 teaspoons ground cinnamon

¼ teaspoon grated nutmeg

¼ teaspoon ground cloves

¼ teaspoon ground allspice

1 raw carrot (100 grams) cut into 1-inch chunks, including peel

¼ tart apple, unpeeled, cored (45 grams)

Zest of ½ orange

1 inch fresh ginger, chopped or grated, or ¼ teaspoon ground

½ tablespoon pure vanilla extract

¼ cup chopped nuts, soaked if possible (see page 10)

1. Preheat the oven to 350°F (if you want your cupcakes to dome, follow the instructions on page 27). Grease and flour or line with cupcake liners twenty-four compartments of a mini cupcake pan or ten compartments of a regular cupcake pan.

2. In a bowl, stir the flaxseeds with the eggs and let them soak for 10 minutes.

3. In a dry food processor fitted with the "S" blade, grind the sweetener until it is a very fine powder.

4. Add the shredded coconut to the sweetener in the food processor. Spin it for a minute until a very fine powder. Open the lid, stir the bottom, replace the lid, and grind again until the powder is uniformly fine.

5. To the ingredients in the food processor, add the arrowroot, baking soda, salt, cinnamon, nutmeg, cloves, and allspice. Mix well.

6. To the dry ingredients in the food processor, add the flaxseed mixture, carrot, apple, orange zest, ginger, and vanilla. Mix briefly and thoroughly until the carrot pulp is mostly liquefied and evenly distributed.

7. Add the nuts and pulse briefly so they remain in large chunks.

8. Fill the cupcake pans about three-quarters full. Bake mini cupcakes for 12 to 14 minutes, regular cupcakes for 18 to 20 minutes. Do not peek!

9. Let cool for 1 hour in the pan. Frost and serve. Leftover cupcakes will keep at room temperature for several days, or longer in the refrigerator.

# Chocolate Cupcakes

*When I feel a need for chocolate cupcakes, I go for these dark beauties. They have a rich, chocolaty flavor and use both 100% cacao and carob for a deep mahogany color. Beaten egg whites give them a better rise and smoother texture. Frost them with Chocolate Crème Cheese Frosting (page 181), Chocolate Buttercream Frosting (page 177), or Chocolate Espresso Buttercream Frosting (page 178). For best results, follow this recipe exactly.*

**[ YIELD: 12 regular cupcakes • EQUIPMENT NEEDED: A food processor; any style blender; a standing mixer or handheld mixer; and a digital scale, as apples vary in size ]**

2¼ cups Just Like Sugar Table Top natural chicory root sweetener (not Baking). A second choice is 3 cups Organic Zero Erythritol.

1½ cups medium-shredded unsweetened coconut flakes (not coconut flour)

¼ cup arrowroot powder

¾ cup pure cacao powder

¼ cup carob powder

1 teaspoon baking soda

¼ teaspoon plus a pinch unprocessed salt

6 large eggs, at room temperature, separated

½ tart apple, unpeeled, cored and cut into chunks (75 grams)

Zest of 1 orange

1 tablespoon pure vanilla extract

1 teaspoon apple cider vinegar

1½ cups thick unsweetened coconut milk, or ¾ cup thin

1 tablespoon *raw* yacón syrup (for caramel flavor)

1. Preheat the oven to 350°F (if you want your cupcakes to dome, follow the instructions on page 27). Line a twelve-cupcake pan, or grease and dust with cacao powder.

2. In a dry food processor fitted with the "S" blade, grind the sweetener to a very fine powder.

3. Add the shredded coconut to the sweetener in the food processor. Spin it for a minute until a very fine powder. Open the lid, stir the bottom, replace the lid, and grind again until the powder is uniformly fine.

4. To the ingredients in the food processor, add the arrowroot, cacao powder, carob powder, baking soda, and salt. Mix well until the color is consistent, and pour into a large mixing bowl.

5. A blender is best for the wet ingredients. Place in any style blender the egg yolks, apple, orange zest, vanilla, vinegar, coconut milk, and yacón syrup. Blend until the apple pieces are completely liquefied, and set aside.

6. In a medium-size mixing bowl or a standing mixer, beat the egg whites until stiff but not dry, just until peaks form when you lift the beaters.

7. Add the apple mixture to the dry mixture in the large mixing bowl. Mix briefly but well enough so no lumps remain. Then fold in the beaten egg whites in three parts. Fold slowly and do not stir.

**continues . . .**

8. Pour the batter into the prepared cupcake pan. Bake for 20 to 22 minutes, or
   until a toothpick inserted into the center comes out clean. Let cool for 30
   minutes in the pan on a rack.

> **variation German Chocolate Cupcakes:** Frost with Coconut Frosting (page 183).

# Fluffy Lemon Cupcakes

*These Fluffy Lemon Cupcakes are delicate and light, filled with tangy citrus flavor. They're perfect when paired with Lemon Buttercream Frosting (page 176) or Lemon Crème Cheese Frosting (page 180). For perfect results, follow this recipe exactly.*

**[ YIELD: 12 regular cupcakes • EQUIPMENT NEEDED: A food processor ]**

1⅔ cups Just Like Sugar Table Top natural chicory root sweetener (not Baking). A second choice is 2¼ cups Organic Zero Erythritol.

1⅔ cups medium-shredded unsweetened coconut flakes (not coconut flour)

3 tablespoons arrowroot powder

½ teaspoon baking powder

½ teaspoon baking soda

¼ teaspoon unprocessed salt

Zest of 2 lemons

¼ cup freshly squeezed lemon juice

4 large eggs, at room temperature

1½ teaspoons pure vanilla extract

1. Preheat the oven to 350°F (if you want your cupcakes to dome, follow the instructions on page 27). Grease a twelve-cupcake pan and dust with coconut flour or arrowroot powder.

2. In a dry food processor fitted with the "S" blade, grind the sweetener to a very fine powder.

3. Add the shredded coconut to the sweetener in the food processor. Spin it for a minute until a very fine powder. Open the lid, stir the bottom, replace the lid, and grind again until the powder is uniformly fine.

4. To the ingredients in the food processor, add the arrowroot, baking powder, baking soda, and salt. Mix well.

5. To the dry ingredients in the food processor, add the lemon zest, lemon juice, eggs, and vanilla. Mix briefly.

6. Pour the batter into the prepared baking pan. Bake for 20 to 24 minutes, or until a toothpick inserted into the center comes out clean. Let cool completely on a rack before removing from the pan. Frost and enjoy!

# Gingerbread Cupcakes

*It doesn't need to be the holidays to enjoy gingerbread. You can enjoy these cupcakes any time of year. They are moist, have a nice ginger zing to them, and are alive with flavor. They taste delish with Maple Crème Cheese Frosting (page 180) or Salted Caramel Buttercream Frosting (page 176). For the best flavor and texture, follow this recipe exactly.*

**[ YIELD: 12 regular cupcakes or one 9-inch square cake • EQUIPMENT NEEDED: A food processor and digital scale, as apples vary in size ]**

3 tablespoons finely ground dark flaxseeds

3 large eggs, at room temperature

1¼ Just Like Sugar Table Top natural chicory root sweetener (not Baking). A second choice is 1⅔ cups Organic Zero Erythritol.

1¾ cups medium-shredded unsweetened coconut flakes (not coconut flour)

¼ cup arrowroot powder

1 teaspoon baking soda

1 tablespoon carob powder (optional, for rich flavor and dark color)

2 teaspoons ground cinnamon

2 teaspoons ground ginger

½ teaspoon ground cloves

¾ teaspoon unprocessed salt

¼ cup *raw* yacón syrup (optional)

2 teaspoons pure vanilla extract

1 teaspoon apple cider vinegar or freshly squeezed lemon juice

¾ tart apple, unpeeled, cored, and cut into chunks (about 150 grams)

½ teaspoon maple flavoring (optional)

1 cup chopped nuts, soaked if possible (see page 10)

1. Preheat the oven to 350°F (if you want your cupcakes or cake to dome, follow the instructions on page 27). Grease a twelve-cupcake pan or 9-inch square pan.

2. In a bowl, stir the ground flaxseeds with the eggs and let them soak for 10 minutes.

3. In a dry food processor fitted with the "S" blade, grind the sweetener to a very fine powder.

4. Add the shredded coconut to the sweetener in the food processor. Spin it for a minute until a very fine powder. Open the lid, stir the bottom, replace the lid, and grind again until the powder is uniformly fine.

5. To the ingredients in the food processor, add the arrowroot, baking soda, carob powder (if using), cinnamon, ginger, cloves, and salt. Mix until the color is uniform.

6. To the dry ingredients in the food processor, add the flaxseed mixture, yacón syrup, vanilla, vinegar, apple, and maple flavoring (if using). Mix very briefly, just until the apple is liquefied.

7. Add the chopped nuts and pulse in very briefly, just a second or two. Pour into the prepared baking pan. Bake regular cupcakes for 20 to 25 minutes, a 9-inch square cake for 35 to 40 minutes, or until a toothpick inserted into the center comes out clean. Let cool for 1 hour in the pan.

*Cooking is like lovemaking. It should be
entered into with abandon or not at all.*
—HARRIET VAN HORNE

# MUFFINS AND BREADS

# Blueberry Muffins with Lemon Streusel Topping

*A classic comfort food for me, these Blueberry Muffins are sweet and fluffy. The lemon streusel topping gives a tart, crunchy addition to this tasty muffin. Or skip the streusel topping and serve with Lemon Crème Cheese Frosting (page 180), if you prefer. Because blueberries soften while baking and sometimes sink to the bottom, I've noticed that it's easier to use cupcake liners and frozen berries. For the best results, follow these instructions exactly.*

**[ YIELD: 12 regular muffins • EQUIPMENT NEEDED: A food processor ]**

**LEMON STREUSEL TOPPING**
1 tablespoon Just Like Sugar Table Top natural chicory root sweetener (not Baking)
Zest of 1 lemon
2 tablespoons medium-shredded unsweetened coconut flakes (not coconut flour)
3 tablespoons diced nuts, soaked if possible (see page 10)
¼ teaspoon grated nutmeg

**MUFFINS**
1 cup plus 2 tablespoons Just Like Sugar Table Top natural chicory root sweetener (not Baking). A second choice is 1½ cups Organic Zero Erythritol.
1 cup plus 2 tablespoons medium-shredded unsweetened coconut flakes (not coconut flour)
3 tablespoons arrowroot powder
½ teaspoon baking soda
¼ teaspoon baking powder
¼ teaspoon unprocessed salt
4 large eggs, at room temperature
2 teaspoons pure vanilla extract
¼ cup thick unsweetened coconut milk, or 2 tablespoons thin
1½ cups frozen blueberries (keep frozen until adding, to stay more intact while baking)

1. Preheat the oven to 350°F (if you want your muffins to dome, follow the instructions on page 27). Line a twelve-cupcake with cupcake liners. You definitely need the liners for this recipe.
2. Make the Lemon Streusel Topping (if using): In a small bowl, stir together the sweetener, lemon zest, coconut, nuts, and nutmeg.
3. For the muffins: In a dry food processor fitted with the "S" blade, grind the sweetener to a fine powder.
4. Add the shredded coconut to the sweetener in the food processor. Spin it for a minute until a very fine powder. Open the lid, stir the bottom, replace the lid, and grind again until the powder is uniformly fine.
5. To the ingredients in the food processor, add the arrowroot, baking soda, baking powder, and salt. Mix well and place a mixing bowl.
6. Place in the empty food processor the eggs, vanilla, and coconut milk, and mix well. Add the wet ingredients to the dry ingredients in the mixing bowl and stir briefly to incorporate. Place the frozen blueberries in last and stir gently until evenly distributed.
7. Fill the cupcake pan about three-quarters full. Sprinkle each with Lemon Streusel Topping (if using). Bake for 20 to 25 minutes, or until a toothpick inserted into the center comes out clean. Let cool completely in the pan on a rack before removing from the pan.

# Flax Muffins

*These spicy muffins are high-fiber, low-carb, nutritious, and totally tasty. Great for breakfast or a sweet pick-me-up, this recipe gives you a choice of three flavors: fresh apple, carrot, or sweet potato, so you can use what is available in your kitchen and suits your mood. These muffins are to die for with Apple Butter (page 187) or Maple Crème Cheese Frosting (page 180). For best results, follow this recipe exactly.*

**[ YIELD: 12 regular muffins • EQUIPMENT NEEDED: A food processor and a digital scale, as apples vary in size ]**

1 cup Just Like Sugar Table Top natural chicory root sweetener (not Baking). A second choice is 1⅓ cups Organic Zero Erythritol.

1¼ cups medium-shredded unsweetened coconut flakes (not coconut flour)

⅔ cup finely ground dark or golden flaxseeds, not soaked

1 teaspoon baking soda

½ teaspoon baking powder

¼ teaspoon unprocessed salt

2 teaspoons ground cinnamon

¼ teaspoon grated nutmeg

3 large eggs, at room temperature

1 teaspoon *raw* yacón syrup

2 teaspoons pure vanilla extract

1 teaspoon apple cider vinegar or freshly squeezed lemon juice

½ teaspoon maple flavoring (optional)

150 grams of your choice: fresh tart apple, unpeeled, cored, and cut into chunks; grated carrot; or (my personal favorite) grated sweet potato (about 1 cup). Or use a mixture of all three.

1 cup chopped nuts, soaked if possible (see page 10)

1. Preheat the oven to 350°F (if you want your muffins to dome, follow the instructions on page 27). Grease a twelve-cupcake pan.
2. In a dry food processor fitted with the "S" blade, grind the sweetener to a very fine powder.
3. Add the shredded coconut to the sweetener in the food processor. Spin it for a minute until a very fine powder. Open the lid, stir the bottom, replace the lid, and grind again until the powder is uniformly fine.
4. To the ingredients in the food processor, add the ground flaxseeds, baking soda, baking powder, salt, cinnamon, and nutmeg. Mix well.
5. To the dry ingredients in the food processor, add the eggs, yacón syrup, vanilla, vinegar, maple flavoring (if using), and your choice of apple, carrot, and/or sweet potato. Mix as briefly as possible, making sure that the apple, carrot, or sweet potato is liquefied.
6. Pour the batter into the prepared pan. Bake for 20 to 24 minutes, or until a toothpick inserted into the center comes out clean. Let cool for 45 minutes in the pan.

# Zucchini Muffins

*Zucchini muffins have always been one of my favorites, even before I went Paleo. Now with this recipe I get the best of both worlds. These muffins are super tasty either plain or with the added chocolate. Zucchini grows like crazy in my garden, and this is my favorite way to enjoy it. I like to serve this with Cinnamon Crème Cheese Frosting (page 180) or basic Coconut Buttercream Frosting (page 175). For the most delicious flavor and texture, follow this recipe exactly.*

[ YIELD: 12 regular muffins or 30 mini muffins • EQUIPMENT NEEDED: A food processor and a digital scale, as zucchini vary in size ]

**ZUCCHINI MUFFINS**
2 tablespoons finely ground golden flaxseeds
4 large eggs, at room temperature
1⅓ cup Just Like Sugar Table Top natural chicory root sweetener (not Baking). A second choice is 1¾ cups Wholesome Sweeteners Organic Zero Erythritol.
1¼ cups medium-shredded unsweetened coconut flakes (not coconut flour)
1 tablespoon arrowroot powder
1 teaspoon baking soda
½ teaspoon baking powder
¼ teaspoon unprocessed salt
2 teaspoons ground cinnamon
¼ teaspoon grated nutmeg
2 teaspoons pure vanilla extract
2 tablespoons *raw* yacón syrup
¾ cup coarsely grated fresh zucchini (200 grams)
1 cup coarsely chopped nuts, soaked if possible (see page 10)

1. Preheat the oven to 350°F (if you want your muffins to dome, follow the instructions on page 27). Grease a twelve-cupcake pan or twenty-four compartments of mini cupcake pans.
2. In a bowl, stir the ground flaxseeds with the eggs and let them soak for 10 minutes.
3. In a dry food processor fitted with the "S" blade, grind the sweetener to a very fine powder.
4. Add the shredded coconut to the sweetener in the food processor. Spin it for a minute until a very fine powder. Open the lid, stir the bottom, replace the lid, and grind again until the powder is uniformly fine.
5. To the ingredients in the food processor, add the arrowroot, baking soda, baking powder, salt, cinnamon, and nutmeg. Mix well.
6. To the dry ingredients in the food processor, add the flaxseed mixture, vanilla, and yacón syrup. Mix as briefly as possible.
7. Add the zucchini and nuts. Pulse very briefly, two to three times, so they remain in huge pieces, otherwise the zucchini will turn to mush.
8. Pour the batter into the prepared pan. Bake regular muffins for 20 to 25 minutes, mini muffins for 14 to 18 minutes, or until a toothpick inserted into the center comes out clean. Let cool for 30 minutes in the pan on a rack before removing from the pan.

**variation Chocolate Zucchini Muffins:** In step 3, add ⅓ cup more Just Like Sugar Table Top sweetener. A second choice is ½ cup more Organic Zero Erythritol. In step 5, add ¼ cup of pure cacao powder, and voilà! You've got chocolate zucchini muffins.

# Banana Bread

*This spice-filled recipe is easy and moist, with lots of cinnamon, nutmeg, and cardamom. I like banana bread in mini loaves. You can also bake it in two 8-inch round cake pans or a twelve-cupcake pan. Whatever size you choose, it is over-the-top delicious with the Banana Crème Cheese Frosting (page 180), Cinnamon Crème Cheese Frosting (page 180), or Banana Buttercream Frosting (page 176). For best results, follow this recipe exactly.*

**[ YIELD: 4 mini loaves • EQUIPMENT NEEDED: A food processor and a digital scale, as bananas vary in size ]**

1 tablespoon finely ground golden flaxseeds

4 large eggs, at room temperature

1½ cups Just Like Sugar Table Top natural chicory root sweetener (not Baking). A second choice is 2 cups Organic Zero Erythritol.

1½ cups medium-shredded unsweetened coconut flakes (not coconut flour)

3 tablespoons arrowroot powder

1 teaspoon baking soda

½ teaspoon baking powder

1 teaspoon nutritional yeast (optional)

¼ teaspoon unprocessed salt

2 teaspoons ground cinnamon

½ teaspoon grated nutmeg

¼ teaspoon ground cardamom

2 inches fresh ginger, chopped or grated (about 20 grams), or ¼ teaspoon ground

¾ cup mashed banana (250 grams)

Zest of ½ orange

1 tablespoon pure vanilla extract

¼ teaspoon maple flavoring (optional)

½ cup coarsely chopped nuts, soaked if possible (see page 10)

1. Preheat the oven to 350°F. Prepare four mini loaf pans about 5¾ by 3¼ inches by lining with strips of parchment paper, with a few inches hanging over the edges as handles for easy removal. Or use two 8-inch round cake pans, or a regular cupcake pan.

2. In a bowl, stir the flaxseeds with the eggs and let them soak for 10 minutes.

3. In a dry food processor fitted with the "S" blade, grind the sweetener to a fine powder.

4. Add the shredded coconut to the sweetener in the food processor. Spin it for a minute until a very fine powder. Open the lid, stir the bottom, replace the lid, and grind again until the powder is uniformly fine.

5. To the ingredients in the food processor, add the arrowroot, baking soda, baking powder, nutritional yeast (if using), salt, cinnamon, nutmeg, cardamom, and ginger. Mix well.

6. To the dry ingredients in the food processor, add the flaxseed mixture, banana, orange zest, vanilla, and maple flavoring (if using). Process briefly until the banana is liquefied. Pulse in the nuts briefly so they remain intact.

7. Pour the batter into the prepared pans. Bake mini muffins for 30 to 45 minutes, 8-inch layers for 30 to 40 minutes, or regular cupcakes for 20 for 23 minutes, or until a toothpick inserted into the center comes out clean. Let cool in the pan before removing.

# Cranberry Nut Bread

*Cranberry Bread is a classic for the holidays and any time of year. This one is moist and alive with a cranberry-orange flavor. Enjoy it plain or with Cinnamon Crème Cheese Frosting (page 180). For the most outstanding flavor and texture, follow this recipe exactly.*

[ **YIELD: One 9 by 5-inch loaf or 3 mini loaves • EQUIPMENT NEEDED: A food processor and a digital scale, as apples vary in size** ]

1¼ cups Just Like Sugar Table Top natural chicory root sweetener (not Baking). A second choice is 1⅔ cups Organic Zero Erythritol.

1 cup medium-shredded unsweetened coconut flakes (not coconut flour)

⅓ cup arrowroot powder

2 teaspoons baking powder

½ teaspoon baking soda

½ teaspoon unprocessed salt

1 teaspoon ground cinnamon

2 large eggs, at room temperature

Zest of 1 orange

¾ tart apple, unpeeled, cored, and cut into chunks (150 grams)

1 teaspoon pure vanilla extract

1 inch fresh ginger, chopped or grated, or ¼ teaspoon ground

1 cup fresh or frozen unsweetened cranberries

⅔ cup coarsely chopped walnuts or pecans, soaked if possible (see page 10)

1. Preheat the oven to 350°F. Line with parchment paper one 9 by 5-inch loaf pan or three mini loaf pans about 5¾ by 3¼ inches.
2. In a dry food processor fitted with the "S" blade, grind the sweetener to a very fine powder.
3. Add the shredded coconut to the sweetener in the food processor. Spin it for a minute until a very fine powder. Open the lid, stir the bottom, replace the lid, and grind again until the powder is uniformly fine.
4. To the ingredients in the food processor, add the arrowroot, baking powder, baking soda, salt, and cinnamon. Mix together well.
5. To the ingredients in the food processor, add the eggs, orange zest, apple, vanilla, and ginger. Process as briefly as possible until the apple is liquefied. Do not overmix.
6. Add the cranberries and walnuts. Pulse them in very briefly so they remain intact.
7. Pour the batter into the prepared pan(s). Bake a 9 by 5-inch loaf for 45 to 55 minutes, mini loaves for 20 to 23 minutes, or until a toothpick inserted into the center comes out clean. Let cool for at least 1 hour in the pan, then cover and refrigerate in the pan. The bread is easier to slice when chilled.

# Pumpkin Bread

*I love this simple Pumpkin Bread for dessert or a snack. It is super quick and healthy, made with fresh raw pumpkin or squash. Spicy and rich, it is delicious with Apple Butter (page 187), Maple Crème Cheese Frosting (page 180), or Salted Caramel Buttercream Frosting (page 176). For best results, follow the recipe exactly.*

**[ YIELD: 4 mini loaves, one 9-inch square loaf, or 8 regular muffins • EQUIPMENT NEEDED: A food processor and a digital scale, for the pumpkin ]**

2 tablespoons finely ground dark or golden flaxseeds

4 large eggs, at room temperature

1½ cups Just Like Sugar Table Top natural chicory root sweetener (not Baking). A second choice is 2 cups Organic Zero Erythritol.

1½ cups medium-shredded unsweetened coconut flakes (not coconut flour)

3 tablespoons arrowroot powder

½ teaspoon baking soda

¼ teaspoon baking powder

1 teaspoon nutritional yeast (optional)

¼ teaspoon unprocessed salt

1 tablespoon ground cinnamon

¼ teaspoon ground cloves

¼ teaspoon grated nutmeg

¼ teaspoon ground cardamom

2 inches fresh ginger, chopped or grated (about 20 grams), or ½ teaspoon ground

Zest of ½ orange

1 tablespoon pure vanilla extract

½ teaspoon maple flavoring (optional)

1 tablespoon *raw* yacón syrup (optional)

¾ cup cubed and lightly steamed pumpkin or squash (250 grams well-drained) (I find butternut squash is sweeter, smoother, and more convenient. I peel and cube the squash or buy a prepack of cubed squash.)

1 cup coarsely chopped nuts, soaked if possible (see page 10)

1. Preheat the oven to 350°F. Prepare four mini loaf pans about 5¾ by 3¼ inches, or a 9-inch square pan, lined with parchment paper, with a few inches hanging over the edges for easy removal. Or prepare eight to nine compartments of a twelve-cupcake pan with grease or cupcake liners.

2. In a bowl, stir the ground flaxseeds with the eggs and let them soak for 10 minutes.

3. In a dry food processor fitted with the "S" blade, grind the sweetener to a very fine powder.

4. Add the shredded coconut to the sweetener in the food processor. Spin it for a minute until a very fine powder. Open the lid, stir the bottom, replace the lid, and grind again until the powder is uniformly fine.

5. To the ingredients in the food processor, add the arrowroot, baking soda, baking powder, nutritional yeast (if

**continues . . .**

# Pumpkin Bread (continued)

using), salt, cinnamon, cloves, nutmeg, cardamom, and ginger. Mix well and pour into a large mixing bowl.

6. Place in the empty food processor the flaxseed mixture, orange zest, vanilla, maple flavoring (if using), yacón syrup (if using), and pumpkin. Mix very well so the pumpkin is liquefied into tiny pieces.

7. Add the wet ingredients to the dry ingredients in the mixing bowl. Add the nuts (optional). Stir very briefly.

8. Pour the batter into the prepared pan(s). Bake mini loaves for 35 to 45 minutes, a square loaf for 30 minutes, or regular muffins for 20 minutes, or until a toothpick inserted into the center comes out clean. Let cool for 1 hour in the pan, then cover and refrigerate in the pan. Bread is easier to slice when chilled.

# COOKIES AND BARS

**C**ookies are my ultimate hunt-and-gather food. And as everyone knows, the critical question in eating cookies is this: Crispy or chewy?

Fortunately, I have a solution, no matter what your answer.

If you like your cookies chewy, keep all the ingredients at room temperature, especially the shortening. The cookies will spread more in the oven, bake faster, and be chewier.

For crispier cookies, chill the dough before baking. When the dough is cold, they'll bake more slowly on the inside.

I suggest a good timer with a bell for cookies because it's far too easy to overbake gluten-free flours, as they do not brown as much as wheat flour does. In addition, cookies continue to bake after they have been removed from the oven. If overbaked, they can be dry or hard (never a good thing).

Also, I recommend using a heavy cookie sheet so the temperature stays uniform and the cookies don't burn on the bottom.

# Chocolate Chip Cookies

*Watch out, there's a new cookie in town. These Chocolate Chip Cookies are sure to blow your Paleo mind. As a suggestion, the first time you make these, consider cutting into pieces a store-bought 100% cacao chocolate bar (see page 7) for your chocolate chips. In the future, you can take the next step of making your own Homemade Chocolate Chips (page 108). They're even yummier than a chocolate bar, plus they're easy to make ahead of time and freeze. Follow this recipe exactly, and you'll be pleased with the results.*

**[ YIELD: About 26 cookies • EQUIPMENT NEEDED: A food processor and a digital scale, as apples vary in size ]**

2 cups Just Like Sugar Table Top natural chicory root sweetener (not Baking). A second choice is 2⅔ cups Organic Zero Erythritol.

1¾ cups medium-shredded unsweetened coconut flakes (not coconut flour)

3 tablespoons arrowroot powder

½ teaspoon baking powder

½ teaspoon unprocessed salt

1 teaspoon nutritional yeast (optional)

2 large eggs

⅓ tart apple, unpeeled, cored, and cut into large chunks (75 grams)

½ teaspoon maple flavoring

1 tablespoon *raw* yacón syrup (optional)

1 tablespoon pure vanilla extract

1½ cups coarsely chopped nuts, soaked if possible (see page 10)

Frozen chocolate pieces (keep in freezer until adding): 1 cup unsweetened 100% cacao chocolate bar, cut into pieces; 1 cup Homemade Chocolate Chips (page 108); or ½ cup 100% unsweetened cacao nibs

1. Preheat the oven to 350°F. Line two cookie sheets with parchment paper.
2. In a dry food processor fitted with the "S" blade, grind the sweetener to a fine powder.
3. Add the shredded coconut to the sweetener in the food processor. Spin it for a minute until a very fine powder. Open the lid, stir the bottom, replace the lid, and grind again until the powder is uniformly fine.
4. To the ingredients in the food processor, add the arrowroot, baking powder, salt, and nutritional yeast (if using). Mix well.
5. To the dry ingredients in the food processor, add the eggs, apple, maple flavoring, yacón syrup (if using), and vanilla. Mix well until the apple is liquefied and the dough fully sticks together. Pulse in the chopped nuts very briefly so they're in large pieces.
6. Place the dough in a bowl and chill for 15 minutes. Remove from the refrigerator. Stir in the frozen chips. Spoon into 1½-inch rounds spaced 2 inches apart on the prepared cookie sheets. These cookies do not spread or rise, so I suggest you press them flat with your hands; grease your palms with coconut oil to keep them from sticking to the dough.
7. Bake for 18 to 24 minutes, until glossy and just starting to brown around the edges. Remove from the oven, let cool on the pan, and enjoy!

# Chocolate Haystack Cookies

*These Chocolate Haystack Cookies are super quick and delicious, which in my opinion is the best combination ever. In fact, there's no need to bake these cookies. Just mix them, roll them, and eat them. They're a great lunch treat or snack, and a fun recipe to make with children. Use any nut butter, such as almond butter, hazelnut butter, coconut butter, or your favorite. For the most delicious flavor and texture, follow this recipe exactly.*

**[ YIELD: About 24 cookies • EQUIPMENT NEEDED: None ]**

3 tablespoons smooth or crunchy roasted almond butter or your favorite nut butter

3 tablespoons melted coconut oil (place jar in lukewarm water to melt oil)

¾ cup Just Like Sugar Table Top natural chicory root sweetener (not Baking). I do not recommend any other sweetener for this.

1 tablespoon *raw* yacón syrup (optional)

¼ cup pure cacao powder

1 teaspoon pure vanilla extract

Pinch of unprocessed salt

2 tablespoons filtered water

1 cup medium-shredded unsweetened coconut flakes (not coconut flour; see note)

1. In a medium-size mixing bowl stir the almond butter, melted coconut oil, sweetener, yacón syrup (if using), cacao powder, vanilla, salt, and water until smooth. Sweeten to taste.
2. Add the coconut and mix in gently.
3. Using a spoon or a melon baller, form 1-inch balls and place on a serving plate.
4. Enjoy immediately or chill to firm up.

**Tip:** *I find these cookies crispier and more flavorful when the shredded coconut is lightly toasted. Before you start, place the shredded coconut on a dry baking sheet and bake at 350°F for 5 to 8 minutes. Watch it carefully and remove from the oven just as it starts to turn golden brown. But take care; it burns easily!*

# Coconut Macaroons

*These Coconut Macaroons offer the best of both worlds—crunchy on the outside and soft on the inside. To up the macaroon ante and make luscious chocolate-covered macaroons, just whisk together the quick chocolate sauce (recipe follows) and dip them.*

**[ YIELD: 30 large or 60 small macaroons • EQUIPMENT NEEDED: None ]**

½ cup medium to thick unsweetened coconut milk

1½ cups Just Like Sugar Table Top natural chicory root sweetener (not Baking). A second choice is 2 cups Organic Zero Erythritol.

¼ teaspoon unprocessed salt

2 teaspoons pure vanilla extract

2 large egg whites

3½ cups medium-shredded unsweetened coconut flakes (not coconut flour)

¼ teaspoon almond extract (optional)

1. Preheat the oven to 375°F. Line two cookie sheets with parchment paper.
2. By hand in a large mixing bowl, or in any style blender, food processor, or mixer, mix well the coconut milk, sweetener, salt, vanilla, egg white, ½ cup of the coconut flakes, and almond extract (if using). If mixed electronically, pour into a large mixing bowl.
3. Add the remaining 3 cups of coconut flakes and stir well by hand.
4. Chill the dough in the same bowl for 10 minutes. This allows the coconut to soak up the sweetness, and makes the cookies crispy on the outside and soft in the middle.
5. With a teaspoon and your fingers, drop mounds of batter spaced 1 inch apart onto the prepared cookie sheets. Press each mound a bit so it stays intact. The cookies can be anywhere from 1 to 2 inches in diameter, and slightly irregular and shaggy.
6. Bake for 16 to 20 minutes, turning the pans after 10 minutes, so all sides are evenly toasted and golden brown. When they are a beautiful golden brown, remove from the oven and transfer to a rack to cool.

> **variation Chocolate-Dipped Macaroons**

**continues . . .**

# Chocolate-Dipped Macaroons (variation)

## variation Chocolate-Dipped Macaroons:

1 recipe Coconut Macaroons

$\frac{1}{3}$ cup Just Like Sugar Table Top natural chicory root sweetener (not Baking).
  A second choice is $\frac{1}{2}$ cup Organic Zero Erythritol.

$2\frac{1}{2}$ tablespoons boiling filtered water

1 tablespoon melted coconut oil (place jar in lukewarm water to melt oil)

2 teaspoons pure vanilla extract

3 tablespoons pure cacao powder

1. Prepare the Coconut Macaroons and let cool.
2. Meanwhile, in a 1-cup glass measuring cup or heatproof small bowl, use a small whisk or spoon to mix the sweetener, boiling water, coconut oil, and vanilla. Mix until smooth and the sweetener is dissolved. (This depends a bit on your sweetener. If you are using erythritol, you need to keep the mixture a bit warmer. In that case, I suggest mixing the chocolate in a heatproof shallow pan over a pan of boiling water.)
3. Add the cacao powder and mix until smooth. The mixture should be quite thick so it sticks to the cookies. (You can thin it out with a bit more boiling water if necessary, or thicken it with a bit more cacao powder.)
4. When the macaroons have cooled, dip them upside down into the chocolate coating so the top third of the cookie is covered. Let any excess chocolate drip back into the cup.
5. Place the coated cookies on a serving plate. The chocolate will harden at room temperature in 15 minutes, or sooner in the refrigerator.

# Double Chocolate Chip Espresso Cookies

*These cookies are for serious chocoholics, much like the classic Chocolate Chip Cookies (page 65), except they're dark chocolate with a strong coffee flavor. The first time you make them, consider cutting into pieces a store-bought 100% cacao chocolate bar (see page 7) for your chocolate chips. However, you can eventually taste for yourself that these are better with Homemade Chocolate Chips (page 108). For best results, follow this recipe exactly.*

[ YIELD: 32 cookies • EQUIPMENT NEEDED: A food processor and a digital scale, as apples vary in size ]

2½ cups Just Like Sugar Table Top natural chicory root sweetener (not Baking). A second choice is 3⅓ cups Organic Zero Erythritol.

1¾ cups medium-shredded unsweetened coconut flakes (not coconut flour)

6 tablespoons pure cacao powder

1½ teaspoons finely ground instant decaffeinated coffee powder or crystals

3 tablespoons arrowroot powder

½ teaspoon baking powder

½ teaspoon unprocessed salt

1 teaspoon nutritional yeast (optional)

3 large eggs

⅓ tart apple, unpeeled, cored, and cut into large pieces (75 grams)

1 tablespoon any unsweetened coconut milk

½ teaspoon maple flavoring

1 tablespoon *raw* yacón syrup (optional)

1 tablespoon pure vanilla extract

1½ cups coarsely chopped nuts, soaked if possible (see page 10)

Frozen chocolate pieces (keep in freezer until adding): 1 cup unsweetened 100% chocolate bar, cut into pieces; 1 cup Homemade Chocolate Chips (page 108); or ½ cup 100% unsweetened cacao nibs

1. Preheat the oven to 350°F. Line two cookie sheets with parchment paper.

2. In a dry food processor fitted with the "S" blade, grind the sweetener to a fine powder.

3. Add the shredded coconut to the sweetener in the food processor. Spin it for a minute until a very fine powder. Open the lid, stir the bottom, replace the lid, and grind again until the powder is uniformly fine.

4. To the ingredients in the food processor, add the cacao powder, coffee powder, arrowroot, baking powder, salt, and nutritional yeast (if using). Mix well.

5. To the dry ingredients in the food processor, add the eggs, apple, coconut milk, maple flavoring, yacón syrup (if using), and vanilla. Mix well until the apple is liquefied and the dough fully sticks together. Pulse in the chopped nuts very briefly so they're in large pieces.

**continues . . .**

6. Place the dough in a bowl and chill for 15 minutes. Remove from the refrigerator. Stir in the frozen chips. Spoon into 1½-inch rounds spaced 2 inches apart on the prepared cookie sheets. These cookies do not spread or rise, so I suggest you press them flat with your hands; grease your palms with coconut oil to keep them from sticking to the dough.

7. Bake for 18 to 24 minutes, until glossy and just starting to brown around the edges. Remove from the oven, let cool for a few minutes on the pan, and enjoy!

# Hazelnut Butter Cookies

*There's nothing better than coming home to the aroma of these fresh-baked cookies. They taste a lot like a classic peanut butter cookie, but peanuts are a legume and not permitted on the Paleo diet, so this is a nice alternative. I really like hazelnuts because they have an intense and distinctive flavor. You can also make these with almond butter or your favorite nut butter; however, the flavor will be milder. For best results, follow this recipe exactly.*

[ YIELD: 55 to 60 cookies • EQUIPMENT NEEDED: A food processor and a digital scale, as apples vary in size ]

1½ cups Just Like Sugar Table Top natural chicory root sweetener (not Baking). A second choice is 2 cups Organic Zero Erythritol.

1¼ cups medium-shredded unsweetened coconut flakes (not coconut flour)

¼ cup arrowroot powder

½ teaspoon baking powder

1 teaspoon nutritional yeast (optional)

¾ teaspoon unprocessed salt (if your nut butter is unsalted)

2 large eggs

2 teaspoons pure vanilla extract

¼ tart apple, unpeeled, cored, and cut into chunks (50 grams)

¾ cup smooth or crunchy roasted hazelnut butter

1 tablespoon *raw* yacón syrup (optional)

1. Preheat the oven to 350°F. Line two cookie sheets with parchment paper, if desired.
2. In a dry food processor fitted with the "S" blade, grind the sweetener to a very fine powder.
3. Add the shredded coconut to the sweetener in the food processor. Spin it for a minute until a very fine powder. Open the lid, stir the bottom, replace the lid, and grind again until the powder is uniformly fine.
4. To the ingredients in the food processor, add the arrowroot, baking powder, nutritional yeast (if using), and salt (if using).
5. To the dry ingredients in the food processor, add the eggs, vanilla, apple, nut butter, and yacón syrup (if using). Mix well until the dough sticks together well.
6. Remove the container from the processor base, take out the "S" blade, and chill the dough uncovered for 15 to 30 minutes in the processor bowl.
7. Form the dough into 1-inch balls spaced about 1 inch apart on the prepared cookie sheets. Handle them as little as possible, as the coconut oil will melt from the heat of your hands. Press them with the tines of a fork to create crisscross marks.
8. Bake for 13 to 15 minutes. Do not overbake or they will be dry, as these do not brown. When they're done, they'll still be soft; they will get crispier as they cool. Remove from the oven and cool on a rack for 15 minutes.

**continues . . .**

variations **Almond Butter Cookies:** Instead of hazelnut butter, use roasted almond butter.

**Chocolate Hazelnut Butter Cookies:** Add 4 additional tablespoons of sweetener (or 6 tablespoons of erythritol total); add 3 tablespoons pure cacao powder to the dry ingredients; and add 1 tablespoon filtered water to the wet ingredients.

# Mexican Wedding Cookies

*Mexican Wedding Cookies are a scrumptious treat for the holidays or any time of year, for that matter. These delicate morsels will melt in your mouth and can satisfy almost any cookie craving. For best results, follow the recipe closely.*

**[ YIELD: 36 to 40 cookies • EQUIPMENT NEEDED: A food processor ]**

1 cup Just Like Sugar Table Top natural chicory root sweetener (not Baking). A second choice is 1⅓ cups Organic Zero Erythritol.

1¼ cups medium-shredded unsweetened coconut flakes (not coconut flour)

3 tablespoons arrowroot powder

¼ teaspoon unprocessed salt

2 large eggs

1 teaspoon pure vanilla extract

¼ teaspoon almond extract

¾ cup coarsely chopped pecans, soaked if possible (see page 10)

¾ cup granulated sweetener, ground finely, for rolling after baking (erythritol works best for this; see tip)

1. Preheat the oven to 325°F. Line two cookie sheets with parchment paper.
2. In a dry food processor fitted with an "S" blade, grind the sweetener several minutes to a very fine powder.
3. Add the coconut, arrowroot, and salt. Grind again until very fine. Open the lid, stir the bottom, replace the lid, and grind again until the powder is uniformly fine.
4. Add the eggs, vanilla, and almond extract. Mix well.
5. Add the pecans last and pulse gently to mix in evenly.
6. Chill the dough for 15 minutes. (I use the same container.)
7. Gently shape the dough without pressing into smooth ¾-inch balls. Place them 1 inch apart on the prepared cookie sheets. The dough will be soft. It helps to coat your hands with a bit of arrowroot powder to keep them from getting too sticky. If they do get sticky, wash and dry them before continuing.
8. Bake for 18 to 20 minutes. They will not brown, so take care not to overbake.
9. While still warm, roll the delicate cookies very gently in ground granulated sweetener. The cookies will continue to firm up as they cool.

**Tip:** *Erythritol works best for this, as it grinds down more finely and will stay adhered to cookies. Grind it in a food processor or coffee grinder.*

# No-Oatmeal No-Raisin Cookies

*These cookies are crunchy on the outside and soft in the middle. Instead of oatmeal, which is considered a Neolithic (Stone Age) grain, this Paleo recipe uses buckwheat, a plant related to rhubarb. Buckwheat has a texture similar to that of oatmeal. It is flavorful, easy to digest, and high in protein and fiber. Sometimes called kasha or groats, it needs to be soaked for 6 to 8 hours before you use it. To protect your blood sugar levels, this recipe uses no raisins, which are high in carbs. For best results, follow this recipe exactly.*

[ YIELD: 24 cookies • EQUIPMENT NEEDED: A food processor and a digital scale, as apples vary in size ]

1¼ cups raw buckwheat

2 tablespoons finely ground golden flaxseeds

1 large egg, at room temperature

1¼ cups Just Like Sugar Table Top natural chicory root sweetener (not Baking). A second choice is 1⅔ cups Organic Zero Erythritol.

¾ cup medium-shredded unsweetened coconut flakes (not coconut flour)

2 tablespoons arrowroot powder

½ teaspoon unprocessed salt

½ teaspoon baking powder

½ teaspoon ground cinnamon

1 teaspoon nutritional yeast (optional)

1 teaspoon pure vanilla extract

¼ tart apple, unpeeled, cored, and cut into large pieces (50 grams)

1 tablespoon *raw* yacón syrup (optional)

½ cup coarsely chopped nuts, soaked and crisped if possible (see page 10)

1. Soak the buckwheat in salted filtered water for 6 hours or more. Rinse and drain very well.

2. In a bowl, stir the ground flaxseeds with the eggs and let them soak for 10 minutes.

3. Preheat the oven to 350°F. Line two cookie sheets with parchment paper.

4. In a dry food processor fitted with the "S" blade, grind the sweetener to a very fine powder.

5. Add the shredded coconut to the sweetener in the food processor. Spin it for a minute until a very fine powder. Open the lid, stir the bottom, replace the lid, and grind again until the powder is uniformly fine.

6. To the ingredients in the food processor, add the arrowroot, salt, baking powder, cinnamon, and nutritional yeast (if using). Mix well.

7. To the dry ingredients in the food processor, add the flaxseed mixture, vanilla, apple, and yacón syrup (if using). Mix well until the apple is liquefied.

8. Add the drained buckwheat and chopped nuts. Pulse briefly until the buckwheat is partially ground but much of it remains whole. You want a pleasantly rough textured dough similar to that of oatmeal. If you mix longer, the buckwheat will get mushy and soggy.

**continues . . .**

9. Drop spoonfuls of dough spaced about 2 inches apart onto the prepared cookie sheets.
10. Bake for 12 to 20 minutes, depending on the size of your cookies. Let cool on a rack.

> **variation No-Oatmeal Chocolate Chip Cookies:** Pulse in ½ cup of chopped 100% cacao chocolate bar or frozen Homemade Chocolate Chips (page 108), or ¼ cup of unsweetened cacao nibs, along with the buckwheat and nuts in step 8.

# Rugelach

*Rugelach, a traditional Jewish delicacy, is made with a crispy cream cheese dough filled with nuts and jam. This Paleo version uses lemon and coconut to simulate cream cheese, and fresh apple in the filling. The dough is rolled out, spread with filling, and then rolled into cookies. There are several ways to roll them. I find it is simplest to roll the dough out into a square, spread the filling, and roll it up like a jelly roll. Then, I cut the roll crosswise into cookies. Or you can roll them the way your mother taught you. For the most delicious flavor and texture, you're going to want to follow this recipe exactly.*

[ YIELD: 36 pieces • EQUIPMENT NEEDED: A food processor and a digital scale, as apples can vary in size ]

### DOUGH

1 cup Just Like Sugar Table Top natural chicory root sweetener (not Baking). A second choice is 1⅓ cups Organic Zero Erythritol.
3½ cups medium-shredded unsweetened coconut flakes (not coconut flour)
⅓ cup arrowroot powder
½ teaspoon baking powder
¼ teaspoon unprocessed salt
2 teaspoons nutritional yeast (optional)
2 large eggs
2 tablespoons freshly squeezed lemon juice
2 teaspoons pure vanilla extract

### FILLING

1 cup walnuts, soaked if possible (see page 10) and toasted lightly (see page 11)
½ tart apple, unpeeled, cored, and cut into chunks (80 grams)
½ cup Just Like Sugar Table Top natural chicory root sweetener (not Baking). A second choice is ¾ cup Organic Zero Erythritol.
2 teaspoons ground cinnamon
1 teaspoon ground allspice
Pinch of unprocessed salt
1 tablespoon arrowroot powder

2 teaspoons apple cider vinegar
1 teaspoon pure vanilla extract
Zest of 1 lemon
½ tablespoon *raw* yacón syrup (optional)
2 tablespoons melted coconut oil (place jar in lukewarm water to melt oil), for brushing
Ground cinnamon, for dusting

1. For the dough: In a dry food processor fitted with the "S" blade, grind the sweetener to a very fine powder.
2. Add the shredded coconut to the sweetener in the food processor. Spin it for a minute until a very fine powder. Open the lid, stir the bottom, replace the lid, and grind again until the powder is uniformly fine.
3. Add to the ingredients in the food processor the arrowroot, baking powder, salt, and nutritional yeast (if using). Mix well.

**continues . . .**

4. Add to the dry ingredients in the food processor the eggs, lemon juice, and vanilla. Mix briefly to form a cohesive dough.

5. Form the dough into six equal logs and flatten to about ½ inch thick. Wrap in plastic wrap and refrigerate for at least 30 minutes to firm up.

6. For the filling: In a food processor, grind the walnuts coarsely. Remove ⅓ cup of the nuts and set aside.

7. Add to the food processor the apple, sweetener, cinnamon, allspice, salt, arrowroot, vinegar, vanilla, lemon zest, and yacón syrup (if using). Mix to a fine paste.

8. To assemble: Preheat the oven to 350°F. Line two cookies sheets with parchment paper.

9. Remove the chilled dough from the refrigerator. Roll out each piece of dough between two pieces of parchment paper into a square about 8½ inches wide. Dust with arrowroot powder to prevent sticking. Spread one-sixth of the filling onto the center of the square with a rubber spatula, leaving a ½-inch border on the top and bottom of the dough. Sprinkle with some of the chopped walnuts you had set aside in step 6.

10. To make a roll, lift up the parchment paper and carefully roll up the dough very tightly from bottom to top, like a jelly roll. If the dough breaks, just squeeze it together to repair it.

11. Brush the entire roll with a bit of melted coconut oil and dust with cinnamon. Using a sharp knife, slice the roll crosswise into small pieces, about ¾ inches wide.

12. Place the cookies 1 inch apart on the prepared cookie sheets. The cookies can be facing upward or sideways. Repeat with the remaining dough.

13. Bake for about 20 minutes, until golden brown. Let cool for 30 minutes on a rack.

# Thumbprint Cookies

*Whether it's a holiday treat, a special day of the year, or just because you want to bake them, everyone will give a thumbs-up to these cookies. My favorite thumbprint filling is bright red Raspberry "Jam" (page 192). Plain or rolled in chopped pecans, these sweet, crunchy morsels will melt in your mouth. For best results, follow this recipe exactly.*

[ YIELD: 40 cookies • EQUIPMENT NEEDED: A food processor ]

1 recipe Raspberry "Jam" (page 192)

1 cup Just Like Sugar Table Top natural chicory root sweetener (not Baking). A second choice is 1⅓ cups Organic Zero Erythritol.

1¼ cups medium-shredded unsweetened coconut flakes (not coconut flour)

3 tablespoons arrowroot powder

¼ teaspoon unprocessed salt

2 large eggs

1 teaspoon pure vanilla extract

¼ teaspoon almond extract

¾ cup coarsely chopped pecans, soaked if possible (see page 10)

2 egg whites, gently beaten in a small bowl

1 cup pecans, unsoaked and coarsely chopped, for coating (optional)

1. Prepare the Raspberry "Jam."
2. Preheat the oven to 350°F. Line two cookie sheets with parchment paper.
3. In a dry food processor fitted with the "S" blade, grind the sweetener to a very fine powder.
4. Add the shredded coconut to the sweetener in the food processor. Spin it for a minute until a very fine powder. Open the lid, stir the bottom, replace the lid, and grind again until the powder is uniformly fine.
5. To the ingredients in the food processor, add the arrowroot and salt. Mix well.
6. To the dry ingredients in the food processor, add the eggs, vanilla, and almond extract. Mix well.
7. Add the chopped, soaked pecans last and pulse gently to mix them in evenly without grinding.
8. Refrigerate the dough for 15 minutes. (I use the same container.)
9. If baking without the optional coating, gently shape the dough without pressing too hard into smooth ¾-inch balls and roll them in the beaten egg whites. Place them 1 inch apart on the prepared cookie sheets. The dough will be soft. It helps to coat your hands with a bit of arrowroot powder. If your hands get sticky, wash and dry them. Press your thumb deeply into the center of each ball to make plenty of room for the yummy filling.

**continues . . .**

## Thumbprint Cookies (continued)

10. If you desire to coat the cookies in chopped pecans, gently shape the dough without pressing too hard into smooth ¾-inch balls. Roll each ball in the beaten egg whites, and then roll them in the pecans. Place them 1 inch apart on the prepared cookie sheets. Press your thumb deeply into the center of each ball to make plenty of room for the yummy filling.

11. Bake for 15 to 18 minutes, until the bottom of the cookies is barely light brown. Refresh the thumbprint if necessary with a thumb-size tool, such as a round wooden spoon handle. Not with your thumb, though; the cookies are hot!

12. Let cool for 30 minutes on a wire rack. Use a spoon or a kitchen squeeze bottle to fill the centers with the Raspberry "Jam." Place the cookies on a serving plate and watch them disappear!

# Trail Mix Cookies

*A breakfast, meal, or snack, these Trail Mix Cookies are crispy and delectable, and filled with homemade trail mix. The crunchy texture is from buckwheat, a flavorful seed that is neither a grain nor grass and is related to the rhubarb family. Find raw buckwheat groats in any healthy grocery. For the best flavor and texture, follow this recipe exactly.*

**[ YIELD: 30 cookies • EQUIPMENT NEEDED: A food processor and a digital scale, as apples vary in size ]**

⅓ cup raw buckwheat

½ recipe (2 cups) Trail Mix (page 146)

2 tablespoons finely ground flaxseeds

⅓ cup filtered water

1¾ cups Just Like Sugar Table Top natural chicory root sweetener (not Baking). A second choice is 2⅓ cups Organic Zero Erythritol.

1 cup medium-shredded unsweetened coconut flakes (not coconut flour)

¼ cup arrowroot powder

¼ teaspoon baking soda

½ teaspoon unprocessed salt

1 tablespoon nutritional yeast (optional)

½ tart apple, unpeeled, cored, and cut into large pieces (100 grams)

½ teaspoon maple flavoring

1 tablespoon *raw* yacón syrup (optional)

1 tablespoon pure vanilla extract

¼ cup 100% pure cacao nibs or Homemade Chocolate Chips (page 108)

1. Soak the raw buckwheat in filtered water for 4 to 6 hours, or overnight. Rinse and drain well.
2. Prepare ½ recipe of Trail Mix.
3. In a bowl, stir the finely ground flaxseeds with the ⅓ cup filtered water and let soak for 10 minutes.
4. Preheat the oven to 350°F. Line two cookie sheets with parchment paper.
5. In a dry food processor fitted with the "S" blade, grind the sweetener to a very fine powder.
6. Add the shredded coconut to the sweetener in the food processor. Spin it for a minute until a very fine powder. Open the lid, stir the bottom, replace the lid, and grind again until the powder is uniformly fine.
7. Add to the ingredients in the food processor the arrow-root, baking soda, salt, and nutritional yeast (if using). Mix well.
8. Add to the dry ingredients in the food processor the soaked flaxseeds with their water, apple, maple flavoring, yacón syrup (if using), and vanilla. Mix to a cohesive dough.
9. Place the dough in a large mixing bowl. Add the drained buckwheat, Trail Mix, and cacao nibs. Mix briefly with a rubber spatula to incorporate.
10. Spoon the dough in 1½-inch rounds spaced 2 inches apart on the prepared cookie sheets. Flatten each cookie gently with a spatula or your hands.
11. Bake for 16 to 20 minutes, until glossy and just starting to brown around the edges. Remove from the oven, let cool on the pan, and enjoy!

# Biscotti

*Biscotti are a traditional breakfast in Italy, where every home has its own recipe. These Paleo biscotti are crispy, easy to make, and fantastic for dipping in your Paleo Caffè (page 210). Personally, I think they taste even better than the Italian ones. For best results, follow this recipe exactly.*

[ YIELD: About 30 biscotti • EQUIPMENT NEEDED: A food processor and a digital scale, as apples vary in size ]

1 cup raw nuts, soaked if possible (see page 10)

1½ cups Just Like Sugar Table Top natural chicory root sweetener (not Baking). A second choice is 2 cups Organic Zero Erythritol.

3 cups medium-shredded unsweetened coconut flakes (not coconut flour)

1 cup arrowroot powder

2 teaspoons baking powder

½ teaspoon unprocessed salt

1 teaspoon nutritional yeast (optional)

4 large eggs, at room temperature

2 teaspoons pure vanilla extract

Zest of ½ orange

1½ teaspoons almond extract (optional)

½ teaspoon ground aniseeds (optional)

1. Preheat the oven to 300°F. Line two baking sheets with parchment paper. Chop the nuts coarsely in the food processor or by hand, and set aside.
2. In a dry food processor fitted with the "S" blade, grind the sweetener to a very fine powder.
3. Add the shredded coconut to the sweetener in the food processor. Spin it for a minute until a very fine powder. Open the lid, stir the bottom, replace the lid, and grind again until the powder is uniformly fine.
4. To the ingredients in the food processor, add the arrowroot, baking powder, salt, and nutritional yeast (if using).
5. To the dry ingredients in the food processor, add the eggs, vanilla, orange zest, almond extract (if using), and aniseeds (if using). Mix briefly.
6. Add the nuts and pulse them several times briefly so they remain in large pieces.
7. Remove the dough from food processor. Divide it into two equal parts and place on the prepared baking sheets. Coat your hands with a bit of coconut oil and knead each piece briefly to distribute the nuts evenly, while you shape each piece into a log about 10 inches long, 2 inches wide, and 1 inch thick at the thickest point.
8. Bake for 20 minutes. If they begin to crack, remove from the oven before they crack deeply. Let cool for 15 minutes in the pans.

**continues . . .**

9. With a sharp, serrated knife on a cutting board, carefully slice each log diagonally into ½-inch-thick biscotti. Place each piece flat on its side on the baking sheets. Bake for 20 minutes at 300°F.

10. Turn over each slice and bake for 15 additional minutes, until golden brown on the top. Transfer to a wire rack to cool. Keep in an airtight container for several weeks. *Buon appetito!*

# Blueberry Lemon Cheesecake Bars

*High-antioxidant Blueberry-Lemon Cheesecake Bars are delightfully creamy and taste refreshing. The secret to their rich flavor and cheesecake texture is fresh lemon and pure coconut butter. For best results, follow this recipe exactly.*

[ YIELD: 36 bars • EQUIPMENT NEEDED: A food processor, any style blender, and a digital scale, to weigh the coconut butter ]

**CRUST**
½ cup Just Like Sugar Table Top natural chicory root sweetener (not Baking). A second choice is ⅔ cups Organic Zero Erythritol (however, you may taste crystals of the latter if the bars are refrigerated).
1 cup medium-shredded unsweetened coconut flakes (not coconut flour)
1 large egg
Zest of ½ lemon

3 tablespoons coconut oil
1 teaspoon pure vanilla extract
¼ teaspoon unprocessed salt
1 cup raw nuts, soaked if possible (see page 10)

**FILLING**
1 cup thick unsweetened coconut milk, or ½ cup thin
3 large eggs
Zest of 1½ lemons
2 lemons, peeled, sliced, and seeded

1 cup same sweetener as used for crust
1 tablespoon pure vanilla extract
⅛ teaspoon unprocessed salt
200 grams (about 1 cup tightly packed pure coconut butter (not coconut oil), at room temperature
2 cups fresh or frozen blueberries (if frozen, keep in freezer until adding, for less color bleeding)

1. Preheat the oven to 325°F. Grease and flour a 9 by 13-pan with a removable bottom, if available. Or you can cover the bottom of a regular 9 by 13-inch pan with parchment paper wide enough to make handles on both sides for easy removal.

2. For the crust: In a food processor fitted with the "S" blade (or whisk together in a mixing bowl) mix the sweetener, coconut, egg, lemon zest, coconut oil, vanilla, and salt. Mix until it is a smooth batter. Add the nuts and pulse briefly so they are chopped coarsely but not mushy. Press the dough into the bottom of the prepared pan. Bake for 20 minutes.

3. For filling: Place in any style blender the coconut milk, eggs, lemon zest, lemons, sweetener, vanilla, and salt. Blend well until smooth and creamy. Add the coconut butter last and blend until smooth.

4. Pour the filling into the baked crust. Sprinkle the blueberries over the top. They will sink into the filling slightly, but should be partly exposed.

5. Bake for 30 to 35 minutes, or until the center is quite firm and jiggles only slightly. Remove from the oven and let cool in the pan. Refrigerate for 3 hours, until set, then remove from the pan and slice six by six into three dozen bars.

# Granola Bars

*Whether it's for breakfast, a snack, or dessert, granola bars are one of my favorite foods. Many granola bars are loaded with syrups and dried fruit, both high in sugars. My goal with this recipe is to give you a tasty, chewy fruit-nut bar with zero impact on your blood sugar. These delicious granola bars use tart apple, nut butter, and buckwheat. You can cut these into bars easily, and they store well in the refrigerator or freezer. For best results, follow this recipe exactly.*

[ YIELD: 24 bars • EQUIPMENT NEEDED: A food processor and a digital scale, as apples vary in size

1 cup raw buckwheat

2½ cups Trail Mix (page 146)

1 tablespoon finely ground flaxseeds

¼ cup filtered water

1¼ cups Just Like Sugar Table Top natural chicory root sweetener (not Baking). A second choice is 1⅔ cups Organic Zero Erythritol (however, you may taste crystals of the latter if the bars are refrigerated).

⅓ cup medium-shredded unsweetened coconut flakes (not coconut flour)

2 tablespoons arrowroot powder

1 teaspoon unprocessed salt

1 teaspoon nutritional yeast (optional)

2 teaspoons ground cinnamon

¾ teaspoon maple flavoring (optional)

1 tablespoon *raw* yacón syrup (optional)

1 cup nut butter of your choice

1 tart apple, unpeeled, cored, and cut into chunks (200 grams)

1½ tablespoons pure vanilla extract

¼ cup 100% cacao nibs, or Homemade Chocolate Chips (page 108) (optional)

1. Soak the buckwheat in the filtered water for 4 to 6 hours and drain well.
2. Prepare the Basic Trail Mix.
3. In a bowl, stir the ground flaxseeds with the ¼ cup of filtered water and let soak for 10 minutes.
4. Preheat the oven to 350°F. Line a 9 by 13-inch pan with a wide strip of parchment paper, allowing it to hang over the sides for easy removal.
5. In a dry food processor fitted with the "S" blade, grind the sweetener to a fine powder.
6. Add the shredded coconut to the sweetener in the food processor. Spin it for a minute until a very fine powder. Open the lid, stir the bottom, replace the lid, and grind again until the powder is uniformly fine.
7. To the ingredients in the food processor, add the arrowroot, salt, nutritional yeast (if using), and cinnamon. Mix well.
8. To the dry ingredients in the food processor, add the maple flavoring (if using), yacón syrup (if using), nut butter, apple, vanilla, and soaked flaxseeds with their water. Mix well until it is a smooth paste and the apple is liquefied.
9. Add the drained buckwheat to the mixture in the food processor and pulse in several times so it is a cohesive dough. Add the cacao nibs (if using). Pulse in very briefly so these remain in large pieces.

**continues . . .**

10. Spoon the dough into the prepared baking pan and spread flat firmly with a rubber spatula.

11. Bake for 30 to 40 minutes, until browned around the edges. The granola may seem underbaked, but will get firmer as it cools. (You can also dehydrate the dough in your oven or in a dehydrator at about 115°F for 9 to 12 hours, until dried. If you choose to do this, you'll need to cut the mixture into squares and flip over midway through to dry the other side.)

12. Let cool for 1 hour in the pan on a rack. Then lift the block onto a cutting board by the parchment handles. Chill for 30 minutes on the board; these are so much easier to cut when cold. Cut four by six into rectangular bars. Store refrigerated in an airtight container or freeze them for later.

# Lemon Bars

*These Lemon Bars are sweet and refreshing, and every bite explodes with citrus flavor. They're easy to make and the lemon cream filling is loaded with healthy vitamins, antioxidants, and bioflavonoids. For the most perfect flavor and texture, follow this recipe exactly.*

**[ YIELD: 20 bars • EQUIPMENT NEEDED: A food processor; any style blender; and a digital scale, as lemons vary in size ]**

1 recipe Minute Piecrust (page 113)

**LEMON CREAM FILLING**
3 lemons (about 415 grams before zesting or cutting)
Zest of 1 orange
½ cup unsweetened coconut milk (thicker is better, but thin will work as well)
1¾ cups Just Like Sugar Table Top natural chicory root sweetener (not Baking). I do not recommend erythritol for this portion of the recipe.
½ teaspoon pure vanilla extract
⅛ teaspoon unprocessed salt
⅓ cup melted coconut oil (place jar in lukewarm water to melt oil)
2 tablespoons agar flakes
½ cup any unsweetened coconut milk, to cook agar
¼ cup medium-shredded unsweetened coconut flakes (not coconut flour; optional, for garnish)

1. Prepare the Minute Piecrust. Press into a 9-inch square pan and chill.
2. For the lemon filling: Zest two of the lemons, then peel all three lemons with a knife to remove the white pith. Slice and seed them with the tip of a knife. Place the zest and pulp in any style blender. Add to the blender the orange zest, coconut milk, sweetener, vanilla, and salt. Liquefy completely until very smooth. Sweeten to taste, if desired, with additional sweetener. Add the coconut oil slowly and blend well.
3. In a shallow nonstick pan over medium heat, stir the agar into the ½ cup of coconut milk. Cook and stir gently for 2 to 3 minutes, until it is bubbling and gummy, and the flakes begin to dissolve. Add the agar mixture to the blender immediately and blend well to remove any lumps. (Makes 3 cups lemon curd.)
4. Pour the filling into the chilled crust. Chill the bars for several hours until the filling becomes firm.
5. Remove from the refrigerator, slice four by five into twenty bars, and garnish the bars with the coconut flakes (if using).

Mexican Wedding Cookies, Page 73

Berry Cobbler with Whipped Crème Topping, Page 138

Easy Chocolate Mousse with Whipped Crème Topping, Page 151

Spicy Carrot Ginger Cake with Crème Cheese Frosting, Page 40

Strawberry Shortcake, Page 42

Awesome Fudge Brownies with Chocolate Buttercream Frosting, Page 91

Belgian Waffles with Maple-Flavored Syrup, Whipped Crème Topping, fresh fruit, and cacao nibs, Page 142

Cherry Pie, Page 118

Chocolate Cake with Raspberry Filling and Instant Mocha Buttercream Frosting, Page 33

Chocolate Chip Cookies and Double Chocolate Chip Espresso Cookies with Homemade Chocolate Chips, Pages 65, 69

Chocolate Cupcake with Chocolate Crème Cheese Frosting, Page 50

Chocolate Marble Cheesecake with Chocolate Sauce, Page 130

Dark Chocolate Truffles, Page 109. Top of page diagonally to right: Hawaiian, Orange, Almond. Middle row diagonally to right: Chocolate Rose, Brazilian Brigadeiros, Mayan. Far left diagonally to right: Chai, Classic with Pistachio Nuts, Classic.

Dutch Apple Pie with Streusel Topping and Whipped Crème, Page 116

Blueberry Harmony, Red Heart and Digestive Healing, and Minty Green Uplift and Clarity Smoothies, Pages 201, 206, 204

Red Velvet Cupcakes with Crème Cheese Frosting, Page 39

Banana, Strawberry, and Chocolate Milk Shakes, Pages 196, 199, 197

Fluffy Lemon Cupcakes with Lemon Buttercream Frosting, Page 51

Lemon-Berry Parfait, Page 154

Pumpkin Pie with Whipped Crème Topping, Page 123

Ice-Cream Sandwiches, Page 168

# Raspberry Crumble Bars

*These Raspberry Crumble Bars are sweet and satisfying. Alive with flavor and nutrition, this is an easy breakfast or dessert. This recipe has a nutty crust that is used for both the bottom and the top portions of the bar. The top crust has crunchy nuts added to it, so it makes a crispy streusel topping. Serve plain or garnish with 1-Minute Whipped Crème Topping (page 173). For the best flavor and texture, follow this recipe exactly.*

**[ YIELD: 12 to 20 bars • EQUIPMENT NEEDED: A food processor and a digital scale, as apples vary in size ]**

### CRUST

⅔ cup Just Like Sugar Table Top natural chicory root sweetener (not Baking). A second choice is ¾ cup Organic Zero Erythritol.

1¼ cups medium-shredded unsweetened coconut flakes (not coconut flour)

½ teaspoon unprocessed salt

2 large eggs, at room temperature

1 teaspoon pure vanilla extract

2 tablespoons filtered water

1 cup raw nuts, soaked if possible (see page 10)

### STREUSEL TOPPING

¼ cup Just Like Sugar Table Top natural chicory root sweetener (not Baking). A second option is ⅓ cup Organic Zero Erythritol.

⅓ cup medium-shredded unsweetened coconut flakes (not coconut flour)

1 tablespoon ground cinnamon

¼ teaspoon grated nutmeg

½ cup raw nuts, soaked if possible (see page 10)

2 tablespoons melted coconut oil (place jar in lukewarm water to melt oil)

### FILLING

½ cup Just Like Sugar Table Top natural chicory root sweetener (not Baking). A second choice is ⅔ cup Organic Zero Erythritol (if the berries are very sour, you may want to add more sweetener to taste).

2 tablespoons arrowroot powder

1 teaspoon ground cinnamon

Pinch of unprocessed salt

10 ounces (1 cup) fresh or frozen raspberries, well drained

Zest of 1 orange

1 tablespoon freshly squeezed lemon juice (if the berries are tart, skip this addition)

**continues . . .**

1. Preheat the oven to 350°F. Line a 9-inch square pan with parchment paper hanging over the sides for easy removal.

2. For the crust: In a dry food processor fitted with the "S" blade, grind the sweetener to a fine powder.

3. Add the shredded coconut to the sweetener in the food processor. Spin it for a minute until a very fine powder. Open the lid, stir the bottom, replace the lid, and grind again until the powder is uniformly fine.

4. Add to the dry ingredients in the food processor the salt, eggs, vanilla, and water. Mix until it is a smooth batter. Add the nuts and pulse briefly so they are coarsely chopped but not mushy.

5. Place two-thirds of the dough in the baking pan. With a rubber spatula, press the dough evenly into the bottom of the pan. Bake for 20 minutes.

6. For the streusel topping: To the mixture remaining in the food processor, add the sweetener, coconut, cinnamon, nutmeg, nuts, and melted coconut oil. Pulse in very briefly, just for 5 seconds, so they remain in coarse pieces.

7. For the filling: In a large mixing bowl, stir together the sweetener, arrowroot, cinnamon, and salt. Add the berries to the mixing bowl with the orange zest and lemon juice. Mix gently to coat the berries evenly. Crush the berries with a fork or a pastry cutter so they are in small pieces.

8. Pour the filling into the partially baked crust and smooth flat. Sprinkle the streusel topping over the filling, covering it evenly, and press it in. Bake for 20 to 25 minutes more, until the topping is slightly browned. Let cool for 30 minutes on a rack before cutting. Cut three by four or four by five into bars and serve warm.

# CHOCOLATE DESSERTS

● ● ● ● ● ● ● ● ● ● ● ● ● ● ● ● ● ● ● ● ● ● ● ● ● ● ● ● ● ● ● ● ● ● ● ● ● ● ● ● ● ● ● ● ● ● ●

**P**ure 100% cacao chocolate is my favorite food in the world. And for good reason. Raw, unsweetened chocolate is said to be *the number one most antioxidant food on Earth*, according to the oxygen radical absorbance capacity (ORAC) measure by the USDA. In fact, pure unsweetened chocolate is higher in antioxidants than grapes, blueberries, or green tea. Maybe that's why ancient cultures revered it as a medicine, calling it "the food of the gods."

Chocolate contains key substances that alter body chemistry and lift the spirits. Theobromine is a natural mood elevator. Tryptophan is an amino acid and precursor to serotonin, which is involved in the transmission of pleasure. Phenethylamine, often called the "Love Chemical," is a neurotransmitter that evokes feelings of passion. Caffeine, a stimulant, is also present in chocolate, in small amounts. All in all, chocolate is quite a sweet cocktail.

Not all chocolate is ideal for these recipes. See page 7 for my discussion of what to use. You can substitute carob in any of these recipes for a milder, zero caffeine alternative.

Shaved chocolate strips are a beautiful garnish for desserts. To make them, all you need is a bar or block of 100% cacao chocolate and a vegetable peeler. Shave flat, thin strips from the narrow side of the chocolate. And voilà! You've got yourself perfect chocolate garnish.

# Awesome Fudge Brownies

*Moist and chewy, these dark chocolate brownies will satisfy the most serious craving. This recipe is unique in that it calls for adding sweetener to the dry ingredients, and again to the wet ingredients. Which makes these brownies delightfully soft and gooey. Do not overbake. They'll seem wet, but they continue to bake after they're out of the oven. These brownies are luscious with Instant Mocha Buttercream Frosting (page 184), or just dusted with powdered erythritol. For the most delicious flavor and texture, follow this recipe exactly.*

[ YIELD: 20 rich brownies • EQUIPMENT NEEDED: A food processor ]

1½ cups walnuts or pecans, soaked and crisped if possible (see page 10)

3 cups Just Like Sugar Table Top natural chicory root sweetener (not Baking). A second choice is 4 cups Organic Zero Erythritol.

1 cup medium-shredded unsweetened coconut flakes (not coconut flour)

¾ cup pure cacao powder

1 tablespoon roasted carob powder (optional)

1½ teaspoons coffee powder

½ teaspoon unprocessed salt

½ teaspoon baking powder

1 teaspoon nutritional yeast (optional, for butter flavor)

½ cup warm filtered water or unsweetened coconut milk

3 large eggs, at room temperature

1½ teaspoons chocolate extract (optional)

1 tablespoon pure vanilla extract

½ cup roasted almond butter

2 tablespoons *raw* yacón syrup (optional)

⅓ cup coconut oil

Powdered Organic Zero Erythritol, for dusting (optional)

1. Preheat the oven to 350°F. Line a 9-inch square pan with parchment paper that overhangs on the sides for easy removal. Chop the nuts coarsely in the food processor and place them in a large mixing bowl.

2. In the dry food processor fitted with the "S" blade, grind 1 cup of the Just Like Sugar Table Top sweetener to a very fine powder. If using Organic Zero Erythritol, grind 1⅓ cups of that sweetener.

3. Add the shredded coconut to the sweetener in the food processor. Spin it for a minute until a very fine powder. Open the lid, stir the bottom, replace the lid, and grind again until the powder is uniformly fine.

4. To the ingredients in the food processor, add the cacao powder, roasted carob powder (if using), coffee powder, salt, baking powder, and nutritional yeast (if using). Mix well, place in the mixing bowl with the nuts, and mix again.

5. Place in the empty food processor the remaining 2 cups of Just Like Sugar Table Top Sweetener (or 2⅔ cups of Organic Zero Erythritol) and grind it to a fine powder. Then add the ½ cup of warm filtered water through the hole at the top. Mix until the sweetener is dissolved. Add the eggs, chocolate extract (if using), vanilla, almond butter, yacón syrup (if using), and coconut oil. Mix well until totally incorporated.

**continues . . .**

6. Pour the wet ingredients into the dry mixture. Stir briefly. The batter will be very thick.

7. Spoon the batter into the prepared baking pan and spread evenly.

8. Bake for 24 to 25 minutes. Let cool completely, 1 to 2 hours, in the pan on a rack. Use the paper handles to lift the cake onto a cutting board. Dust with powdered erythritol (optional). Cut four by five into twenty squares and enjoy!

# Black Forest Cake

*This luscious Black Forest Cake has two layers of dark chocolate cake. The 5-Minute Whipped Crème Topping and cherry sauce are luscious between each layer and on top. And if that wasn't yummy enough already, you'll finish it off with chocolate shavings as a garnish. Traditionally, this style of cake contains 2 tablespoons of kirsch liqueur in the cherry sauce, but I've omitted that here because it's not Paleo. Besides, this cake is delicious without it. For the best flavor and texture, follow the recipe exactly.*

[ YIELD: One double-layer 8-inch round cake • EQUIPMENT NEEDED: Any style blender and a food processor ]

2 cups 5-Minute Whipped Crème Topping (page 174)
1 recipe Devil's Food Double Chocolate Cake (page 97)
2 (10-ounce) bags frozen cherries, or 3 cups fresh
⅓ to ¾ cup Just Like Sugar Table Top natural chicory root sweetener (not Baking). I do not recommend erythritol, as you may taste the crystals when the sauce is chilled. (Sweeten to taste depending on the flavor of your cherries.)
2 tablespoons arrowroot powder
¼ teaspoon unprocessed salt
2 teaspoons freshly squeezed lemon juice
1 teaspoon pure vanilla extract
1 tablespoon melted coconut oil (place jar in lukewarm water to melt oil)
2 tablespoons finely grated fresh beet (optional, needed only if your cherries are not red)
1 ounce 100% cacao unsweetened baking chocolate, shaved (see tip), or ¼ cup pure unsweetened cacao nibs, for garnish

1. Prepare 2 cups of 5-Minute Whipped Crème Topping.
2. Prepare the Devil's Food Double Chocolate Cake in two 8-inch round layers.
3. Drain the cherries and reserve ½ cup of juice. In a small saucepan, whisk together the reserved cherry juice, sweetener, arrowroot powder, salt, lemon juice, vanilla, coconut oil, and beet (if using). Stir over medium heat until the arrowroot thickens. Add the cherries and cook 2 for 3 minutes, until the sauce becomes thick. Sweeten to taste, as cherries vary widely in sweetness. If the sauce is too thick, add a bit more cherry juice. Remove from the heat, pour into a bowl, and chill.
4. To assemble: With a thin knife, release the edges of the pan and gently allow the cake to pull away. Place one layer on a serving plate. Spread with half of the Whipped Crème, and pour half the cherry sauce over the topping so that it drips over the sides. Release the second cake layer from the pan, flip it on top of the first layer, and spread the remaining whipped topping over it. Top with the rest of the cherry sauce and garnish with shaved chocolate or cacao nibs. Keep the cake cold until serving.

**Tip:** *To make chocolate shavings for a garnish, start with a square of chocolate at room temperature. With a vegetable peeler, shave flat, thin strips from the narrow side of the chocolate.*

# Chocolate Lava Cake

*This lava cake is 100 percent irresistible chocolate decadence with a velvety smooth texture like a flourless dark chocolate soufflé. You'd never guess it takes just a few minutes to make. The secret to its luscious texture is beaten egg whites. Serve cold in thin wedges either plain, with fresh raspberries, or 1-Minute Whipped Crème Topping. Follow this recipe exactly, and you'll be pleased with the results.*

**[ YIELD: One 9- or 8-inch round cake • EQUIPMENT NEEDED: A food processor or high-speed blender such as Blendtec or Vitamix, and a handheld or standing mixer ]**

2 cups Just Like Sugar Table Top natural chicory root sweetener (not Baking). A second choice is 2⅔ cups Organic Zero Erythritol (be aware that the latter will not have a perfectly smooth texture and you may taste crystals).

1 cup pure cacao powder

1 teaspoon finely ground instant decaffeinated coffee powder or crystals (optional)

2 pinches of unprocessed salt

Zest of 1 orange

1 tablespoon pure vanilla extract

6 large eggs, at room temperature, separated

½ cup warm (not boiling) filtered water

½ cup melted coconut oil (place jar in lukewarm water to melt oil)

1. Preheat the oven to 325°F. Grease a 9- or 8-inch round pan. It is best to use a springform or removable-bottom pan. Dust it with cacao powder. Position a rack in the center of the oven.
2. In a dry food processor fitted with the "S" blade or a high-speed blender, grind the sweetener until it is a very fine powder.
3. To the ingredients in the food processor, add the cacao powder, coffee powder, and salt. Mix well.
4. To the dry ingredients in the food processor, add the orange zest, vanilla, egg yolks, warm water, and coconut oil. Mix very well several times until it is completely combined and all the sweetener crystals are dissolved. Pour this lavalike mixture into a large mixing bowl. You'll want to eat the whole thing at this point. But wait, it gets better!
5. In a large mixing bowl, with an electric mixer, beat the egg whites until soft peaks form. Do not beat until dry. With a rubber spatula, gently fold the egg whites into the chocolate mixture in three parts. Fold slowly and do not stir.
6. Pour the batter into the prepared baking pan. Bake for 30 to 35 minutes.
7. Remove from the oven and let cool for 1 hour in the pan. The cake will fall like a custard. This is normal. Chill the cake for 2 hours. Remove the sides of the pan, and serve.

# Dark Chocolate Cheesecake

*Chocolate cheesecake is a necessity of life. And this recipe does just the trick. Imagine luscious New York cheesecake merging with dark chocolate truffles. Sounds like heaven, right? Only this recipe is easy to make* and *totally dairy-free, of course. The cream-cheesy texture comes from blended lemons and coconut butter (who woulda thought?!). For the best flavor and texture, follow this recipe exactly.*

**[ YIELD: One 10-inch cheesecake • EQUIPMENT NEEDED: A food processor; any style blender (a high-speed blender such as Blendtec or Vitamix will give a smoother result); and a digital scale as lemons vary in size ]**

1 recipe 1-Minute Whipped Crème Topping (page 173)
1 recipe Minute Piecrust, Chocolate variation (page 113)
2 cups unsweetened coconut milk, as thick as possible (Lite coconut milk and coconut milk beverage in a carton will not work, as they are too thin.)
2¾ cups Just Like Sugar Table Top natural chicory root sweetener (not Baking). I do not recommend any other sweetener for this.

2 to 3 lemons, peeled and seeded (about 180 grams pulp) (Meyer lemons are my favorite.)
1 tablespoon pure vanilla extract
⅛ teaspoon plus a pinch unprocessed salt
1½ cups pure cacao powder
1 teaspoon finely ground instant decaffeinated coffee powder or crystals (optional)
200 grams (about 1 cup, packed tight) pure coconut butter (not coconut oil)
¼ cup melted coconut oil

(place jar in lukewarm water to melt oil)
1 tablespoon agar flakes
⅓ cup any unsweetened coconut milk, to cook agar
Unsweetened cacao nibs or shaved 100% cacao chocolate (see tip, page 93), for garnish

1. Prepare 1 cup of 1-Minute Whipped Crème Topping.
2. Make the Minute Piecrust, Chocolate variation. Press into a 10-inch springform pan and chill.
3. In a blender, combine the 2 cups of coconut milk, sweetener, lemons, vanilla, and salt. Blend until smooth and creamy.
4. Add the cacao powder, coffee powder (if using), and coconut butter. Blend again until smooth.
5. Add the coconut oil last and blend again. Add a tablespoon more coconut milk if necessary to blend.
6. In a shallow nonstick pan over medium heat, stir the agar into the ⅓ cup of coconut milk. Cook and stir gently

continues . . .

for 2 to 3 minutes until it is bubbling and gummy, and the flakes begin to dissolve. Add the agar mixture to the blender immediately and mix well to remove any lumps. Sweeten to taste. This is moderately sweet, and you may want it sweeter.

7. Pour the filling into the chilled crust. Refrigerate for 3 to 5 hours. You can chill it faster by placing it in the freezer for 30 minutes. However, be careful not to freeze longer than that because then it will be too difficult to cut.

8. Pour the Whipped Crème over the pie after the filling has chilled well and is firm. Chill the whole pie again. The topping will firm up in 30 minutes. Serve cold, garnished with unsweetened cacao nibs or shaved 100% cacao chocolate.

variations **Chocolate Raspberry Cheesecake:** Follow the recipe for Dark Chocolate Cheesecake. Make Raspberry "Jam" (page 192). Spread the Raspberry Jam on top of the chilled cheesecake. Garnish with fresh raspberries and shaved chocolate.

**German Chocolate Cheesecake:** Follow the recipe for Dark Chocolate Cheesecake, using the Minute Piecrust, German Chocolate version (page 114). Garnish the finished cheesecake with toasted coconut and pecans.

# Devil's Food Double Chocolate Cake

*The secret to this rich and luscious chocolate layer cake is beaten egg whites, which help it rise and stay moist. I use both 100% cacao and carob, which has a sweet, mild flavor and gives the cake a dark mahogany color. Follow this recipe exactly and you'll be pleased with the results. This double-layer cake is delicious with Chocolate Buttercream Frosting or Chocolate Crème Cheese Frosting.*

[ YIELD: One double-layer 8-inch cake • EQUIPMENT NEEDED: A food processor, any style blender; a standing or handheld mixer; and a digital scale, as apples vary in size ]

1 recipe Chocolate Buttercream Frosting (page 177) or Chocolate Crème Cheese Frosting (page 181)

2¼ cups Just Like Sugar Table Top natural chicory root sweetener (not Baking). A second choice is 3 cups Organic Zero Erythritol.

1½ cups medium-shredded unsweetened coconut flakes (not coconut flour)

¼ cup arrowroot powder

¾ cup pure cacao powder

¼ cup carob powder

1 teaspoon baking soda

¼ teaspoon plus a pinch unprocessed salt

6 large eggs, at room temperature, separated

About ½ tart apple, peeled and cored, cut into chunks (75 grams)

Zest of 1 orange

1 tablespoon pure vanilla extract

1 teaspoon apple cider vinegar

1½ cups thick unsweetened coconut milk, or ¾ cup thin

1 tablespoon *raw* yacón syrup (for caramel flavor)

1. Prepare the frosting and chill.
2. For the cake: Preheat the oven to 350°F. Line two 8-inch round cake pans with parchment paper.
3. In a dry food processor fitted with the "S" blade, grind the sweetener to a very fine powder.
4. Add the shredded coconut to the sweetener in the food processor. Spin it for a minute until a very fine powder. Open the lid, stir the bottom, replace the lid, and grind again until the powder is uniformly fine.
5. To the ingredients to the food processor, add the arrowroot powder, cacao powder, carob powder, baking soda, and salt. Mix until the color is consistent. Pour into a large mixing bowl.
6. A blender is best for wet ingredients. Place in any style blender the egg yolks, apple, orange zest, vanilla, vinegar, coconut milk, and yacón syrup. Blend until the apple pieces are completely liquefied, and then let the mixture sit while you beat the egg whites.
7. In a medium-size mixing bowl or a standing mixer, beat the egg whites until stiff but not dry—just until peaks form when you lift the beaters.
8. Add the liquid apple mixture to the dry mixture. Mix briefly but well enough so no lumps remain. Then fold in the beaten egg whites in three parts. Fold slowly and do not stir.
9. Pour the batter into the prepared baking pans. Bake for 30 to 35 minutes, let cool for 1 hour in the pans, then remove from the pans and frost.

# German Chocolate Cake

*This luscious dessert has three moist layers of cake with a sweet, gooey caramel frosting. A traditional classic, the flavor is so spectacular my friends can't believe it's Paleo. For best results, follow the recipe exactly.*

[ YIELD: One triple-layer 8-inch cake • EQUIPMENT NEEDED: A food processor; any style blender; a standing mixer or handheld mixer; and a digital scale, as apples vary in size ]

1 recipe Coconut Pecan Frosting (page 183)
2¼ cups Just Like Sugar Table Top natural chicory root sweetener (not Baking). A second choice is 3 cups Organic Zero Erythritol.
1½ cups medium-shredded unsweetened coconut flakes (not coconut flour)
¼ cup arrowroot powder
¾ cup pure cacao powder
¼ cup carob powder
1 teaspoon baking soda
¼ teaspoon plus a pinch unprocessed salt
6 large eggs, at room temperature, separated
½ tart apple, peeled and cored, cut into chunks (75 grams)
Zest of 1 orange
1 tablespoon pure vanilla extract
1 teaspoon apple cider vinegar
1½ cups thick unsweetened coconut milk, or ¾ cup thin
1 tablespoon *raw* yacón syrup (for caramel flavor)

1. Prepare the Coconut Pecan Frosting and chill.
2. Preheat the oven to 350°F. Line three 8-inch round cake pans with parchment paper. Grease the paper with coconut oil and dust with cacao powder.
3. In a dry food processor fitted with the "S" blade, grind the sweetener to a very fine powder.
4. Add the shredded coconut to the sweetener in the food processor. Spin it for a minute until a very fine powder. Open the lid, stir the bottom, replace the lid, and grind again until the powder is uniformly fine.
5. To the ingredients in the food processor, add the arrowroot powder, cacao powder, carob powder, baking soda, and salt. Mix until the color is consistent. Pour the dry mixture into a large mixing bowl.
6. A blender is best for the wet ingredients. Place in any style blender the egg yolks, apple, orange zest, vanilla, vinegar, coconut milk, and yacón syrup. Blend until the apple pieces are completely liquefied and then let the mixture sit while you beat the egg whites.
7. In a medium-size mixing bowl or a standing mixer, beat the egg whites until stiff but not dry—just until peaks form when you lift the beaters.
8. Add the liquid apple mixture to the dry mixture. Mix briefly and well enough so no lumps remain. Then fold in the beaten egg whites in three parts. Fold slowly and do not stir.

continues . . .

9. Pour the batter into the baking pans. Bake for 35 to 40 minutes, or until a toothpick inserted into the center comes out clean. Let cool well in the pans, at least an hour.

10. To assemble the cake: Using a thin knife, release the edges of each pan and gently allow the cake to pull away. Place one layer on a serving plate. Tuck a few strips of parchment paper under the edges of the cake to keep the plate clean while you frost it. Spread the cake layer with 1 cup of the Coconut Pecan Frosting. Release the second cake layer from the pan, place on top of the first layer, and spread with 1 cup of frosting. Repeat for the top layer, frosting the top and sides. Serve!

# Chocolate Bavarian Cream Filling or Mousse

*A rich and decadent filling or a dessert by itself, traditional Bavarian Cream is made with heavy cream and gelatin. This supereasy recipe is made with coconut milk and thickened with agar. As a creamy, smooth chocolate mousse, it melts in your mouth. Use it between cake layers or serve it in dessert cups. This recipe is also an excellent filling for Tiramisu (page 43), pies, cakes, or cupcakes. Follow this recipe exactly, and you will be quite pleased. I promise.*

**[ YIELD: 4 cups or 4 servings • EQUIPMENT NEEDED: Any style blender ]**

2 (14-ounce) cans (3½ cups) unsweetened coconut milk, as thick as possible (Lite coconut milk and coconut milk beverage in a carton will not work, as they are too thin.)

1 cup Just Like Sugar Table Top natural chicory root sweetener (not Baking). I do not recommend any other sweetener.

4 egg yolks, at room temperature (optional)

⅛ teaspoon unprocessed salt

1 tablespoon pure vanilla extract

¼ cup coconut oil

6 tablespoons pure cacao powder

1 teaspoon finely ground instant decaffeinated coffee powder or crystals (optional)

2 tablespoons *raw* yacón syrup (optional, for a lovely caramel flavor)

2 tablespoons agar flakes

½ cup any unsweetened coconut milk, to cook agar

1. In any style blender, blend the thick coconut milk, sweetener, egg yolks (if using), salt, vanilla, coconut oil, cacao powder, coffee crystals (if using), and yacón syrup (if using), until smooth and creamy. Do a taste test and then sweeten to taste.

2. In a shallow nonstick pan over medium heat, stir the agar flakes into the ½ cup of coconut milk. Cook and stir gently for 2 to 3 minutes, until it is bubbling and gummy, and the flakes begin to dissolve. Add the agar mixture to the blender immediately and blend well to remove any lumps.

3. Pour into four dessert cups or a bowl, cover, and chill for 2 hours or until firm before serving or using as a filling.)

# Chocolate Cream Pie

*Who doesn't love a creamy, dark chocolate cream pie? Just the name evokes memories of the sweet, smooth filling, and crispy crust. It's easy to make: Just blend a smooth chocolate mousse, place in a pie shell, and top with 5-Minute Whipped Crème Topping. For the best flavor and texture, follow the recipe exactly.*

[ YIELD: One 9-inch pie • EQUIPMENT NEEDED: A food processor and any style blender (a high-speed blender such as Blendtec or Vitamix will give you a smoother result) ]

2 cups 5-Minute Whipped Crème Topping (page 174)

1 recipe any single Paleo piecrust, such as either the Flaky Baked Piecrust (page 115) or the Minute Piecrust (page 113)

1¾ cups medium to thick unsweetened coconut milk (do not use thin)

1 cup Just Like Sugar Table Top natural chicory root sweetener (not Baking). I do not recommend any other sweetener for this.

2 teaspoons pure vanilla extract

5 tablespoons pure cacao powder

¼ teaspoon unprocessed salt

¼ cup melted coconut oil (place jar in lukewarm water to melt oil)

1½ tablespoons agar flakes

⅓ cup thick unsweetened coconut milk, to cook agar

Pure unsweetened cacao nibs, 100% cacao unsweetened baking chocolate, shaved (see tip, page 93), or pure cacao powder, for garnish

1. Prepare 2 cups of 5-Minute Whipped Crème Topping. Prepare the piecrust recipe of your choice, place in a 9-inch pie pan, and chill.
2. In a blender, combine 1¾ cups of coconut milk, sweetener, vanilla, cacao powder, and salt. Blend well until smooth and creamy. Sweeten to taste and mix again.
3. Add the barely warm coconut oil, and blend again until smooth.
4. In a shallow nonstick pan over medium heat, stir the agar flakes into the ⅓ cup of coconut milk. Cook and stir gently for 2 to 3 minutes, until it is bubbling and gummy, and the flakes begin to dissolve. Add the agar mixture to the blender immediately and blend well to remove any lumps.
5. Pour the blended filling into the piecrust and chill well until firm. Before serving, pour the Whipped Crème on top and spread it smooth. Garnish with unsweetened cacao nibs or shaved 100% cacao chocolate, or dust with pure cacao powder.

variation **German Chocolate Cream Pie:** Follow the recipe above. For the crust use the Minute Piecrust, German Chocolate variation (page 114).

# Coffee Toffee Pie

*This luscious chocolate mocha mousse has a sweet crunchy crust and creamy topping that will sat-*
*isfy the most passionate chocoholic. The Paleo recipe is adapted from Rudi's Country Kitchen in*
*Big Indian, New York. For the most delicious flavor and texture, follow this recipe exactly.*

**[ YIELD: One 9- or 10-inch pie • EQUIPMENT NEEDED: A food processor and any style blender ]**

## TOPPING
1 cup 5-Minute Whipped Crème Topping (page 174)
2 tablespoons instant decaffeinated coffee powder
¼ cup Just Like Sugar Table Top natural chicory root sweetener (not Baking).

## CRUST
½ cup Just Like Sugar Table Top natural chicory root sweetener (not Baking).
   I do not recommend any other sweetener for this.
¼ cup medium-shredded unsweetened coconut flakes (not coconut flour)
¼ cup pure cacao powder
½ teaspoon ground cinnamon
¼ teaspoon unprocessed salt
¼ cup pure coconut butter (not coconut oil)
1 teaspoon pure vanilla extract
½ teaspoon maple flavoring (optional)
⅔ cup raw nuts, soaked if possible (see page 10)
3 tablespoons filtered water

## FILLING
3 cups unsweetened coconut milk, as thick as possible (Lite coconut milk and coconut milk beverage in a carton will not work, as they are too thin.)
1 cup Just Like Sugar Table Top natural chicory root sweetener (not Baking).
1 teaspoon ground cinnamon
2 teaspoons pure vanilla extract
⅛ teaspoon unprocessed salt
½ cup pure cacao powder
2 teaspoons instant decaffeinated coffee powder
2 tablespoons *raw* yacón syrup (optional, for a lovely caramel flavor)
6 tablespoons coconut oil
2 tablespoons agar flakes
½ cup any unsweetened coconut milk, to cook agar
Unsweetened cacao powder or shaved 100% cacao chocolate (see tip, page 93), for garnish

**continues . . .**

1. Prepare 1 cup of 5-Minute Whipped Crème Topping, adding to the blender the coffee powder and sweetener. Blend well and chill.

2. For the crust: Get out a 9- or 10-inch springform pan (your choice!).

3. In a dry food processor fitted with the "S" blade, grind the sweetener until it is a very fine powder.

4. Add the shredded coconut to the sweetener in the food processor. Spin it for a minute until a very fine powder. Open the lid, stir the bottom, replace the lid, and grind again until the powder is uniformly fine.

5. To the ingredients to the food processor, add the cacao powder, cinnamon, salt, coconut butter, vanilla, and maple flavoring. Mix well.

6. Add the nuts and pulse in very briefly so they remain in pieces and are not mushy. Then, add the filtered water and mix again very briefly until it forms a cohesive dough.

7. Pour the filling into the springform pan. With a rubber spatula, press the filling evenly into the crust. If you prefer a crispier crust, you may bake it for 20 minutes at 350°F. Baking is optional, as the crust is delicious raw. (I like the crispy crust myself.) Chill well.

8. For the filling: In a blender, combine the 3 cups of coconut milk, sweetener, cinnamon, vanilla, salt, cacao powder, coffee powder, yacón syrup (if using), and coconut oil. Blend well until it is completely smooth and creamy. (The original Rudi's recipe had 2 tablespoons of coffee liqueur; however, we know this is not Paleo, and so it is omitted from this recipe.)

9. In a shallow nonstick pan over medium heat, stir the agar into the ½ cup of coconut milk. Cook and stir gently for 2 to 3 minutes until it is bubbling and gummy, and the flakes begin to dissolve. Add the agar mixture to the blender immediately and blend well to remove any lumps.

10. Pour the filling into the chilled crust. Refrigerate for 3 to 5 hours. You can chill it faster in the freezer for 30 minutes; however, freezing completely will make it too hard to cut.

11. To finish the pie: Pour the Whipped Crème onto the pie after the filling has chilled. Chill the whole pie again, and the topping will firm up in about 30 minutes. Serve cold, garnished with unsweetened cacao powder or shaved 100% cacao chocolate.

# Chocolate Fudge

*This creamy fudge is for extreme chocolate lovers. It has an intense, rich flavor of dark chocolate, along with a crunchy texture of toasted pecans.* And *it's amazingly quick to make in any style blender—just blend, chill, and serve! For best results, follow this recipe exactly.*

**[ YIELD: About 60 pieces • EQUIPMENT NEEDED: Any style blender ]**

1 cup raw nuts, soaked if possible (see page 10)

⅔ cup unsweetened coconut milk, as thick as possible (Lite coconut milk and coconut milk beverage in a carton will not work, as they are too thin.)

1¼ cups Just Like Sugar Table Top natural chicory root sweetener (not Baking).
I do not recommend any other sweetener for this.

1 tablespoon pure vanilla extract

⅛ teaspoon unprocessed salt

2 tablespoons *raw* yacón syrup (optional)

¼ cup pure cacao powder

75 grams (about ⅓ cup tightly packed) pure coconut butter (not coconut oil)

½ cup melted coconut oil (place jar in lukewarm water to melt oil)

1. Preheat the oven to 350°F. Line a 9-inch square pan with parchment paper so it hangs over the edges for easy removal.
2. Chop the nuts coarsely by hand or in a food processor. Then toast them in a dry, shallow baking pan with the timer set for 10 minutes. Take care not to burn them. Remove them from the oven and allow to cool.
3. In a blender, combine the coconut milk, sweetener, vanilla, salt, yacón syrup (if using), and cacao powder. Blend until smooth and creamy.
4. Add the coconut butter and blend again until smooth and creamy.
5. Add the melted oil last, and blend until smooth and creamy.
6. Remove the blender from its stand. Add the nuts and stir them in by hand with a rubber spatula.
7. Pour the molten mixture into the prepared pan. Chill for 4 hours or overnight. Remove from pan and place the whole block of fudge on a cutting board. Cut eight by eight into about sixty square pieces and enjoy. Keep chilled.

> **variation Chocolate Hazelnut Fudge:** Add ⅓ cup of roasted hazelnut butter to the blender in step 3.

# Superfood Black Fudge

*This creamy chocolate fudge is a real energy booster as a snack or dessert. I call it Superfood Black Fudge because it is loaded with nutrients. The dark color comes from pure cacao, carob, and green chlorella powder, a mild-flavored green algae high in protein and nutrients. Buy it in your local healthy grocery or online. Try the recipe once as written so you'll experience this amazing flavor combination. After that, you can omit any of the superfoods, or substitute your own. But be careful, as many green powders are really bitter.*

**[ YIELD: About 60 pieces • EQUIPMENT NEEDED: Any style blender (a high-speed blender will give a smoother result) and a digital scale, for the coconut butter ]**

2 cups raw nuts, soaked if possible (see page 10)

⅔ cup unsweetened coconut milk, as thick as possible (Lite coconut milk and coconut milk beverage in a carton will not work, as they are too thin.)

1½ cups Just Like Sugar Table Top natural chicory root sweetener (not Baking). I do not recommend erythritol as it does not give a smooth texture.

1 tablespoon pure vanilla extract

¼ teaspoon unprocessed salt

3 tablespoons *raw* yacón syrup (optional)

¼ cup pure cacao powder

1 teaspoon finely ground instant decaffeinated coffee powder or crystals (optional)

2 teaspoons ground cinnamon

⅔ cup melted coconut oil (place jar in lukewarm water to melt oil)

**SUPERFOODS**

2 teaspoons chlorella powder

2 tablespoons roasted carob powder

2 tablespoons raw hemp seeds

1 teaspoon bee pollen

1 tablespoon maca powder

100 grams (about ½ cup) pure coconut butter (not coconut oil)

1. Preheat the oven to 350°F. Line a 9-inch square pan with parchment paper so it hangs over the edges for easy removal.

2. Chop the nuts coarsely by hand or in a food processor. Then toast them in a shallow baking pan, setting the timer for 10 minutes. Take care not to burn them. Remove from the oven and let cool.

3. In a blender, combine the coconut milk, sweetener, vanilla, salt, and yacón syrup (if using). Blend well until the sweetener dissolves.

4. Add the cacao powder, coffee powder (if using), and cinnamon, and blend again.

5. Add the melted oil and blend until smooth and creamy.

**continues . . .**

6. Now add the chlorella, roasted carob powder, hemp seeds, bee pollen, and maca powder. Blend until smooth and creamy.

7. Add the coconut butter last, and blend until smooth.

8. Remove the blender from its stand. Add the chopped nuts and stir them in by hand with a rubber spatula.

9. Pour the fudge into the prepared pan and smooth it flat. Chill for 4 hours up to overnight, or freeze for 2 hours if you're in a hurry. Remove from the pan, remove the paper, and transfer to a cold cutting board. Cut into ¾-inch squares and place them on a serving plate. Store covered in the refrigerator.

# Chocolate-Covered Strawberries

*As most everyone knows, Chocolate-Covered Strawberries equal love, and this simple recipe is no exception.*

**[ YIELD: 20 chocolate-covered strawberries • EQUIPMENT NEEDED: A double boiler, or a smaller pan that fits on top of a larger one ]**

20 fresh strawberries
4 ounces (118 grams) 100% cacao unsweetened baking chocolate
1½ cups Just Like Sugar Table Top natural chicory root sweetener (not Baking). I do not recommend any other sweetener for this.
½ cup any unsweetened coconut milk or water
2 teaspoons pure vanilla extract
2 tablespoons carob powder
2 tablespoons melted coconut oil (place jar in lukewarm water to melt oil)

1. Wash the strawberries gently and dry thoroughly with a soft towel. Line a plate with waxed paper or parchment paper for the strawberries.
2. Melt the chocolate in a double boiler (or a smaller pan set on top of a larger pan of hot water). When the water begins to boil, turn down the heat to a low simmer.
3. When the chocolate melts, add the sweetener and stir with a rubber spatula until completely dissolved. Add the coconut milk, vanilla, and carob powder. Stir until the chocolate mixture is completely smooth.
4. While the mixture is warm but not very hot, add the melted coconut oil and stir with a rubber spatula until it is completely mixed in. Coconut oil is delicate, so it's important that both temperatures be similar—moderately warm.
5. When the mixture is smooth, you're ready to dip the strawberries. Make sure they are dry or the chocolate will not adhere properly. Keep the double boiler at a simmer so the chocolate is slightly warm. Check the thickness of the mixture by dipping the first strawberry. If it is too thick, you can stir in a tiny bit more coconut milk or water. If is too thin, wait a few minutes and it will evaporate to the perfect consistency.
6. Dip each strawberry halfway into the melted chocolate. Place it, either upside down or on its side, on the prepared plate. Chill well. When they're cold, transfer the strawberries to a serving plate, and enjoy!

# Homemade Chocolate Chips

*I can't live without chocolate chips. These Paleo chocolate chips are easy: You melt the ingredients together, then freeze the mixture in a flat pan. Once frozen, it's quick to cut the chocolate into tiny cubes. Keep them on hand in the freezer to use in cookies, ice cream, or cheesecake. Most store-bought chocolate chips are filled with refined sugar and dairy. But not these! Instead, you're eating pure dark chocolate, strictly Paleo and delicious. If you don't have time to make your own chips, you can cut any 100% cacao chocolate bar into tiny pieces . . . but they will be bitter. This recipe makes your Paleo chocolate chips sweet. For best results, follow this recipe exactly.*

**[ YIELD: 2 cups chips • EQUIPMENT NEEDED: A double boiler, or a smaller pan that fits on top of a larger one ]**

4 ounces 100% cacao unsweetened baking chocolate or cacao paste (118 grams)

1¼ cups Just Like Sugar Table Top natural chicory root sweetener (not Baking). I do not recommend any other sweetener for this.

1 teaspoon pure vanilla extract

1 tablespoon any unsweetened coconut milk

1 teaspoon instant decaffeinated coffee powder or crystals (optional)

2 tablespoons melted coconut oil (place jar in lukewarm water to melt oil)

1. Line with parchment paper a flat tray or pan that fits in your freezer.
2. Melt the chocolate in a double boiler (or a smaller pan set on top of a larger pan of hot water). When the water begins to boil, turn down the heat to a low simmer.
3. With a rubber spatula, stir in the sweetener, vanilla, coconut milk, and coffee powder (if using). Stir gently until smooth.
4. While the mixture is warm but not hot, add the melted coconut oil, and stir with a rubber spatula until it is mixed in. Coconut oil is delicate, so it is important that both temperatures be similar—moderately warm.
5. Pour the chocolate into the prepared pan and freeze for 1 hour, until solid. Place your cutting board in the freezer, too, so it will be nice and cold and the chocolate will stay firm while you cut.
6. Remove the chocolate and cutting board from the freezer, and place the slab of chocolate on your chilled cutting board. With a sharp knife, cut the chocolate into ⅛- to ¼-inch strips vertically. Then cut them the same size horizontally, into tiny cubes. (Do pop a few in your mouth just to make sure they're tasty.) Store the chips in a sealed container in the freezer. When adding to cookie dough, add them frozen, so they will stay intact better while baking.

# Dark Chocolate Truffles

*They taste divine. They look totally luscious and decadent. They make a beautiful dessert or gift. It's hard to believe they're so easy! These rich, dark chocolate truffles are made with melted 100% cacao chocolate and coconut milk. Choose from a delicious variety of flavors and coatings. For the most wonderful flavor and texture, please follow this recipe exactly.*

[ YIELD: About 30 truffles • EQUIPMENT NEEDED: A food processor ]

**BASIC FILLING**

4 ounces 100% cacao unsweetened baking chocolate or raw cacao paste (118 grams)

½ cup unsweetened coconut milk, as thick as possible (Lite coconut milk and coconut milk beverage in a carton will not work, as they are too thin.)

1¼ to 1½ cups Just Like Sugar Table Top natural chicory root sweetener (not Baking). I do not recommend any other sweetener for the filling. (I like truffles moderately sweet.

If you like them quite sweet, use the larger amount of sweetener.)

2 teaspoons pure vanilla extract

**SUGGESTED COATINGS**

**Choose your favorite, or be adventurous and do them all:**

½ cup raw nuts, soaked if possible (see page 10), chopped finely and toasted lightly (see page 11)

¼ cup medium-shredded unsweetened coconut (not coconut flour), raw or toasted (see page 120)

Pure cacao powder

¼ cup *raw* yacón syrup and chopped nuts (roll in the syrup, then in the nuts)

¼ cup *raw* yacón syrup and pure unsweetened cacao nibs (my personal favorite) (roll in the syrup, then in the nibs)

3 tablespoons finely ground Wholesome Sweeteners Organic Zero Erythritol (grind in a blender, food processor, or home coffee grinder)

Spices, such as ground cinnamon, ground cardamom, or ground ginger

1. Weigh out the chocolate and cut it into large chunks. In a food processor, chop it into tiny pieces.

2. In a small saucepan over medium heat, slowly heat the coconut milk, sweetener, and vanilla. Stir until the sweetener dissolves and the mixture is hot but not boiling.

3. Remove from the heat and immediately add the chopped chocolate. Stir with a small whisk until smooth and creamy. If it cools too fast it may get lumps; if this happens, put the pan on the heat briefly to soften it

gently, but do not boil. Low heat is enough to melt the chocolate. Stir until perfectly smooth. Then pour the mixture into a bowl and chill for 2 hours, until firm. Get out a heavy serving plate, and chill it.

4. To form the truffles: Use a spoon to measure out small portions of the soft chocolate, and then roll into ¾-inch balls between your hands. Coat in the coatings of your choice. Arrange them on your cold serving plate. Keep the finished truffles refrigerated. Serve and enjoy!

**continues . . .**

variations

**Almond Chocolate Truffles:** Prepare the basic filling, adding ⅓ cup of almond butter in step 2. Roll in chopped almonds.

**Brazilian Chocolate Brigadeiros:** Prepare the basic filling, adding ½ teaspoon of ground cinnamon and ½ teaspoon of instant decaffeinated coffee powder or crystals in step 2. Roll in *raw* yacón syrup and coat with small raw cacao nibs.

**Chocolate Chai Truffles:** Prepare the basic filling, adding ½ teaspoon of ground cinnamon, ¼ teaspoon of ground cardamom, and ¼ teaspoon of ground ginger in step 2. Roll in pure cacao powder.

**Chocolate Hawaiian Truffles:** Prepare the basic filling, adding ½ teaspoon of ground ginger in step 2. Roll in unsweetened coconut flakes or chopped macadamia nuts.

**Chocolate Hazelnut Truffles:** Prepare the basic filling, adding ⅓ cup of hazelnut butter in step 2. Roll in finely chopped hazelnuts.

**Chocolate Orange Truffles:** Prepare the basic filling, adding the zest of ½ orange and 3 drops of food-safe sweet orange aromatherapy oil (optional) in step 2. Roll in Chocolate Sauce (page 189) or medium-shredded unsweetened coconut flakes (not coconut flour).

**Chocolate Rose Truffles:** Prepare the basic filling, adding 4 drops of food-safe rose absolute or aromatherapy oil in step 2. Roll in ¼ cup of finely ground Organic Zero Erythritol.

**Classic Chocolate Truffles:** Prepare the basic filling, then roll in Chocolate Sauce (page 189).

**Mayan Chocolate Truffles:** Prepare the basic filling, adding ½ teaspoon of ground cinnamon, ½ teaspoon of instant decaffeinated coffee powder, and a pinch of cayenne in step 2. Roll in pure cacao powder with a pinch of ground cinnamon.

*If you want to make an apple pie from scratch,*
*you must first create the universe.*

—CARL SAGAN

# PIES AND TARTS

∙∙∙∙∙∙∙∙∙∙∙∙∙∙∙∙∙∙∙∙∙∙∙∙∙∙∙∙∙∙∙∙∙∙∙∙∙∙∙∙∙∙∙∙∙∙∙∙∙∙∙∙∙∙∙∙∙∙∙∙∙∙∙∙∙∙∙∙∙

**I** am so excited to share these Paleo pie recipes with you, because they include some amazing and delicious discoveries. There's nothing more wonderful than a hot baked pie, but a flaky piecrust without grain seemed an impossible task. After about ten attempts, I found the perfect combination of coconut, arrowroot powder, and egg—and the Flaky Baked Piecrust (page 115) is the result. I couldn't believe my eyes—it rolls easily, bakes beautifully, and tastes absolutely crisp and delicious, whether it's Pecan Pie (page 122) or Cherry Pie (page 118). Try it!

The Minute Piecrust recipe (page 113) is so easy, it's a boon to any kitchen—and tastes absolutely luscious. You can choose from myriad flavor variations, such as Almond Streusel Piecrust (page 113) and German

Chocolate Piecrust (page 114). Another useful discovery is the Cheesecake (page 128) without cheese. Instead, this recipe calls for pure 100% coconut butter with lemon juice. It has a smooth, creamy and tart flavor, so much like cream cheese that my guests can't tell the difference. Again, the recipe has many variations so you can have cheesecake practically every day and it will always be new. If you're feeling adventurous, try the Finger Tarts (page 127), a fabulous recipe for entertaining: individual bite-size treats for everybody. For those who prefer to savor the classic traditional pies, there's Pumpkin Pie (page 123), Dutch Apple Pie (page 116), and more, all made with 100 percent whole Paleo foods.

# Minute Piecrust

*This simple piecrust recipe is my go-to favorite. Make it in a minute. Literally, one minute. Modify it a hundred ways and discover that no matter what you do—it's always delicious. Just mix these few ingredients, press into the pan, and serve. There's no need to roll it out or bake it. If you can soak the nuts beforehand, it's even better. For best results, follow this recipe exactly.*

**[ YIELD: One single 9-inch piecrust • EQUIPMENT NEEDED: A food processor ]**

1½ cups raw nuts, soaked if possible (see page 10)

⅓ cup Just Like Sugar Table Top natural chicory root sweetener (not Baking). I do not recommend any other sweetener for this.

3 tablespoons coconut oil

1 teaspoon pure vanilla extract

¼ teaspoon unprocessed salt

1 to 2 tablespoons filtered water, only if needed

1. Place in a food processor the nuts, sweetener, coconut oil, vanilla, and salt. Mix well until the texture resembles a paste. If your nuts are very dry, you may need to slowly add a bit of filtered water. Sweeten to taste.
2. Press into a 9-inch pie pan and chill briefly while you make the filling. Easy, breezy!

---

### variations

**Almond Streusel Piecrust:** For the nuts, use 1½ cups of almonds, soaked if possible (see page 10). Add ½ teaspoon of ground cinnamon, ¼ teaspoon of grated nutmeg, and a pinch of ground cloves.

**Chocolate Piecrust:** Add ¼ cup of pure cacao powder, ½ teaspoon of ground cinnamon, and ⅓ cup more Just Like Sugar Table Top sweetener.

**Chocolate Hazelnut Piecrust:** Use 1½ cups of hazelnuts only. Add ¼ cup of pure cacao powder, ½ teaspoon of ground cinnamon, ⅓ cup more Just Like Sugar Table Top sweetener, ¼ teaspoon of maple flavoring, and a pinch of nutmeg.

**Coconut Piecrust:** Instead of nuts, substitute 3 cups of toasted medium-shredded unsweetened coconut flakes (not coconut flour). Use only 1 tablespoon of coconut oil, instead of three.

**Coconut Cashew Piecrust:** Use 1 cup of soaked cashews (see page 10) and substitute 1 cup of toasted, medium-shredded unsweetened coconut flakes for the remaining nuts.

**continues . . .**

## Minute Piecrust (variations)

**German Chocolate Piecrust:** For the nuts, use 1 cup of toasted pecans, soaked if possible (see page 10) and 1 cup of toasted, medium-shredded unsweetened coconut flakes (not coconut flour).

**Lemon Ginger Piecrust:** Add the grated zest of 1 lemon and 1½ inches of fresh ginger, chopped or grated.

**Macadamia Nut Piecrust:** Use 2 cups of raw, unsalted macadamia nuts and a pinch of nutmeg.

# Flaky Baked Piecrust

*This baked piecrust will quickly become your favorite because it is so simple to make and goes perfectly with any pie recipe. Perfect for Dutch Apple Pie (page 116) or Pumpkin Pie (page 123), it is crispy and sweet, and you can roll it out or press it into the pan with your fingers. My guests love this crust, and never guess that it's completely grain-free. For the most delicious flavor and texture, follow this recipe exactly.*

**[ YIELD: One single or double 9-inch piecrust • EQUIPMENT NEEDED: A food processor ]**

**SINGLE PIECRUST**
3 tablespoons Just Like Sugar Table Top natural chicory root sweetener (not Baking). A second choice is ¼ cup Organic Zero Erythritol.
3 cups medium-shredded unsweetened coconut flakes (not coconut flour)
⅓ cup arrowroot powder
½ teaspoon unprocessed salt
1 teaspoon pure vanilla extract
2 large eggs

**DOUBLE PIECRUST**
6 tablespoons Just Like Sugar Table Top natural chicory root sweetener (not Baking). A second choice is ½ cup Organic Zero Erythritol.
4½ cups medium-shredded unsweetened coconut flakes (not coconut flour)
½ cup arrowroot powder
¾ teaspoon unprocessed salt
1½ teaspoons pure vanilla extract
3 medium to large eggs

1. In a dry food processor fitted with the "S" blade, grind the sweetener to a very fine powder.
2. Add the shredded coconut to the sweetener in the food processor. Spin it for a minute until a very fine powder. Open the lid, stir the bottom, replace the lid, and grind again until the powder is uniformly fine.
3. To the ingredients in the food processor, add the arrowroot and salt. Mix well.
4. To the dry ingredients in the food processor, add the vanilla and eggs. Mix again until it becomes a soft, uniform dough.
5. Form the dough into a ball (or two balls, if a double crust). Flatten it with your hands to about ½ inch thick. Wrap in plastic or a damp cloth, and chill for 30 minutes to firm up.
6. Preheat the oven to 300°F. Roll out each ball of dough between two pieces of parchment paper to about ⅛ inch thick and 13 to 14 inches round, depending on the pan size.
7. Remove the top layer of parchment paper, and use the bottom layer to flip the dough gently over onto the pie pan. Repair any rips and flute or crimp the edges with your fingers.
8. Prick the bottom of the pie with a fork in a few places and prebake for 25 minutes at 300°F. Allow the crust to cool completely before using.
9. If baking a double crust, follow the recipe directions for the top crust.

# Dutch Apple Pie

*This Paleo Apple Pie puts a new spin on an old favorite. It tastes just like my mom's traditional pie, except that it's grain-free. I'm told that Paleolithic apples were tart, something like our crab apples today. So you can make it Paleo-friendly by using tart apples, such as Granny Smith, Fuji, and Pink Lady (which are also lower in carbs). Serve with 1-Minute Whipped Crème Topping (page 173). For the best flavor and texture, follow this recipe exactly.*

**[ YIELD: One 9-inch pie • EQUIPMENT NEEDED: A food processor ]**

1 recipe single-crust Flaky Baked Piecrust (page 115)
6 tart apples (6 to 7 cups when sliced)
2 tablespoons freshly squeezed lemon juice
⅔ cup Just Like Sugar Table Top natural chicory root sweetener (not Baking). A second choice is ¾ cup Organic Zero Erythritol.
3½ tablespoons arrowroot powder
2 teaspoons ground cinnamon

⅛ teaspoon grated nutmeg
⅛ teaspoon ground cloves
⅛ teaspoon unprocessed salt
Zest of ½ orange
2 tablespoons melted coconut oil (place jar in lukewarm water to melt oil)
1 to 2 tablespoons *raw* yacón syrup (optional, for caramel taste)

**STREUSEL TOPPING**
⅓ cup medium-shredded unsweetened coconut flakes (not coconut flour)

⅓ cup Just Like Sugar Table Top natural chicory root sweetener (not Baking). A second choice is ½ cup Organic Zero Erythritol.
¼ teaspoon unprocessed salt
1 teaspoon ground cinnamon
¼ teaspoon grated nutmeg
⅓ cup chopped nuts, soaked if possible (see page 10)
2 tablespoons melted coconut oil (place jar in lukewarm water to melt oil)

1. Preheat the oven to 300°F. Prepare the single-crust Flaky Baked Piecrust, place in a 9-inch pie pan, and prebake for 20 minutes. When it finishes, increase the oven temperature to 350°F.

2. For the filling: Core and slice the apples into very thin slices, about ⅛ inch, by hand or using the slicer of a food processor. Peeling is optional. Personally, I love to eat the peels. Being in thin slices help the peels to soften. Place the apples in a large mixing bowl and toss with the lemon juice to coat.

3. Sprinkle on the apples and stir in the sweetener, arrowroot powder, cinnamon, nutmeg, cloves, salt, orange zest, coconut oil, and yacón syrup (if using). Adjust the sweetness and spices to taste. Set the apples aside to rest for 15 minutes.

4. For the streusel: In a small bowl, stir together the coconut, sweetener, salt, cinnamon, nutmeg, nuts (if using), and coconut oil.

5. Pour the apples into the baked crust and press tightly so they are level. Spread the streusel on top and poke holes in it with a spoon handle, to help it to sink in. Press it firmly with your hands.

6. Put the pie pan on a baking sheet to catch leaks. Bake for 55 to 75 minutes. Let cool for 1 to 3 hours in the pan on a rack. Serve warm.

# Banana Cream Pie

*Simple ingredients make this banana cream pie a classic: smooth vanilla pudding and sliced bananas, all covered with fluffy coconut whipped cream, like a delicious ambrosia. Everyone loves this dessert. For the best flavor and texture, follow the recipe exactly.*

**[ YIELD: One 9-inch pie • EQUIPMENT NEEDED: A food processor and any style blender (a high-speed blender such as Blendtec or Vitamix will make it smoother) ]**

2 cups 5-Minute Whipped Crème Topping (page 174)

1 recipe any single Paleo piecrust, such as the Flaky Baked Piecrust (page 115) or Minute Piecrust (page 113)

4 ripe bananas

2½ cups medium to thick unsweetened coconut milk (not thin)

1 to 1⅓ cups Just Like Sugar Table Top natural chicory root sweetener (not Baking). I do not recommend any other sweetener for this.

1 tablespoon pure vanilla extract

2 teaspoons freshly squeezed lemon juice

¼ teaspoon unprocessed salt

⅓ cup melted coconut oil (place jar in lukewarm water to melt oil)

2 tablespoons agar flakes

½ cup unsweetened coconut milk, to cook agar

1. Prepare 2 cups of the 5-Minute Whipped Crème Topping and chill.

2. Prepare your choice of piecrust. Press into a 9-inch pie pan and chill.

3. In a blender, combine two of the bananas, the 2½ cups of coconut milk, the sweetener, vanilla, lemon juice, and salt. Blend well until smooth and creamy. Sweeten to taste.

4. Add the barely warm coconut oil and blend again until smooth.

5. In a shallow nonstick pan over medium heat, stir the agar into the ½ cup of coconut milk. Cook and stir gently for 2 to 3 minutes, until it is bubbling and gummy, and the flakes begin to dissolve. Add the agar mixture to the blender immediately and blend well to remove any lumps.

6. Slice the remaining two bananas into thin disks and line the bottom of the chilled piecrust with them. Pour the blended filling on top and chill for 2 hours, until firm. Before serving, spread with the Whipped Crème. Serve cold.

# Cherry Pie

*Cherry Pie with a lattice top is one of my favorite desserts. I'm told Paleolithic cherries were not as sweet as our cherries, so if you can hunt and gather some sour cherries, you'll be right in step with our ancestors. This recipe works for all types of cherries, sour or sweet. In fact, it works for any berry pie or fruit pie. One of the secrets to a great cherry pie is to achieve the perfect level of sweetness to enhance the natural cherries. As sweetness levels vary widely, you will need to adjust the sweetener to taste, depending on the type of cherries. The second secret to cherry pie is to make a filling that is thick and juicy, but not too runny. Cherries vary in liquid content. Some cherries are compact and dry. Other cherries are juicier, including frozen cherries. Some of the excess juice may need to be drained off. This recipe guides you through the steps to a successful pie with every type of cherry. Cherries combine beautifully with chocolate, and the Black Forest Cherry Pie variation that follows adds a truly delicious flavor rush. To pit fresh cherries, use a decorator tip: stand it on end and push the cherry down onto the tip. It's that easy. Or use a cherry pitter, an inexpensive tool similar to a paper punch. Don't miss the variation that follows for berry pie. For best results, follow this recipe exactly. Serve warm or cold with 1-Minute Whipped Crème Topping (page 173).*

[ YIELD: One 9-inch pie • EQUIPMENT NEEDED: A food processor and a decorator tip or cherry pitter ]

1 recipe double-crust Flaky Baked Piecrust (page 115)

4 (10-ounce) bags frozen cherries, or 8 cups fresh pitted

½ to 3 cups Just Like Sugar Table Top natural chicory root sweetener (not Baking). A second choice is ⅔ to 2 cups Organic Zero Erythritol. (Sweeten to taste, depending on your cherries.)

3½ tablespoons arrowroot powder

¼ teaspoon unprocessed salt

1 tablespoon freshly squeezed lemon juice

1 teaspoon pure vanilla extract

1 tablespoon melted coconut oil (place jar in lukewarm water to melt oil)

2 tablespoons Microplane-grated fresh beet (optional, needed only if your cherries are not red)

1. Prepare the double-crust Flaky Baked Piecrust. Divide the dough into two equal balls. Wrap them in plastic or parchment paper. Press them flat to ½ inch thick so they'll chill evenly, and refrigerate for 30 minutes.

2. Preheat the oven to 425°F. Get out a 9-inch pie pan.

3. Place the cherries in a food processor. Pulse them three or four times briefly, to gently break them up into pieces and release the juices, but without turning them to mush. Pour them into a colander over a large mixing bowl and press firmly to squeeze out their excess juice. Drain the cherries very well, reserving ½ cup of the juice. (If you don't get any juice, substitute ½ cup of filtered water.) Place the strained cherries in a large mixing bowl.

**continues . . .**

4. Place in the empty food processor the ½ cup of cherry juice, ½ cup of sweetener, arrowroot powder, salt, lemon juice, vanilla, coconut oil, and grated beet (if using). Mix well. Pour this mixture over the cherries in the mixing bowl and stir well by hand. Sweeten to taste by adding the sweetener slowly. You will need to add from ½ to 2½ cups more sweetener if your cherries are sour. Stir and let the filling stand for 15 minutes.

5. Remove one portion of pie dough from the refrigerator. It is important to keep the dough cool. Even your warm hands can melt the coconut oil. Roll out the dough between two pieces of parchment paper to about ⅛ inch thick and 13 to 14 inches round.

6. Remove the top layer of parchment paper, and use the bottom layer to flip the dough gently over onto the pie pan. Trim the edges.

7. Between two fresh pieces of parchment paper, roll out the remaining dough for the lattice top of the pie to ⅛ inch thick and 13 to 14 inches round. With a knife, cut the dough into strips ½-inch wide. Pour the cherry filling into the piecrust and carefully place strips horizontally ½ inch apart over the pie. Then place more strips vertically over the pie, creating a simple lattice. Repair any rips. Crimp or flute the edges with your fingers. Brush the edges with water to retard browning.

8. Put the pie pan on a baking sheet to catch leaks. Bake at 425°F for 20 minutes. Lower the temperature to 350°F and continue baking for 30 to 40 minutes. When it is finished, the juices should be bubbling, the arrowroot must be completely dissolved, the cherries soft, and crust golden brown. Let cool completely if you want pretty pieces. However, this pie is delicious warm with Paleo Vanilla Ice Cream (page 161), and nobody will care how it looks.

---

variations

**Black Forest Cherry Pie:** Follow the recipe above. Add to the blended filling 3 tablespoons of pure cacao powder; ⅓ cup of thick coconut milk, or 3 tablespoons thin; and ¼ cup more Just Like Sugar Table Top sweetener, or ⅓ cup Organic Zero Erythritol, or to taste. Serve with 1-Minute Whipped Crème Topping (page 173) and a sprinkling of unsweetened cacao nibs.

**Berry Pie:** Make your favorite berry pie with blueberries, marionberries, chokeberries, elderberries, blackberries, gooseberries, or any berry you like. Follow the Cherry Pie recipe, substituting 8 cups of berries. If you're using frozen berries, follow the instructions to drain them very well. You'll need to adjust the sweetener to taste, depending on your berry.

# Coconut Cream Pie

*This pie has a rich, smooth coconut filling in a crispy crust. The key to its sumptuous flavor is creamy coconut milk with lightly toasted coconut, which is a bit crunchy and adds a rich sweetness to each bite. It's so easy to prepare: Just make a Minute Piecrust, blend the filling, and chill. For the ideal flavor and texture, follow this recipe exactly.*

[ **YIELD: One 9-inch pie** • **EQUIPMENT NEEDED: Any style blender (a high-speed blender such as Blendtec or Vitamix will give you a smoother pie)** ]

2 cups 5-Minute Whipped Crème Topping (page 174)

Minute Piecrust, Coconut variation (page 113)

1 cup medium-shredded unsweetened coconut (not coconut flour)

2½ cups medium to thick unsweetened coconut milk (not thin)

1 to 1⅓ cups Just Like Sugar Table Top natural chicory root sweetener (not Baking). I do not recommend any other sweetener.

1 tablespoon pure vanilla extract

¼ teaspoon unprocessed salt

⅓ cup melted coconut oil (place jar in lukewarm water to melt oil)

2½ tablespoons agar flakes

½ cup thick unsweetened coconut milk, to cook agar

1. Preheat the oven to 300°F. Prepare the 5-Minute Whipped Crème Topping and the Minute Piecrust. You may toast the coconut flakes for the crust and filling together on one shallow baking pan: Toast for 15 to 20 minutes, stirring every 5 minutes until they are barely golden brown. Set the timer and watch carefully, as they burn easily. Let cool completely. Reserve ¼ cup of coconut.

2. In a blender, combine the 2½ cups of coconut milk, sweetener, vanilla, and salt. Blend well until smooth and creamy. Sweeten to taste.

3. Add the barely warm coconut oil, and blend again until smooth.

4. In a shallow nonstick pan over medium heat, stir the agar into the ½ cup of coconut milk. Cook and stir gently for 2 to 3 minutes until it is bubbling and gummy, and the flakes begin to dissolve. Add the agar mixture to the blender immediately and mix well to remove any lumps.

5. Spread the ¾ cup of toasted coconut flakes in the bottom of the chilled piecrust. Pour the blended filling over the flakes and chill for 2 hours, until the pie is firm. Before serving, sprinkle the reserved ¼ cup of toasted coconut flakes on top.

**variation Chocolate Coconut Cream Pie:** Prepare one recipe of warm Chocolate Sauce (page 189). Follow the Coconut Cream Pie recipe above. Before pouring the filling into the pie shell, pour the warm chocolate sauce into the bottom of the shell so that it lines the entire shell evenly. Sprinkle the ¾ cup of coconut flakes over the sauce. Pour the filling on top and chill per the instructions above.

# Key Lime Pie

When I tasted this pie I couldn't believe how delicious it was (and I'm pretty sure you'll have the same reaction as well!). The filling is made with fresh lime juice and a surprise ingredient: creamy avocado. Smooth, cool, and refreshing, mild avocado adds richness to this Key Lime Pie without affecting the flavor. Garnish with lime slices and 1-Minute Whipped Crème Topping (page 173). For best results, follow this recipe exactly.

**[ YIELD: One 9-inch pie • EQUIPMENT NEEDED: A food processor and any style blender ]**

1 recipe Minute Piecrust (page 113)

1⅓ cups unsweetened coconut milk, as thick as possible (Lite coconut milk and coconut milk beverage in a carton will not work, as they are too thin.)

Zest of ½ lime

⅓ cup freshly squeezed lime juice (2 to 3 limes)

1 ripe avocado, pitted and peeled

1 cup Just Like Sugar Table Top natural chicory root sweetener (not Baking). I do not recommend any other sweetener for this.

¼ cup melted coconut oil (place jar in lukewarm water to melt oil)

2 tablespoons agar flakes

⅓ cup unsweetened coconut milk, to cook agar

Lime slices, for garnish

1. Prepare the Minute Piecrust. Press into a 9-inch pie pan and chill.
2. In a blender, combine the 1⅓ cups of coconut milk, lime zest, lime juice, avocado, and sweetener. Mix until smooth and creamy.
3. Add the melted coconut oil and mix again until perfectly smooth. Adjust the sweetener to taste.
4. In a shallow nonstick pan over medium heat, stir the agar into the ⅓ cup of coconut milk. Cook and stir gently for 2 to 3 minutes, until it is bubbling and gummy, and the flakes begin to dissolve. Add the agar mixture to the blender immediately and blend well to remove any lumps.
5. Pour the mixture into the chilled crust. Refrigerate for 3 to 5 hours. You can chill it faster in the freezer for 30 minutes; however, freezing completely will make it too difficult to cut. Garnish with fresh lime slices and enjoy!

# Pecan Pie

*This is the easiest pecan pie recipe I've ever seen (or created, for that matter!). It tastes crispy and divine, with a deep brown sugar flavor from the yacón syrup. (A tablespoon of rum is traditional in this recipe; however, that is not Paleo. And the pie is so delicious without it, that most people don't miss it.) If you've never tasted pecan pie with soaked and toasted pecans, you're in for a treat. Serve plain or with 1-Minute Whipped Crème Topping (page 173). For the most delicious flavor and texture, follow this recipe exactly.*

**[ YIELD: One 9-inch pie • EQUIPMENT NEEDED: A food processor or any style blender ]**

3 cups pecan halves, soaked if possible (see page 10)

1 recipe single-crust Flaky Baked Piecrust (page 122)

2 cups Just Like Sugar Table Top natural chicory root sweetener (not Baking). A second choice is 2⅔ cups Organic Zero Erythritol.

½ teaspoon unprocessed salt

½ cup warm (not boiling) filtered water

3 large eggs

1 tablespoon pure vanilla extract

1 teaspoon apple cider vinegar

½ teaspoon maple flavoring

2 tablespoons *raw* yacón syrup (optional)

¼ cup melted coconut oil (place jar in lukewarm water to melt oil)

1. Position a rack in the center of the oven. Preheat the oven to 350°F. Toast the pecans in a dry, shallow baking pan with the timer set for 10 minutes. Take care not to burn them. Remove them from the oven and allow to cool.

2. Prepare the Flaky Baked Piecrust and place in a 9-inch pie pan. Heat the pie shell in the oven only until it is hot to the touch (no need to prebake).

3. In a food processor or blender, place the sweetener and salt. Mix well.

4. Add the filtered water, eggs, vanilla, vinegar, maple, yacón syrup (if using), and melted coconut oil. (Rum is traditional here; however, alcoholic beverages are not Paleo.) Mix well until the sugar dissolves.

5. Pulse in 1½ cups of the toasted pecans briefly so they are chopped coarsely.

6. Pour the mixture into the pie shell. Top with the remaining pecan halves. Bake for 40 to 50 minutes, until the edges are firm but the center is barely quivery.

7. Let cool for at least 1 hour in the pan on a rack. Serve warm or at room temperature.

**variation Chocolate Pecan Pie:** For a yummy variation with an added layer of chocolate, follow the recipe above. Prepare one recipe of Chocolate Sauce (page 189). Before pouring the filling into the pie shell, pour the chocolate sauce into the bottom of the shell, and spread it so it lines the entire shell evenly. Pour the filling on top and bake per the instructions above.

# Pumpkin Pie

*This classic Pumpkin Pie is a favorite for the holidays or any time of year. I love pumpkin; however, I find that fresh butternut squash makes a smoother and more flavorful pie. Another advantage is that it's easier to peel, cube, and steam lightly on the stove. This pie is perfect with the Flaky Baked Piecrust (page 115) and 5-Minute Whipped Crème Topping (page 174). For the most delicious flavor and texture, follow this recipe exactly.*

[ YIELD: One 9-inch pie • EQUIPMENT NEEDED: Any style blender, preferably small; a food processor; and a high-speed blender such as Blendtec or Vitamix (optional) ]

1 recipe 5-Minute Whipped Crème Topping (page 174)

1 recipe single-crust Flaky Baked Piecrust (page 115)

½ cup medium to thick unsweetened coconut milk, or ¼ cup thin

⅔ cup Just Like Sugar Table Top natural chicory root sweetener (not Baking). A second choice is ¾ cup Organic Zero Erythritol.

4 large eggs

2 teaspoons pure vanilla extract

½ teaspoon ground cinnamon

½ teaspoon unprocessed salt

Zest of ½ orange

Zest of 1 Meyer lemon

¼ teaspoon ground cloves

¼ teaspoon grated nutmeg

¼ teaspoon ground allspice

¼ teaspoon ground cardamom

2 tablespoons *raw* yacón syrup (optional)

3 tablespoons coconut oil

1½ inches fresh ginger, chopped or grated, or ¼ teaspoon ground

1½ cups butternut squash, peeled, cubed, steamed lightly until soft, and drained very well

1. Prepare the 5-Minute Whipped Crème Topping and chill.
2. Preheat the oven to 300°F. Prepare the Flaky Baked Piecrust and place in a 9-inch pie pan. Prebake for 20 minutes, then increase the oven temperature to 350°F.
3. While the piecrust prebakes, in a food processor fitted with "S" blade or a high-speed blender, place the coconut milk, sweetener, eggs, vanilla, cinnamon, salt, orange zest, Meyer lemon zest, cloves, nutmeg, allspice, cardamom, yacón syrup, coconut oil, and ginger. Mix well. Add the steamed butternut squash and mix until smooth and creamy. Sweeten to taste and adjust the spices so they're yummy.
4. Pour the mixture into the prebaked pie shell.
5. Bake for 45 for 60 minutes. Let cool for 1 hour in the pan on a rack. Then serve and enjoy!

**continues . . .**

**variations**

**Chocolate Marble Pumpkin Pie:** This variation comes out looking beautiful and I think it's the perfect food combination. In a 1-cup pitcher or a small bowl, whisk together one egg, ⅓ cup of Just Like Sugar Table Top (a second choice is ½ cup of Organic Zero Erythritol), 2 tablespoons cacao powder, and 1 teaspoon of pure vanilla, to create a chocolate marble sauce. Mix until smooth and thick like honey. Follow the Pumpkin Pie recipe. At step 4, pour the pumpkin filling into the pie. Pour the chocolate marble sauce over the pie filling in uneven globs. Then with a knife or narrow spatula, stir it into the filling with large circular strokes going around the pie, to create a marbled design. Bake per the recipe.

**Chocolate Sweet Potato Pie:** I couldn't resist sharing this traditional Southern soul food favorite. Prepare one recipe of Chocolate Sauce (page 189). Follow the Pumpkin Pie recipe above, but instead of using butternut squash, substitute 1½ cups of sweet potato or yam, peeled, cubed, steamed lightly, and very well drained. At step 4, pour the Chocolate Sauce into the pie shell and smooth it evenly. Then pour the pie filling over it and bake per the recipe. It's so yummy!

# Apple Tart

*My favorite dessert in Italy, this tart is often suggested for beginners because it always comes out delicious. It is called* torta di mele morbida *(soft apple tart). This recipe is adapted from my friend Giorgia Pistellato in Venice. For best results, follow this recipe exactly.*

**[ YIELD: One 9- to 10-inch tart • EQUIPMENT NEEDED: A food processor ]**

3 tart apples
2 tablespoons freshly squeezed lemon juice
1 cup Just Like Sugar Table Top natural chicory root sweetener (not Baking). A second choice is 1⅓ cups Organic Zero Erythritol.
1½ cups medium-shredded unsweetened coconut flakes (not coconut flour)
⅓ cup arrowroot powder
1½ teaspoons baking powder
¼ teaspoon unprocessed salt
1 teaspoon nutritional yeast (optional, for butter flavor)
3 large eggs
¾ cup any unsweetened coconut milk
Zest of ½ lemon or ½ orange
2 teaspoons pure vanilla extract
2 tablespoons melted coconut oil (place jar in lukewarm water to melt oil)
¼ cup Just Like Sugar Table Top natural chicory root sweetener (not Baking), for sprinkling
1 tablespoon ground cinnamon, for sprinkling

1. Preheat the oven to 350°F. Grease a 9- to 10-inch cake pan, springform pan, or tart pan, and dust it with coconut flour or arrowroot powder. A removable bottom pan is nice, but not required.
2. Core the apples and slice very thinly—⅛ inch thick. Personally, I love to include the peels, so peeling is optional. Place the sliced apples in a bowl. Sprinkle them with the lemon juice and toss gently.
3. In a dry food processor fitted with the "S" blade, grind the sweetener to a very fine powder.
4. Add the shredded coconut to the sweetener in the food processor. Spin it for a minute to become a very fine powder. Open the lid, stir the bottom, replace the lid, and grind again until the powder is uniformly fine.
5. To the ingredients in the food processor, add the arrowroot powder, baking powder, salt, and nutritional yeast (if using). Mix well.
6. To the dry ingredients in the food processor, add the eggs, coconut milk, zest, and vanilla. Mix briefly.
7. Pour half of the batter into the prepared baking pan. Arrange half of the apple slices in a single layer on top of the batter, making a flat fan pattern covering the bottom of the pan. Repeat this process again, pouring the remaining batter on top, spreading it smooth, and cover with the remaining apples in a fan pattern.
8. Drizzle the melted coconut oil over the apples. Sprinkle with sweetener and cinnamon. Bake for 30 to 40 minutes or until a toothpick comes out clean. Cool and enjoy. *Deliziosa!*

# Berry Tart

*This Berry Tart is easy, refreshing, and divinely delicious. Berries are high in antioxidants, so it's a treat and very good for you, too. Be mindful that the color will depend on your berries. What color will you create today? Garnish with 1-Minute Whipped Crème Topping (page 173) and fresh berries. For the most delicious flavor and texture, follow this recipe exactly.*

**[ YIELD: One 9-inch tart • EQUIPMENT NEEDED: A food processor and any style blender ]**

1 recipe Minute Piecrust (page 113)

1¾ cups any unsweetened coconut milk

1¼ cups Just Like Sugar Table Top natural chicory root sweetener (not Baking). I do not recommend any other sweetener for this.

1 cup raw cashews, soaked for 4 to 6 hours (see page 10)

1 cup unsweetened fresh or frozen raspberries or mixed berries

1 lemon, peeled, sliced, and seeded

Zest of 1 orange

¾ orange, peeled, sliced, and seeded

2 inches fresh ginger, chopped or grated

2 teaspoons pure vanilla extract

Pinch of unprocessed salt

1 small slice of beet (optional—I use it to create a beautiful fuchsia color)

⅓ cup melted coconut oil (place jar in lukewarm water to melt oil)

2 tablespoons agar flakes

⅓ cup unsweetened coconut milk, to cook agar

1. Prepare the Minute Piecrust. Press into a 9- to 10-inch springform pan or removable-bottom tart pan, and chill.

2. In a blender, combine the 1¾ cups of coconut milk, sweetener, soaked cashews, berries, lemon, orange zest, orange, ginger, vanilla, salt, and beet slice (if using). Blend well until smooth and creamy. Take your time and blend several times to liquefy completely. Sweeten to taste.

3. Add the melted coconut oil, and blend again.

4. In a shallow nonstick pan over medium heat, stir the agar into the ⅓ cup of coconut milk. Cook and stir gently for 2 to 3 minutes, until it is bubbling and gummy, and the flakes begin to dissolve. Add the agar mixture to the blender immediately and blend well to remove any lumps.

5. Pour into the chilled pie shell. Refrigerate until firm. This pie is also delightful served frozen.

# Finger Tarts

*Okay, so who has heard of a finger tart? No one? Well, you got me—I made it up. A finger tart is a crispy pie dough cookie spread with your favorite creamy filling or frosting, and covered with fresh fruit. It's a perfect dessert to serve at any party, or enjoy as a quick snack. You can prepare them ahead of time. I made them for a gathering recently and they were a huge hit. You can also make them in a mini muffin pan, so be sure to check out the variation that follows. For best results, follow this recipe exactly.*

[ **YIELD:** About 40 small cookie tarts or 24 mini muffin tarts • **EQUIPMENT NEEDED:** Any style blender, a food processor, and a pastry wheel cutter with a crimp blade, if possible (a cookie cutter or a knife will work, too) ]

1 recipe Chocolate Crème Cheese Frosting (page 181), Vanilla Pastry Cream with Cashews (page 185), Vanilla Pastry Cream with Coconut (page 186), 5-Minute Whipped Crème Topping (page 174), or your favorite

1 recipe double-crust Flaky Baked Piecrust (page 115)

¼ cup Cinnamon "Sugar" (page 190)

2 cups any colorful cut fruit, such as strawberries, raspberries, blueberries, grapes, blackberries, papaya, kiwi, apricots, plums, oranges, etc.

1. Make your choice of filling and chill.
2. Preheat the oven to 350°F. Line two to four baking sheets with parchment paper (optional).
3. Make the Flaky Baked Piecrust. Divide the pie dough into three equal balls and press them flat to ½ inch thick. Wrap and chill for 30 minutes.
4. Roll out the dough one piece at a time to ¼ to ⅛ inch thick (no thinner or they could break). With a crimped pastry wheel cutter or plain wheel cutter, cookie cutter, or a knife, cut the dough into pieces. They can be round, square, or rectangular. I cut them into 2-inch squares. Dust the dough generously with Cinnamon Sugar.
5. Place the dough pieces on the prepared baking sheets. Bake for 12 to 15 minutes, until golden brown. Remove from the oven and let cool on the pans on a rack.
6. Cut the fruit in small pieces. To assemble the tarts, spread 1 teaspoon of filling on each tart. Top with an assortment of fruit. Place the tarts on a serving platter.

---

**variation Mini Muffin Tart Shells:** Follow recipe above through step 4, using a 3-inch round cookie cutter to cut the dough and transferring each piece to a mini muffin pan. Press the pastry into each well with your fingers. Bake until the shells are evenly golden and crisp, 15 to 20 minutes, depending on their thickness. Let cool completely in the pan on a rack. They're delicate, so let them cool completely before removing them from the pan or they'll break. Cut colorful fruit into small pieces. To assemble the tarts, fill each shell with 1½ tablespoons of pastry cream. Top with an assortment of fruit. Place the finished tarts on a serving platter. Chill until serving.

# Cheesecake

*My ideal authentic cheesecake is rich, dense, and creamy, with a perfect balance of sweet and tart. This recipe is very similar—tangy, sweet, and creamy, and made with coconut butter and lemons instead of cream cheese. And unlike traditional cheesecake, it's a breeze to prepare—just blend and chill. Be sure to check out the luscious flavor variations that follow. For best results, follow this recipe exactly.*

[ YIELD: One 9- to 10-inch cheesecake • EQUIPMENT NEEDED: Any style blender and a digital scale, for the coconut butter ]

1 recipe Minute Piecrust (page 113)

**BASIC CHEESECAKE FILLING**

1¾ cups unsweetened coconut milk, as thick as possible, at room temperature (Lite coconut milk and coconut milk beverage in a carton will not work, as they are too thin.)

1¼ cups Just Like Sugar Table Top natural chicory root sweetener (not Baking). I do not recommend any other sweetener for this.

2 lemons, peeled, sliced, and seeded (150 grams pulp)

1 tablespoon pure vanilla extract

⅛ teaspoon unprocessed salt

200 grams (about 1 cup, very tightly packed) pure coconut butter (not coconut oil)

⅓ cup melted coconut oil (place jar in lukewarm water to melt oil)

1½ tablespoons agar flakes

⅓ cup unsweetened coconut milk, to cook agar

**COCONUT SOUR CRÈME TOPPING**

½ cup medium to thick unsweetened coconut milk, at room temperature

¼ cup Just Like Sugar Table Top natural chicory root sweetener (not Baking). A second choice is ⅓ cup Organic Zero Erythritol.

1 tablespoon freshly squeezed lemon juice

½ teaspoon apple cider vinegar

1 teaspoon pure vanilla extract

2 tablespoons melted coconut oil (place jar in lukewarm water to melt oil)

1. Make the Minute Piecrust. Press into a 9- or 10-inch springform pan and chill.

2. To make the filling: In a blender, combine the coconut milk, sweetener, lemons, vanilla, and salt. Blend until smooth and creamy.

3. Add the coconut butter. Blend again until smooth.

4. Add the melted coconut oil last, and blend again. Add a tablespoon more of coconut milk if necessary to blend.

5. In a shallow nonstick pan over medium heat, stir the agar into the ⅓ cup of coconut milk. Cook and stir gently for 2 to 3 minutes until it is bubbling and gummy, and the flakes begin to dissolve. Add the agar mixture to the

**continues . . .**

blender immediately and blend well to remove any lumps.

6. Pour the filling into the chilled crust. Refrigerate for 3 to 5 hours. You can chill it faster in the freezer for 30 minutes; however, freezing completely will make it too difficult to cut.

7. For the topping: In a blender, combine the coconut milk, sweetener, lemon juice, vinegar, vanilla, and coconut oil. Blend well. Pour this topping onto the pie after the filling has chilled well and is firm. Chill the whole pie again, and the topping will firm up in about 30 minutes. Serve cold and garnish with fresh fruit.

---

**variations**

**Blueberry Cheesecake:** Prepare the basic Cheesecake recipe through step 5. For the topping: Puree ¾ cup of fresh or frozen blueberries with 2 to 4 tablespoons of Just Like Sugar Table Top sweetener. Pour the cheesecake filling into the crust. Chill until firm. Pour the blueberry puree on top and spread evenly.

**Cherry Cheesecake:** Prepare the basic Cheesecake recipe through step 5. For the topping: Puree 1 cup of fresh or frozen cherries with 2 to 8 tablespoons of Just Like Sugar Table Top sweetener. Sweeten to taste. Pour the cheesecake filling into the crust. Chill until firm. Pour the cherry puree on top and spread evenly.

**Chocolate Caramel Pecan Cheesecake:** Prepare the basic Cheesecake recipe through step 5, using the Minute Piecrust, Chocolate variation (page 113). For the topping: Toast 1 cup of soaked pecans (see page 10). Let cool and chop, reserving ¼ cup of pecan halves for garnish. In a small mixing bowl, stir together until smooth ¼ cup of Just Like Sugar Table Top natural chicory root sweetener (not Baking), 3 tablespoons of boiling filtered water, 2 tablespoons of *raw* yacón syrup, and ⅛ teaspoon of unprocessed salt. Stir in the ¾ cup of pecans. Pour the cheesecake filling into the crust. Fold the pecan mixture into the filling, using circular motions. Chill until firm. Garnish with the reserved pecan halves and drizzle with the *raw* yacón syrup.

**Chocolate Chip Cheesecake:** Prepare the basic Cheesecake recipe through step 5, using the Minute Piecrust, Chocolate variation. Pour the cheesecake filling into the crust (page 113). Stir into the filling ½ cup of Homemade Chocolate Chips (page 108) or ¼ cup of unsweetened cacao nibs. Chill well. Garnish with Homemade Chocolate Chips (page 108) or unsweetened cacao nibs.

**continues . . .**

**Chocolate Marble Cheesecake:** Prepare the basic Cheesecake recipe through step 5, using the Minute Piecrust, Chocolate variation (page 113). Prepare one recipe of Chocolate Sauce (page 189). Pour the cheesecake filling into the crust, then pour two-thirds of the chocolate sauce on top of it in irregular globs. Fold or stir with a knife or spatula, in circular motions, to make a marbled effect. Chill until firm. Garnish with the remaining chocolate sauce and shaved chocolate.

**Marble Berry Cheesecake:** Prepare the basic Cheesecake recipe through step 5. Puree 1 cup of fresh or frozen berries (strawberries, raspberries, blueberries, etc.) with 2 to 6 tablespoons of Just Like Sugar Table Top natural chicory root sweetener (not Baking). Pour the cheesecake filling into the crust. Fold the berry puree into the filling, using circular motions. Chill until firm. Garnish with additional fresh berries.

**Raspberry Cheesecake:** Prepare the basic Cheesecake recipe through step 5. For the topping: Puree 1 cup of fresh or frozen raspberries with 3 to 6 tablespoons of Just Like Sugar Table Top natural chicory root sweetener (not Baking). Pour the cheesecake filling into the crust. Chill until firm. Pour the raspberry puree on top and spread evenly. Garnish with raspberries.

**Strawberry Cheesecake:** Prepare the basic Cheesecake recipe through step 5. For the topping: Puree 1 cup of fresh or frozen strawberries with 3 to 6 tablespoons of Just Like Sugar Table Top natural chicory root sweetener (not Baking). Pour the cheesecake filling into the crust. Chill until firm. Pour the strawberry puree on top and spread evenly. Garnish with strawberries.

# Lemon Cheesecake with Berries

*This cheesecake is refreshing and light. The creamy, luscious consistency comes from blended lemon and coconut butter. Colorful berries, such as raspberries or blueberries, add sweet fruit flavor and a beautiful finish to its tart lemony flavor. If you can find my favorite Meyer lemons, it will be divine and the perfect summertime cheesecake. For best results, follow this recipe exactly.*

[ YIELD: One 9- or 10-inch cheesecake • EQUIPMENT NEEDED: A food processor; any style blender; and a digital scale, for the coconut butter ]

1 recipe Minute Piecrust, Lemon Ginger variation (page 114)

**FILLING**

1 cup unsweetened coconut milk, as thick as possible (Lite coconut milk and coconut milk beverage in a carton will not work, as they are too thin.)

1½ cups Just Like Sugar Table Top natural chicory root sweetener (not Baking). I do not recommend any other sweetener for this.

Zest of 1 lemon

2 lemons, peeled and seeded (150 grams lemon pulp)

2 teaspoons pure vanilla extract

⅛ teaspoon unprocessed salt

200 grams (about 1 cup very tightly packed) pure coconut butter (not coconut oil)

¼ cup melted coconut oil (place jar in lukewarm water to melt oil)

1½ tablespoons agar flakes

⅓ cup unsweetened coconut milk, to cook agar

**COCONUT SOUR CRÈME TOPPING**

½ cup medium to thick unsweetened coconut milk, at room temperature

¼ cup Just Like Sugar Table Top natural chicory root sweetener (not Baking). A second choice is ⅓ cup Organic Zero Erythritol.

1 tablespoon freshly squeezed lemon juice

½ teaspoon apple cider vinegar

1 teaspoon pure vanilla extract

2 tablespoons melted coconut oil (place jar in lukewarm water to melt oil)

1 cup berries, sliced Meyer lemon, or your favorite fruit, for garnish

1. Prepare the Minute Piecrust, Lemon Ginger variation. Press into a 9- or 10-inch springform pan and chill.

2. For the filling: In a blender, combine the 1 cup of coconut milk, sweetener, lemon zest, lemons, vanilla, and salt. Blend until smooth and creamy.

3. Add the coconut butter. Blend again until smooth.

4. Add the coconut oil last, and blend again. Add a tablespoon more coconut milk if necessary to blend.

5. In a shallow nonstick pan over medium heat, stir the agar into the ⅓ cup of coconut milk. Cook and stir gently for 2 to 3 minutes, until it is bubbling and gummy, and the flakes begin to dissolve. Add the agar mixture to the blender immediately and blend well to remove any lumps.

**continues . . .**

6. Pour the filling into the chilled crust. Refrigerate for 3 to 5 hours. You can chill it faster in the freezer for 30 minutes; however, freezing completely will make it too difficult to cut.

7. For the topping: In a blender, combine the coconut milk, sweetener, lemon juice, vinegar, vanilla, and coconut oil. Blend well. Pour this topping onto the pie after the filling has chilled well and is firm. Chill the whole pie again, and the topping will firm up in about 30 minutes. Serve cold, garnished with berries and Meyer lemon zest.

# Pumpkin Cheesecake

*This rich and creamy Pumpkin Cheesecake is always a crowd favorite. People just can't believe it can be so delicious and dairy-free. Wherever I take it, everyone asks for the recipe. And when I tell them it's also grain-free and doesn't have to be baked, they're left speechless. This recipe uses smooth butternut squash instead of pumpkin, because I find it easier to peel and steam, and more flavorful. Make this recipe in three simple steps: the Whipped Crème Topping, crust, and filling. For the best flavor and texture, follow this recipe exactly.*

[ YIELD: One 9- or 10-inch cheesecake • EQUIPMENT NEEDED: A food processor and a digital scale, for the coconut butter ]

1 to 2 cups 5-Minute Whipped Crème Topping (page 174)
1 recipe any Minute Piecrust (page 113)

**FILLING**
1 cup Just Like Sugar Table Top natural chicory root sweetener (not Baking). I do not recommend any other sweetener for this.
2 cups medium-shredded unsweetened coconut flakes (not coconut flour)
1 cup any unsweetened coconut milk
2 lemons, peeled and seeded (about 150 grams or ½ cup plus 2 tablespoons lemon pulp)
¼ cup melted coconut oil (place jar in lukewarm water to melt oil)

1½ cups butternut squash, peeled, cubed, and lightly steamed until soft
1 tablespoon ground cinnamon
¼ teaspoon ground cloves
¼ teaspoon grated nutmeg
¼ teaspoon ground cardamom
⅛ teaspoon unprocessed salt
2-inches fresh ginger, chopped or grated, or 1 teaspoon ground ginger
2 teaspoons pure vanilla extract
Zest of 1 orange
1 tablespoon *raw* yacón syrup (optional)
1½ tablespoons agar flakes
⅓ cup any unsweetened coconut milk, to cook agar
Toasted pecans (see page 11) or *raw* yacón syrup, for garnish

1. For the topping: Make 1 to 2 cups of 5-Minute Whipped Crème Topping. Chill well to thicken.
2. For the crust: Prepare the Minute Piecrust and chill. Press into a 9- or 10-inch pie pan, with a removable bottom if possible, or a springform pan.

3. For the filling: In a dry food processor fitted with the "S" blade, grind the sweetener to a fine powder.
4. Add the shredded coconut to the sweetener in the food processor. Spin it for a minute until a very fine powder. Open the lid, stir the bottom, replace the lid, and grind again until the powder is uniformly fine.

continues . . .

5. To the ingredients in the food processor, add the 1 cup of coconut milk, lemons, coconut oil, squash, cinnamon, cloves, nutmeg, cardamom, salt, ginger, vanilla, orange zest, and yacón syrup (if using). Mix thoroughly until the squash is liquefied and the filling is smooth.

6. In a shallow nonstick pan over medium heat, stir the agar into the ⅓ cup of coconut milk. Cook and stir gently for 2 to 3 minutes until it is bubbling and gummy, and the flakes begin to dissolve. Add the agar mixture to the blender immediately and blend well to remove any lumps. Sweeten to taste.

7. Pour the filling into the chilled crust. Tap the pan on the counter to remove any air bubbles. Chill for 1 to 3 hours, until firm. You can put it in the freezer briefly, but for no longer than 30 minutes or it will be too hard to cut. Remove from the refrigerator. Spread with Whipped Crème and serve. Garnish with toasted pecans or drizzles of *raw* yacón syrup.

*Cookery is not chemistry. It is an art.*
*It requires instinct and taste rather than exact measurements.*

—MARCEL BOULESTIN

# CRISPS, CRUMBLES, AND OTHER TREATS

No dessert book would be complete without my favorite crisps, crumbles, and treats. These recipes are some of the juiciest and most irresistible sweets. Even better, they're also easy to make—from Apple Cranberry Crisp to Pear Ginger Crumble. I discovered how to make tender Crêpes Suzettes so moist and sweet they can rival the original French recipe. Don't miss the Paleo Belgian Waffles and Hazelnut Butter Cups. Lastly, no self-respecting Paleo cookbook could be without a Berry Cobbler and a great Trail Mix. Of course, I had to taste them all! I hope you enjoy them as much as I have.

# Apple Cranberry Crisp

*Apple Cranberry Crisp is one of the easiest desserts to make. This seasonal favorite will warm your home with the scent of baked apples, cinnamon, and orange. Cranberries add a delightful tart flavor. Serve plain or with 1-Minute Whipped Crème Topping (page 173). For the most delicious flavor and texture, follow this recipe exactly.*

**[ YIELD: 8 servings • EQUIPMENT NEEDED: None ]**

**APPLE FILLING**
6 tart apples (such as Granny Smith, Fuji, or Pink Lady)
¾ cup fresh or frozen unsweetened cranberries
2 tablespoons freshly squeezed lemon juice
⅔ cup Just Like Sugar Table Top natural chicory root sweetener (not Baking). A second choice is ⅞ cup Organic Zero Erythritol.
3 tablespoons arrowroot powder
2 teaspoons ground cinnamon
Zest of ½ orange
¼ teaspoon unprocessed salt
2 tablespoons melted coconut oil (place jar in lukewarm water to melt oil) (optional)

**STREUSEL TOPPING**
½ cup medium-shredded unsweetened coconut flakes (not coconut flour)
⅓ cup Just Like Sugar Table Top natural chicory root sweetener (not Baking)
¼ teaspoon unprocessed salt
2 teaspoons ground cinnamon
¼ teaspoon grated nutmeg
½ cup coarsely chopped nuts, soaked if possible (see page 10)
2 tablespoons melted coconut oil (place jar in lukewarm water to melt oil) (optional)

1. Preheat the oven to 350°F. Grease a 9-inch pie pan.
2. Peel the apples, if you desire. Core them, and slice very thinly—⅛ inch thick. Toss the apples in the pie pan with the remaining filling ingredients.
3. In a mixing bowl, combine the Streusel Topping ingredients.
4. Spread the streusel mixture over the apples and press it in firmly. Poke holes in it with a spoon handle so it will mix with the apple juices while baking.
5. Bake until the streusel is golden brown, the juices are bubbling and the apples are tender when pierced, 55 to 65 minutes.

# Berry Cobbler

*A quick, high-antioxidant dessert, Berry Cobbler is a favorite all year round. It's super tasty with any kind of berries—raspberries, blueberries, and/or blackberries. You can also experiment with wild gooseberries, lingonberries, mulberries, or marionberries. This recipe calls for precooking the berries, as they require a longer baking time than the dough. This provides just the right amount of time for perfect blending of flavors and browning for an awesome cobbler. Serve with 1-Minute Whipped Crème Topping (page 173). For best results, follow this recipe exactly.*

**[ YIELD: 9 servings • EQUIPMENT NEEDED: A food processor ]**

### FILLING

½ cup Just Like Sugar Table Top natural chicory root sweetener (not Baking). A second choice is ⅔ cup Organic Zero Erythritol. (If your berries are very sour, you may want to add more sweetener to taste.)

2 tablespoons arrowroot powder

1 teaspoon ground cinnamon, plus extra for sprinkling

Pinch of unprocessed salt

6 cups unsweetened fresh or frozen blueberries, raspberries, blackberries, etc., or any mixture of berries

1 teaspoon grated lemon or lime zest

1 tablespoon freshly squeezed lemon juice

### DOUGH

½ cup Just Like Sugar Table Top natural chicory root sweetener (not Baking). A second choice is ⅔ cup Organic Zero Erythritol.

1½ cups medium-shredded unsweetened coconut flakes (not coconut flour)

½ teaspoon baking soda

¼ teaspoon unprocessed salt

2 tablespoons arrowroot powder

1 teaspoon nutritional yeast (optional, adds butter flavor)

1 egg

1 teaspoon pure vanilla extract

4 tablespoons any unsweetened coconut milk or filtered water

1. Preheat the oven to 350°F. Grease a 9-inch square baking pan.

2. In a large mixing bowl, stir together the sweetener, arrowroot powder, 1 teaspoon of cinnamon, and salt.

3. Wash and drain the berries, and add them to the mixing bowl with zest and lemon juice. Mix gently with a rubber spatula to coat evenly. Pour them into the baking pan and bake them for 20 minutes, then set aside.

4. Prepare the dough: In a dry food processor fitted with the "S" blade, grind the sweetener to a fine powder.

5. To the ingredients in the food processor, add the coconut, soda, salt, arrowroot powder, and nutritional yeast (if using) and grind very fine. Open the lid, stir the bottom, replace the lid, and grind again until uniformly fine.

**continues . . .**

6. To the dry ingredients in the food processor, add the egg, vanilla, and coconut milk. Mix briefly until the batter is smooth.

7. Drop spoonfuls of the batter on top of the berries, one per serving, so the mounds of dough are evenly spaced and do not touch. Be sure to leave room around the edges for expansion. Sprinkle the top with a bit of cinnamon.

8. Bake for about 25 minutes, until golden brown and the fruit is bubbling. Let cool for 20 minutes and serve.

# Pear Ginger Crumble

*This easy Pear Ginger Crumble is a comfort food for me. Subtly spicy and warm, it's perfect as a dessert or a snack. Serve it alone or you can dress it up with 1-Minute Whipped Crème Topping (page 173). For best results, follow the recipe exactly.*

**[ YIELD: 6 servings • EQUIPMENT NEEDED: None ]**

**PEAR GINGER FILLING**

3 tablespoons Just Like Sugar Table Top natural chicory root sweetener (not Baking). A second choice is 4 tablespoons Organic Zero Erythritol.

½ teaspoon ground cinnamon

2 tablespoons arrowroot powder

4 large ripe pears, unpeeled, cored, and cut into pieces about ¼ inches thick and ½ inch long

2 tablespoons freshly squeezed lemon juice

½ teaspoon pure vanilla extract

1 tablespoon grated fresh ginger, or ½ teaspoon ground

½ tablespoon grated lemon or orange zest

2 teaspoons *raw* yacón syrup, ½ teaspoon maple flavoring, or ½ teaspoon ground cardamom (optional)

**TOPPING**

⅓ cup Just Like Sugar Table Top natural chicory root sweetener (not Baking). A second choice is ½ cup Organic Zero Erythritol.

¼ teaspoon unprocessed salt

1 tablespoon ground cinnamon

¼ teaspoon grated nutmeg

3 tablespoons melted coconut oil (place jar in lukewarm water to melt oil)

⅔ cup chopped nuts, soaked if possible (see page 10)

⅓ cup medium-shredded unsweetened coconut flakes (not coconut flour)

1. Preheat the oven to 350°F. Grease a 9-inch square baking dish with coconut oil.

2. For the filling: In a large bowl, whisk together the sweetener, cinnamon, and arrowroot powder. Add the pears, lemon juice, vanilla, ginger, zest, and your additional flavoring of choice (if using). Stir to coat the pears evenly. Place the filling in the baking dish.

3. For the topping: In a dry food processor, place the sweetener, salt, cinnamon, and nutmeg. Mix well.

4. Pulse in briefly the oil, nuts, and coconut so they remain in coarse pieces. Sprinkle this mixture on top of the pears in the baking dish. Press it in a little and poke a few small holes in the streusel so that it can seep into the pears while baking.

5. Bake the crumble for 40 to 45 minutes, or until the pears are tender and the topping is slightly browned. Remove from the oven. Let cool for 20 minutes before serving.

# Paleo Pancakes

*Whether it's for breakfast or dessert, I can't live without pancakes. These Paleo Pancakes are not only scrumptious, they are quick to create and low-carb. You can embellish them with your favorite Paleo toppings and serve with hot Paleo Caffè (page 210). For best results, follow this recipe exactly.*

**[ YIELD: 12 pancakes or 4 servings • EQUIPMENT NEEDED: A food processor ]**

Maple-Flavored Syrup (page 191), fresh fruit, Chocolate Sauce (page 189), chopped nuts, and/or 1-Minute Whipped Crème Topping (page 173), for serving
1 cup Just Like Sugar Table Top natural chicory root sweetener (not Baking). A second choice is 1⅓ cups Organic Zero Erythritol.
1⅓ cups medium-shredded unsweetened coconut flakes (not coconut flour)
6 tablespoons arrowroot powder
1 teaspoon baking powder
⅛ teaspoon plus a pinch unprocessed salt
4 large eggs, at room temperature
2 teaspoons pure vanilla extract
¼ cup thin unsweetened coconut milk, or 2 tablespoons thick plus 2 tablespoons filtered water

1. Set the table and prepare your choice of toppings.
2. In a dry food processor fitted with the "S" blade, grind the sweetener to a fine powder.
3. Add the shredded coconut to the sweetener in the food processor. Spin it for a minute until a very fine powder. Open the lid, stir the bottom, replace the lid, and grind again until the powder is uniformly fine.
4. To the ingredients in the food processor, add the arrowroot powder, baking powder, and salt. Mix well.
5. Heat your griddle or skillet over medium heat. Check that it is ready. Then to the dry ingredients in the food processor, add the eggs, vanilla, and coconut milk. Mix briefly. Slightly lumpy batter is no problem.
6. Pour a few tablespoons of batter onto the griddle for each pancake. The pancakes should be 2 to 4 inches in diameter. Cook until the bottom is browned and you see bubbles coming through the top. Then flip and cook for an additional 2 to 3 minutes.
7. Place the pancakes on a serving plate. Serve hot with your favorite toppings. Yummy!

# Belgian Waffles

*A quick and easy dessert or a special breakfast, these Paleo waffles are crispy and delicious, and can be dressed up in many ways. For another great variation, try the Chocolate Waffles recipe that follows. Then brew some Paleo Caffè (page 210) and enjoy! If you have leftovers, these waffles freeze well. To thaw, just pop them in a toaster. For the best results, follow this recipe exactly.*

**[ YIELD: About 12 waffles • EQUIPMENT NEEDED: A food processor and a waffle iron ]**

Maple-Flavored Syrup (page 191), fresh fruit, Chocolate Sauce (page 189), chopped nuts, and/or 1-Minute Whipped Crème Topping (page 173), to serve

1 cup Just Like Sugar Table Top natural chicory root sweetener (not Baking). A second choice is 1⅓ cups Organic Zero Erythritol.

1⅓ cups medium-shredded unsweetened coconut flakes (not coconut flour)

6 tablespoons arrowroot powder

1 teaspoon baking powder

⅛ teaspoon plus a pinch un-processed salt

4 large eggs, at room temperature

2 teaspoons pure vanilla extract

¼ cup thin unsweetened co-conut milk, or 2 tablespoons thick plus 2 tablespoons fil-tered water

1. Set the table and prepare your choice of toppings. Heat a waffle iron according to the manufacturer's directions.
2. In a dry food processor fitted with the "S" blade, grind the sweetener to a fine powder.
3. Add the shredded coconut to the sweetener in the food processor. Spin it for a minute until a very fine powder. Open the lid, stir the bottom, replace the lid, and grind again until the powder is uniformly fine.
4. To the ingredients in the food processor, add the arrow-root powder, baking powder, and salt. Mix well.
5. Check that your waffle iron is hot. Brush it with a dash of coconut oil. Then to the dry ingredients in the food processor, add the eggs, vanilla, and coconut milk. Mix briefly. Don't worry if your batter is slightly lumpy—it will still turn out just fine.
6. To cook the waffles, pour a small amount of batter into the center of each waffle iron square. It should barely fill its square, allowing space for the waffle to expand. Close the waffle iron and bake per the manufac-turer's instructions. When you can pull the waffles out with a fork, and they are crispy and golden brown, they're done.
7. Place the waffles on a serving plate. Enjoy them hot with your choice of toppings.

**variation Chocolate Belgian Waffles:** Follow the recipe above. Add to the dry ingredients 3 table-spoons more sweetener and 3 tablespoons of pure cacao powder. Add to the wet ingredients 3 table-spoons of thin coconut milk.

# Crêpes Suzettes

*My first true dessert infatuation was for the crêpes suzettes that my mother bought me at a French food fair. The sweet pungent flavor was so indescribably delicious I couldn't imagine ever being able to make them taste just as good. This Paleo recipe tastes just as magical, and is much easier than I imagined, using eggs, coconut, and blended orange. For a truly authentic flavor, follow this recipe exactly.*

[ YIELD: About 15 crepes • EQUIPMENT NEEDED: A food processor, an 8-inch nonstick skillet or sauté pan (I use an 8-inch titanium pan), and any style blender ]

### CREPES
²/₃ cup Just Like Sugar Table Top natural chicory root sweetener (not Baking). A second choice is ¾ cup Organic Zero Erythritol. (For this recipe, erythritol is a wonderful option, as it has a cooling taste.)
1 cup medium-shredded unsweetened coconut flakes (not coconut flour)
6 tablespoons arrowroot powder
⅛ teaspoon unprocessed salt
9 large eggs, at room temperature
¾ cup thin unsweetened coconut milk, or 6 tablespoons thick plus 6 tablespoons filtered water
1 tablespoon pure vanilla extract
Fresh strawberries or orange slices, for garnish
2 tablespoons finely ground sweetener, for sprinkling

### ORANGE SAUCE (BEURRE SUZETTE)
1 orange
½ teaspoon nutritional yeast (for butter flavor)
1 teaspoon freshly squeezed lemon juice
⅓ cup Paleo sweetener (Organic Zero Erythritol is delicious in this)
2 tablespoons cognac or Grand Marnier are traditional; however, alcoholic beverages are not Paleo. The recipe will taste delicious without them.
⅓ cup melted coconut oil (place jar in lukewarm water to melt oil)

1. For the crepes: In a dry food processor fitted with the "S" blade, grind the sweetener to a very fine powder.
2. Add the shredded coconut to the sweetener in the food processor. Spin it for a minute until a very fine powder. Open the lid, stir the bottom, replace the lid, and grind again until the powder is uniformly fine.
3. To the ingredients in the food processor, add the arrowroot powder and salt. Mix well.
4. To the dry ingredients in the food processor, add the eggs, coconut milk, and vanilla. Mix well until smooth.

**continues . . .**

5. To cook the crepes: Preheat over medium heat an 8-inch nonstick skillet or sauté pan. You don't need a fancy crepe pan. Brush the pan with a bit of coconut oil before making each crepe. Use ¼ cup batter or a bit less to make a crepe. Measure the batter into the pan and twirl it around gently to coat the surface. Watch it carefully. Notice when the crepe begins to dry out and you can release the edges a bit with a rubber spatula. When the entire crepe can slide and pull away from the pan, flip it gently by grabbing the edges with your fingers, or use a spatula.

6. After the second side has cooked for half a minute, check the color, and when it is gently browned slip it out of the pan onto a serving plate. Don't be alarmed if the first crepe looks a little strange— it just takes time to fine-tune the heat, amount of batter, and the timing. Adjust the pan heat if necessary and your next few creations should be just fine. Make all the crepes, putting them in a stack under a towel or in the oven at low heat.

7. For the orange butter: Place the orange zest in a blender. Cut away the white pith left on the orange with a sharp knife. Slice the orange and seed it, if necessary. Add the orange to the blender, along with sweetener, nutritional yeast, lemon juice, and coconut oil. Liquefy the ingredients completely. Then pour the sauce into a shallow pan over low heat.

8. To assemble the Crêpes Suzettes: One at a time, place each crepe in the warm sauce for a few seconds to soak up the sauce. Then fold the crepe gently into quarters and arrange on dessert plates, two crepes per plate. Garnish with strawberries or orange slices. Dust with finely ground sweetener and serve immediately. Bon appétit!

# Chocolate Hazelnut Butter Cups

*These little beauties are a dark chocolate version of peanut butter cups. Because peanuts aren't Paleo, I use hazelnut butter instead, and its distinctive flavor blends beautifully with chocolate. You can make them with almond butter or cashew butter as well. They're easy to prepare: Just blend the chocolate, pour into lined mini muffin cups, and chill. For the most amazing flavor and consistency, follow this recipe exactly.*

[ **YIELD: 24 Hazelnut Butter Cups** • **EQUIPMENT NEEDED: Any style blender and a 24-compartment mini muffin pan** ]

## CHOCOLATE

¼ cup thick unsweetened coconut milk, or 2 tablespoons thin

6 tablespoons Just Like Sugar Table Top natural chicory root sweetener (not Baking). I do not recommend any other sweetener for this.

3 tablespoons pure cacao powder

2 teaspoons pure vanilla extract

Pinch of unprocessed salt

½ teaspoon instant decaffeinated coffee powder or crystals (optional)

⅓ cup melted coconut oil (place jar in lukewarm water to melt oil)

## FILLING

3 tablespoons roasted unsweetened hazelnut butter

1 tablespoon finely chopped nuts, soaked if possible (see page 10)

3 tablespoons Just Like Sugar Table Top natural chicory root sweetener (not Baking)

⅛ teaspoon unprocessed salt

1 teaspoon pure vanilla extract

1. For the chocolate: Line the mini muffin pan with paper liners. Have ready all the ingredients at room temperature.
2. In a blender, combine the coconut milk, sweetener, cacao powder, vanilla, salt, coffee powder (if using), and melted coconut oil. Blend until very creamy. The consistency should be smooth and runny.
3. Pour or spoon a small amount (about 1 teaspoon) of the chocolate mixture into each compartment of the prepared pan. Bang the pan on the counter to remove any bubbles. Place in the freezer for 15 to 20 minutes.
4. For the filling: In a small mixing bowl, place the hazelnut butter, nuts, sweetener, salt, and vanilla. Stir until well mixed.
5. Remove the chocolate cups from the freezer. Spoon ½ teaspoon of the filling into each cup with a spoon or melon baller. Keep the filling flat and away from the edges, so there's room for the chocolate to enclose the filling. Pour another layer of chocolate over the top of each cup so the filling is fully covered. Bang the pan again on a hard surface. Freeze for 15 to 20 minutes. Serve cold with or without the liners. They'll disappear fast!

# Trail Mix

*This Trail Mix is a delicious and healthy Paleo snack or dessert topping. I use it to make Trail Mix cookies and energy bars. This recipe is absolutely a breeze to make and it's low-carb (unlike many trail mix recipes). Don't miss the recipes for Crunchy and Spicy Trail Mix that follow, as they are very tantalizing. For best results, follow the recipe exactly. Feel free to play with it and add other ingredients after you've gotten the hang of it.*

**[ YIELD: 4 cups trail mix • EQUIPMENT NEEDED: None ]**

4 cups raw nuts (see tip)
⅛ to ¼ teaspoon unprocessed salt
¼ cup unsweetened cacao nibs or Homemade Chocolate Chips (page 108) (optional)

**Tip:** *Here's my favorite nut mixture: (You can mix any raw nuts.)*
*1 cup raw almonds*
*1 cup raw pecans*
*1 cup raw cashews*
*¼ cup sunflower seeds*
*¼ cup pumpkin seeds*
*¼ cup walnut halves*
*¼ cup any other nut (Brazil nuts, hazelnuts, large coconut flakes, etc., except peanuts)*

1. Soak the nuts if you can (see page 10). Soaking dissolves antinutrients, and makes the nuts less bitter, tastier, and easier to digest. Drain well.
2. Preheat the oven to 350°F. Prepare a large, shallow baking pan or rimmed baking sheet.
3. Place all the nuts in the baking pan. Sprinkle with salt and mix it in.
4. Roast the nuts for 15 minutes, stirring occasionally, until they're slightly crunchy. If they're wet when you put them in, roasting will take a little longer. Keep an eye on them and check every 3 minutes, as they can overbrown very quickly.
5. Remove from the oven. Let cool completely. Add the pure cacao nibs or Homemade Chocolate Chips (if using) and mix them in.
6. That's it! Enjoy, and if there's any left over, store in an airtight container.

**continues . . .**

variation **Crunchy Trail Mix:** This is just like the previous recipe, with the same yield; however, it has a sweet coating that solidifies into a crunchy glaze as the nuts cool. You'll be tempted to eat the whole batch.

6 tablespoons filtered water
3 tablespoons arrowroot powder
1 teaspoon unprocessed salt
$\frac{2}{3}$ to $1\frac{1}{3}$ cups Just Like Sugar Table Top natural chicory root sweetener (not Baking). I do not recommend any other sweetener for this.
1 teaspoon pure vanilla extract
4 cups mixed nuts (see tip, page 146)
$\frac{1}{4}$ cup unsweetened cacao nibs or Homemade Chocolate Chips (page 108) (optional)

1. Preheat the oven to 300°F. Line a cookie sheet with parchment paper.
2. Whisk together in a large mixing bowl the water, arrowroot powder, salt, sweetener, and vanilla. Stir until the mixture is smooth and the sweetener dissolves.
3. Add the nuts to the bowl and mix well to coat them. Spread the coated nuts evenly on the prepared cookie sheet and bake for 40 minutes, stirring every 10 minutes. Set the timer to remind you every 10 minutes, so they'll bake evenly on all sides.
4. Remove from the oven. Let cool for 4 to 5 minutes, until you can just barely handle them. Then with your hands, break the nuts apart. If you let them cool completely, they will solidify and be more difficult to break up. Add the pure cacao nibs or Homemade Chocolate Chips (if using) and mix them in.
5. Place the nuts in a serving bowl or store at room temperature. On second thought, maybe you should hide them! If you leave them out they'll disappear in no time.

variation **Spicy Trail Mix:** This trail mix is to die for! Crunchy and spicy, it is a favorite for the holidays or any time of year. The yield is 4 cups.

1 recipe Crunchy Trail Mix (above)
2 teaspoons ground cinnamon
$\frac{1}{2}$ teaspoon ground allspice
$\frac{1}{2}$ teaspoon ground cloves
$\frac{1}{2}$ teaspoon maple flavoring (optional)
$\frac{1}{4}$ teaspoon ground cumin
2 pinches of cayenne
2 tablespoons pure cacao powder
2 tablespoons melted coconut oil (place jar in lukewarm water to melt oil)

1. Follow the recipe for Crunchy Trail Mix (above), adding these delightful spices and the oil to the wet mixture in step 2.

*Simplicity is the ultimate sophistication.*
—LEONARDO DA VINCI

# PUDDINGS AND MOUSSES

**Y**ou just might melt from the smooth deliciousness of these puddings, whether it's rich chocolate mousse, tart lemon custard,

or oh-so-creamy flan. Easy to make and wonderful to eat, these are a few of my favorite pudding and mousse recipes.

# Easy Chocolate Mousse

*This is the easiest dessert in the world. It is smooth, creamy, chocolaty, and even tastier than the original. Just mix it and chill it for an hour. For best results, follow this recipe exactly.*

[ YIELD: 4 small servings or 2 large ones • EQUIPMENT NEEDED: Any style blender or mixer, or a food processor ]

1 (14-ounce) can unsweetened coconut milk as thick as possible (Lite coconut milk and coconut milk beverage in a carton will not work, as they are too thin.)

7 tablespoons Just Like Sugar Table Top natural chicory root sweetener (not Baking). I do not recommend any other sweetener for this.

¼ cup pure cacao powder

¼ cup melted coconut oil (place jar in lukewarm water to melt oil)

2 teaspoons pure vanilla extract

Pinch of unprocessed salt

1-Minute Whipped Crème Topping (page 173), or medium-shredded unsweetened coconut flakes (not coconut flour), ground cinnamon, or unsweetened cacao nibs, for garnish

1. In any style blender, mixer, or food processor, mix together the coconut milk, sweetener, cacao powder, coconut oil, vanilla, and salt.
2. Taste it and feel free to sweeten to your taste buds' liking.
3. Pour into four small stemmed glasses or two large ones.
4. Refrigerate for 30 to 60 minutes, or until firm.
5. Garnish with Whipped Crème or sprinkle with unsweetened coconut, ground cinnamon, or unsweetened cacao nibs.

---

**Optional Flavorings**

**Orange:** Add the zest of ¼ orange.

**Mocha:** Add ½ teaspoon of instant decaffeinated coffee powder or crystals.

**Mayan Spice:** Add 1 teaspoon of ground cinnamon and a pinch of cayenne.

# Instant Mocha Mousse

*This velvety treat is quick to make and a delight to enjoy immediately. "Way too good" is how my taste testers described this creamy mousse. Avocado lends a beautiful smooth consistency, and its taste disappears in the mix of chocolaty flavors. Although this recipe can be enhanced and modified in myriad ways, I suggest you follow the basic recipe—at least for the first time.*

**[ YIELD: 2 servings • EQUIPMENT NEEDED: Any style blender ]**

1¾ cups medium to thick unsweetened coconut milk

¼ cup Just Like Sugar Table Top natural chicory root sweetener (not Baking). I do not recommend any other sweetener for this.

2 tablespoons coconut oil

1 teaspoon pure vanilla extract

2 tablespoons pure cacao powder

1 teaspoon instant decaffeinated coffee powder or crystals

½ teaspoon ground cinnamon

Pinch of unprocessed salt

1 tablespoon *raw* yacón syrup (optional, gives caramel flavor)

1 ripe avocado, pitted and peeled

1. In a blender, combine the coconut milk, sweetener, coconut oil, vanilla, cacao powder, coffee powder, cinnamon, salt, and yacón syrup (if using). Blend well.
2. Add the avocado last, and blend until smooth.
3. Serve immediately or chill and it will thicken further. Makes 2½ cups.

---

**variation Mocha Mousse with Crunchy Nibs:** Layer the mousse into cups with 2 tablespoons of unsweetened cacao nibs

---

# Raspberry Rose Delight Mousse

*Raspberry Rose Delight is a recipe for LOVE. This intimate dessert for two is a creamy and magical mousse with raspberries and coconut milk, and it is sure to open someone's heart. The secret ingredient is a real rose. The first time I tasted this, we were making a video. It was so breathtaking I almost lost it on camera. Yes, that's how good it is! For the most delicious flavor and consistency, follow this recipe exactly.*

**[ YIELD: 2 servings • EQUIPMENT NEEDED: Any style blender (a high speed blender such as Blendtec or Vitamix will produce the smoothest consistency) ]**

½ orange

⅔ cup thick unsweetened coconut milk (Lite coconut milk or coconut milk beverage in a carton will not work, as they are too thin.)

1 cup fresh, organic raspberries

½ banana

½ cup raw cashews, soaked for 2 hours in filtered water (see page 10)

¼ cup Just Like Sugar Table Top natural chicory root sweetener (not Baking). I do not recommend any other sweetener for this.

1 teaspoon pure vanilla extract

2 tablespoons coconut oil

1 very thin slice of fresh beet, for a deep pink color

9 drops food-grade rose aromatherapy oil (optional)

15 fresh rose petals (from someone's organic garden, not a florist rose, which may be chemically treated)

1 tablespoon agar flakes

¼ cup unsweetened coconut milk, to cook agar

1. Have ready all the ingredients at room temperature. Get out two dessert cups or stemmed glasses.
2. Zest the orange half and reserve the zest. Then peel the orange half or cut away the peel with a knife. Remove the seeds. Place two-thirds of the orange half (one-third of the entire orange) in a blender, along with the ⅔ cup of coconut milk, raspberries, banana, cashews, sweetener, vanilla, coconut oil, and beet slice. Blend well until smooth and creamy.
3. Now for the fun part: Add the rose oil and nine of the rose petals. As you add them, think about that someone special you're making this dessert for. Think wonderful thoughts. Blend well until smooth and creamy.
4. In a shallow nonstick pan over medium heat, stir the agar into the ¼ cup of coconut milk. Cook and stir gently for 2 to 3 minutes, until it is bubbling and gummy, and the flakes begin to dissolve. Add the agar mixture to the blender immediately, and blend well to remove any lumps.
5. Taste your magical pudding and sweeten to taste.
6. Pour into two dessert glasses.
7. Garnish each glass with three rose petals in a triangle, to represent a merging of physical and higher love.
8. Chill for 30 minutes to thicken, and serve. And know that something wonderful is going to happen!

# Lemon-Berry Parfait

*This is an easy and refreshing treat made with lemon cream pudding layered in tall glasses with berries and crunchy nuts or cookies. A traditional chilled custard with heavy cream and eggs, parfait means "perfect" in French. This recipe is made with coconut, cashews, fresh fruit, and nuts instead, so it's Paleo perfect. For the best flavor and texture, follow this recipe exactly.*

**[ YIELD: 2 servings • EQUIPMENT NEEDED: Any style blender ]**

½ cup 1-Minute Whipped Crème Topping (page 173), for garnish

1 lemon, a Meyer lemon if possible

1 orange

1 cup unsweetened coconut milk, as thick as possible (Lite coconut milk or coconut milk beverage in a carton will not work, as they are too thin.)

⅔ cup Just Like Sugar Table Top natural chicory root sweetener (not Baking). I do not recommend any other sweetener for this.

½ cup raw cashews, soaked for 2 hours (see page 10) and well drained

1 teaspoon pure vanilla extract

3 tablespoons melted coconut oil (place jar in lukewarm water to melt oil)

1½ tablespoons agar flakes

⅓ cup unsweetened coconut milk

1 cup mixed berries, cut into bite-size pieces, for layering (All berries are wonderful. I like raspberries, blueberries, and strawberries.)

½ cup raw nuts, soaked if possible (see page10), for layering

1. Prepare ½ cup of Whipped Crème Topping. Have ready all the ingredients at room temperature. Get out four tall glasses for the parfait.

2. Zest the lemon and orange into the blender. With a sharp knife, cut away the outer white pith from both lemon and orange. Slice both fruits, seed them with the tip of a knife, and place in the blender. Add the 1 cup of coconut milk, sweetener, cashews, vanilla, and coconut oil. Blend until smooth and creamy.

3. In a shallow nonstick pan over medium heat, stir the agar into the ⅓ cup of coconut milk. Cook and stir gently for 2 to 3 minutes until it is bubbly and gummy, and the flakes begin to dissolve. Add the agar mixture to the blender immediately, and blend well to remove any lumps.

4. To assemble: In each tall glass, layer the lemon cream pudding with mixed berries and nuts. I usually do two layers of each.

5. Refrigerate the glasses for 1 hour, or until the pudding thickens. Top with Whipped Crème.

# Flan with Dulce de Leche

*Traditional Latino flan is made with cream, eggs, and sugar. This easy flan is one of my favorites because it contains none of those ingredients. And it's so simple—just blend and chill. My Latino guests have been amazed at the custardlike consistency and flavor, especially when they discovered that it's made with cashews and coconut milk. Orange gives this flan zesty flavor and golden color. For best results, follow this recipe exactly.*

**[ YIELD: 4 servings • EQUIPMENT NEEDED: Any style blender (a high-speed blender such as Blendtec or Vitamix will provide an even smoother result) ]**

### FLAN

1 cup any unsweetened coconut milk, at room temperature

¾ cup raw cashews soaked in filtered water for 3 hours or more (see page 10), then drained well

⅓ cup Just Like Sugar Table Top natural chicory root sweetener (not Baking). I do not recommend any other sweetener for this.

2 teaspoons *raw* yacón syrup (optional)

¼ cup coconut oil

2 teaspoons freshly squeezed lemon juice

¼ teaspoon unprocessed salt

2 teaspoons pure vanilla extract

Zest of ½ orange

1 tablespoon agar flakes

¼ cup any unsweetened coconut milk, to cook agar

### DULCE DE LECHE SAUCE

⅓ cup Just Like Sugar Table Top natural chicory root sweetener (not Baking). I do not recommend any other sweetener for this.

1 tablespoon boiling filtered water

3 tablespoons thick unsweetened coconut milk, or 1 tablespoon thin

3 to 4 tablespoons *raw* yacón syrup (optional; adds a wonderful caramel taste)

¼ teaspoon maple flavoring (optional)

1 teaspoon pure vanilla extract

⅛ teaspoon unprocessed salt, or to taste

1 tablespoon melted coconut oil (place jar in lukewarm water to melt oil)

1. Get out four ramekins.
2. Blend the 1 cup of coconut milk, cashews, sweetener, yacón syrup (if using), coconut oil, lemon juice, salt, vanilla, and orange zest until very smooth.
3. In a shallow nonstick pan over medium heat, stir the agar flakes into the ¼ cup of coconut milk. Cook and stir gently for 2 to 3 minutes until it is bubbly and gummy, and the flakes begin to dissolve. Add the agar mixture to the blender immediately, and blend well to remove any lumps. Sweeten to taste.
4. Pour into the ramekins. Chill for 1 hour to thicken.

continues . . .

5. For the Dulce de Leche Sauce: Place the sweetener in a small, heatproof serving pitcher and pour the tablespoon of boiling filtered water over it. Stir until the crystals dissolve. Add the coconut milk, yacón syrup (if using), maple flavoring (if using), vanilla, and salt. Whisk until very creamy. When completely smooth, gently add the melted coconut oil and stir until smooth. Makes about 1 cup of sauce.

6. Remove the chilled flan from the refrigerator. Pour the sauce over the flan and enjoy!

# Gell-o with Fruit and Whipped Crème

*This refreshing dessert is blended fruit puree gell-o layered with bite-size fresh fruit, and is served in a tall glass with Whipped Crème. This gell-o is made with agar—an amazing clear and tasteless seaweed plant with real binding power. It's easy to make, and holds just as well as commercial Jell-O, but it is unprocessed and plant-based. You should be able to find it in most grocery stores or online. Some fruits that are high in acids or enzymes require more agar. If you are using citrus fruits, strawberry, papaya, kiwi, peach, or mango, I suggest using 1½ tablespoons of agar flakes. I like to cut my fruit into pretty bite-size pieces that will go into the bottom of the cup, then any odd-shaped pieces can be used for the puree. For best results, follow this recipe exactly.*

**[ YIELD: 4 servings • EQUIPMENT NEEDED: Any style blender ]**

1 cup fresh, colorful fruit (raspberry, banana, grape, melon, cherry, blueberry, blackberry, apricot, etc.), cut into bite-size pieces

1½ cups fresh fruit, for puree (Transparent fruit, such as watermelon, plum, apple, grape, raspberry, etc., is prettier for the puree.)

⅓ cup or more Just Like Sugar Table Top natural chicory root sweetener (not Baking). I do not recommend any other sweetener for this.

1 tablespoon agar flakes

3 tablespoons filtered water, to cook agar

Chopped nuts or 1-Minute Whipped Crème Topping (page 173), for garnish (optional)

1. Get out four dessert cups or stemmed glasses. Place the 1 cup of bite-size fruit into the bottom of the four dessert cups.
2. Place 1½ cups of the fruit for the puree into any style blender, along with the sweetener, and blend until smooth. Taste your puree and sweeten to taste; the sweetener amount will depend on the fruit chosen.
3. In a shallow nonstick pan over medium heat, stir the agar into the 3 tablespoons of filtered water. Cook and stir gently for 2 to 3 minutes, until it is bubbling and gummy, and the flakes begin to dissolve. Add the agar mixture to the blender quickly, and blend well to remove any lumps.
4. Pour the blended fruit mixture into the dessert cups. Refrigerate for 30 minutes to allow it to gel. Serve plain, or with chopped nuts or Whipped Crème.

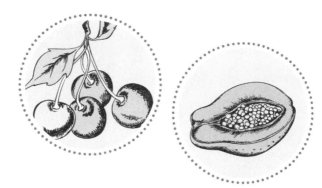

*Without ice cream, there would be darkness and chaos.*
—DON KARDONG

# FROZEN DESSERTS

oconut milk ice creams are delicious and easy to make because you simply blend and freeze. There's no cooking required. These recipes are completely dairy-free, and I personally think they're just as luscious as the ones made with cream and eggs. You can use any coconut milk you like. The final thickness and texture of the ice cream will depend on the thickness of the coconut milk. I prefer thick canned coconut milk for these ice creams. However, you can use "lite" coconut milk or coconut milk beverage in a carton, and these will come out more like ice milk, which is equally delicious. Just make sure the coconut milk is unsweetened. Most of these ice-cream recipes are easy because they use one entire 14-ounce can (1¾ cups) of coconut milk: Use 1¼ cups in the first blending, and the remaining ¼ cup to cook the agar, which thickens to a beautiful creamy texture.

These ice creams do not have whipped air in them so common in commercial ice creams. Therefore they will freeze quite hard. Just leave them out to soften at room temperature for 3 to 5 minutes before serving. If stored in shallow containers, they are easier to serve.

Make these recipes in an electric ice-cream machine or an old-fashioned hand-cranked machine, or whip with an electric mixer. But just so you're aware (and I've tried this all ways)—an ice-cream machine is the easiest option. Follow the instructions that come with the machine. I suggest chilling the blended mixture in the refrigerator thoroughly for 2 to 4 hours before putting it into the machine. How's that for simple?

To make your ice cream with an electric mixer, follow these steps:

1. Prepare the recipe as written. Instead of putting it in an ice-cream maker,

place the mixture in a deep, freezer-safe mixing bowl and refrigerate for 4 hours. After 4 hours, mix with an electric mixer until smooth and put in the freezer for 1 hour.

2. After one hour, remove the ice cream from the freezer every 30 minutes to mix it again, so you can break up any ice crystals and keep it smooth. Place back in the freezer and repeat this process every 30 minutes.

3. If you plan to add chopped nuts or fruit at the end, these must be chilled or frozen first so they don't melt the ice cream. Be careful not to freeze the fruit into a single block.

4. Continue this process every 30 minutes, until the ice cream reaches your desired texture. When finished, add chopped nuts or fruit, mix quickly and place the ice cream into serving bowls.

5. If you're storing the ice cream, place it quickly in a shallow freezing container and cover the surface of the ice cream with plastic wrap to prevent ice crystals from forming.

# Vanilla Ice Cream

*This creamy vanilla ice cream is super easy. You can use this recipe for ice-cream sandwiches if you freeze it in a 9-inch square pan. For best results, follow this recipe exactly.*

[ YIELD: 2 cups ice cream • EQUIPMENT NEEDED: Any style blender (a high-speed blender such as Blendtec or Vitamix will give you a smoother ice cream) and an ice-cream machine (easiest) or electric mixer ]

1½ cups any unsweetened coconut milk

½ to ⅔ cup Just Like Sugar Table Top natural chicory root sweetener (not Baking). I do not recommend any other sweetener for this.

2 teaspoons pure vanilla extract

1 fresh vanilla bean, sliced lengthwise to scrape out the tiny seeds (optional)

⅛ teaspoon unprocessed salt

¼ cup melted coconut oil (place jar in lukewarm water to melt oil)

1 tablespoon agar flakes

¼ cup thick unsweetened coconut milk, to cook agar

1. In a blender, combine the 1½ cups of coconut milk, sweetener, vanilla, vanilla bean (if using), and salt. Blend well until smooth. Sweeten to taste.
2. Add the barely warm coconut oil, and blend again until smooth.
3. In a shallow nonstick pan over medium heat, stir the agar into the ¼ cup of coconut milk. Cook and stir gently for 2 to 3 minutes, until it is bubbling and gummy, and the flakes begin to dissolve Add the agar mixture to the blender immediately and blend well to remove any lumps.
4. Pour the mixture into a bowl and chill for several hours in the refrigerator.
5. Next, pour the mixture into an ice-cream maker and process, or follow the instructions for using an electric mixer (page 159).
6. Freeze in flat containers, covered with plastic wrap to prevent the formation of crystals.

**Tip:** *If you're in a hurry, just chill for at least 30 minutes and serve this as a pudding.*

# Chocolate Chip Ice Cream

*Why do I love Chocolate Chip Ice Cream? That's easy—because I enjoy sweet, creamy, crunchy, and chocolate all together in the same bite. Check out the recipe for Homemade Chocolate Chips (page 108), or you can also use pure unsweetened cacao nibs. For best results, follow this recipe exactly.*

[ YIELD: 2 cups ice cream • EQUIPMENT NEEDED: Any style blender (a high-speed blender such as Blendtec or Vitamix will give you a smoother ice cream) and an ice-cream machine (easiest) or electric mixer ]

1½ cups any unsweetened coconut milk

½ to ⅔ cup Just Like Sugar Table Top natural chicory root sweetener (not Baking). I do not recommend any other sweetener for this.

2 teaspoons pure vanilla extract

⅛ teaspoon unprocessed salt

¼ cup melted coconut oil (place jar in lukewarm water to melt oil)

1 tablespoon agar flakes

¼ cup thick unsweetened coconut milk, to cook agar

½ cup Homemade Chocolate Chips (page 108), or ¼ cup unsweetened cacao nibs

1. In a blender, combine the 1½ cups of coconut milk, sweetener, vanilla, and salt. Blend well until smooth. Sweeten to taste.

2. Add the barely warm coconut oil, and blend again until smooth.

3. In a shallow nonstick pan over medium heat, stir the agar into the ¼ cup of coconut milk. Cook and stir gently for 2 to 3 minutes, until it is bubbling and gummy, and the flakes begin to dissolve. Add the agar mixture to the blender immediately and blend well to remove any lumps.

4. Pour the mixture into a bowl and chill for several hours in the refrigerator.

5. Next, pour the mixture into an ice-cream maker and process, or follow the instructions for using an electric mixer (see page 159).

6. When the ice cream is almost finished, stir in the frozen Homemade Chocolate Chips or cacao nibs.

7. Freeze in flat containers, covered with plastic wrap to prevent the formation of crystals.

**Tip:** *If you're in a hurry, just chill for at least 30 minutes and serve this as a pudding.*

# Chocolate Ice Cream

*This rich and creamy chocolate ice cream takes just a few minutes to make in any style blender. Try the variation below with cacao nibs or chocolate chips, for an extra chocolate punch. For best results, follow this recipe exactly.*

[ YIELD: 2 cups ice cream • EQUIPMENT NEEDED: Any style blender (a high-speed blender such as Blendtec or Vitamix will give you a smoother ice cream) and an ice-cream machine (easiest) or electric mixer ]

1½ cups any unsweetened coconut milk

¾ cup Just Like Sugar Table Top natural chicory root sweetener (not Baking). I do not recommend any other sweetener for this.

1 tablespoon pure vanilla extract

3 tablespoons pure cacao powder

⅛ teaspoon unprocessed salt

1 tablespoon *raw* yacón syrup (optional)

¼ cup melted coconut oil (place jar in lukewarm water to melt oil)

1 tablespoon agar flakes

¼ cup thick unsweetened coconut milk, to cook agar

1. In a blender, combine the 1½ cups of coconut milk, sweetener, vanilla, cacao powder, salt, and yacón syrup (if using). Blend well until smooth. Sweeten to taste.
2. Add the barely warm coconut oil, and blend again until smooth. Sweeten to taste.
3. In a shallow nonstick pan over medium heat, stir the agar into the ¼ cup of coconut milk. Cook and stir gently for 2 to 3 minutes, until it is bubbling and gummy, and the flakes begin to dissolve. Add the agar mixture to the blender immediately and blend well to remove any lumps.
4. Pour the mixture into a bowl and chill for several hours in the refrigerator.
5. Next, pour the mixture into an ice-cream maker and process, or follow the instructions for using an electric mixer (see page 159).
6. Freeze in flat containers, covered with plastic wrap to prevent the formation of crystals.

**Tip:** *If you're in a hurry, just chill for at least 30 minutes and serve this as a pudding.*

**variation Double Chocolate Chip Ice Cream:** Follow the recipe above. Freeze ½ cup of Homemade Chocolate Chips (page 108) or ¼ cup of unsweetened cacao nibs. When the ice cream is almost finished, stir in the frozen chocolate pieces. Yum!

# Cappuccino Ice Cream

Cappuccino *means "little hat" in Italian, a name inspired by the robes of sixteenth-century Capuchin monks, which were brown with a white hood. Now it's a coffee with milk and it will give you a nice caffeine jolt. This creamy ice cream is heavenly and kind to your nervous system—it's made with decaffeinated coffee powder. For best results, follow this recipe exactly.*

[ YIELD: 2 cups ice cream • EQUIPMENT NEEDED: Any style blender (a high-speed blender such as Blendtec or Vitamix will give you a smoother ice cream) and an ice cream machine (easiest) or electric mixer ]

1½ cups any unsweetened coconut milk

¾ cup Just Like Sugar Table Top natural chicory root sweetener (not Baking). I do not recommend any other sweetener for this.

1½ teaspoons pure cacao powder

2¼ teaspoons instant decaffeinated coffee powder, or 2½ teaspoons crystals

¼ teaspoon ground cinnamon

1 teaspoon pure vanilla extract

⅛ teaspoon unprocessed salt

¼ cup melted coconut oil (place jar in lukewarm water to melt oil)

1 tablespoon agar flakes

¼ cup thick unsweetened coconut milk, to cook agar

1. In a blender, combine the 1½ cups of coconut milk, sweetener, cacao powder, coffee, cinnamon, vanilla, and salt. Blend well until smooth. Sweeten to taste.
2. Add the barely warm coconut oil and blend again until smooth.
3. In a shallow nonstick pan over medium heat, stir the agar into the ¼ cup of coconut milk. Cook and stir gently for 2 to 3 minutes, until it is bubbling and gummy, and the flakes begin to dissolve. Add the agar mixture to the blender immediately and blend well to remove any lumps.
4. Pour into a bowl and chill for several hours in the refrigerator.
5. Next, pour the mixture into an ice-cream maker and process, or follow the instructions for using an electric mixer (see page 159).
6. Freeze in flat containers, covered with plastic wrap to prevent the formation of crystals.

> **variation Chocolate Chip Cappuccino Ice Cream:** Follow the recipe above. Freeze ½ cup of Homemade Chocolate Chips (page 108) or ¼ cup of unsweetened cacao nibs. When the ice cream is almost finished, stir in the frozen chocolate pieces.

# Mint Grasshopper Ice Cream

*This is a rich and refreshing ice cream with a light crème de menthe flavor. Its creamy green color comes from blended mint and spinach leaves. I was amazed to discover that fresh spinach leaves add a beautiful green color, high nutrition, and a mild flavor with no impact on the refreshing mint taste. Go ahead and try it—I think you'll be pleased.*

*Don't miss the variation below with nibs or chocolate chips—it's awesome. For best results, follow this recipe exactly.*

[ **YIELD: 2 cups ice cream** • **EQUIPMENT NEEDED: Any style blender (a high-speed blender such as Blendtec or Vitamix will give you a smoother ice cream) and an ice-cream machine (easiest) or electric mixer** ]

1½ cups any unsweetened coconut milk

½ cup Just Like Sugar Table Top natural chicory root sweetener (not Baking). I do not recommend any other sweetener for this.

10 to 20 medium-size fresh mint leaves

10 small leaves fresh spinach

1¼ teaspoons peppermint extract

½ teaspoon pure vanilla extract

⅛ teaspoon unprocessed salt

¼ teaspoon chocolate extract (optional)

⅓ cup melted coconut oil (place jar in lukewarm water to melt oil)

1 tablespoon agar flakes

¼ cup thick unsweetened coconut milk, to cook agar

1. In a blender, combine the 1½ cups of coconut milk, sweetener, mint leaves, spinach leaves, peppermint extract, vanilla, salt, and chocolate extract (if using). Blend well until smooth and the leaves are as liquefied as possible. Sweeten to taste.
2. Add the barely warm coconut oil, and blend again until smooth.
3. In a shallow nonstick pan over medium heat, stir the agar into the ¼ cup of coconut milk. Cook and stir gently for 2 to 3 minutes, until it is bubbling and gummy, and the flakes begin to dissolve. Add the agar mixture to the blender immediately and blend well to remove any lumps.
4. Pour the mixture into a bowl and chill for several hours in the refrigerator.
5. Next, pour the mixture into an ice-cream maker and process, or follow the instructions for using an electric mixer (see page 159).
6. Freeze in flat containers, covered with plastic wrap to prevent the formation of crystals.

**Tip:** *If you're in a hurry, just chill for at least 30 minutes and serve this as a pudding. It's awesomely delicious.*

variation **Mint Chocolate Chip Ice Cream:** Follow the recipe above. Freeze ½ cup of Homemade Chocolate Chips (page 108) or ¼ cup of unsweetened cacao nibs. When the ice cream is almost finished, stir in the frozen chocolate pieces.

# Strawberry Rose Ice Cream

*This creamy strawberry ice cream is delicate, divine, a beautiful pink color with chunks of strawberries. Rose aromatherapy oil and fresh orange zest add a subtle and magical zing to the flavor. Look for rose oil that is food grade with no added ingredients. For best results, follow this recipe exactly.*

[ YIELD: 3 cups ice cream • EQUIPMENT NEEDED: Any style blender (a high-speed blender such as Blendtec or Vitamix will give you a smoother ice cream) and an ice-cream machine (easiest) or electric mixer ]

10 to 18 fresh or frozen strawberries

1½ cups any unsweetened coconut milk

½ cup Just Like Sugar Table Top natural chicory root sweetener (not Baking). I do not recommend any other sweetener for this.

Zest of ½ orange

1 tablespoon freshly squeezed lemon juice

3 to 6 drops pure food-grade aromatherapy rose oil or rose absolute oil (from your favorite healthy grocery)

1 teaspoon pure vanilla extract

⅛ teaspoon unprocessed salt

¼ cup melted coconut oil (place jar in lukewarm water to melt oil)

1 tablespoon agar flakes

¼ cup thick unsweetened coconut milk, to cook agar

1. Slice half of the strawberries into ¼-inch pieces and reserve in the refrigerator.
2. In a blender, combine the 1½ cups of coconut milk, sweetener, the unsliced strawberries, and the orange zest, lemon juice, rose oil, vanilla, and salt. Blend well until smooth, and sweeten to taste.
3. Add the barely warm coconut oil and blend again.
4. In a shallow nonstick pan over medium heat, stir the agar into the ¼ cup of coconut milk. Cook and stir gently for 2 to 3 minutes, until it is bubbling and gummy, and the flakes begin to dissolve. Add the agar mixture to the blender immediately and blend well to remove any lumps.
5. Pour into a bowl and chill for several hours in the refrigerator.
6. Next, pour the mixture into an ice-cream maker and process, or follow the instructions for using an electric mixer (see page 159).
7. When the ice cream is almost finished, mix in the chilled strawberries.
8. Freeze in flat containers, covered with plastic wrap to prevent the formation of crystals. Remove from the freezer 30 to 60 minutes before serving, to soften.

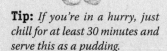

**Tip:** *If you're in a hurry, just chill for at least 30 minutes and serve this as a pudding.*

# Açaí Berry Lavender Ice Cream

*A new and refreshing flavor, açaí berries, from Central and South America, are recognized as one of the world's highest antioxidant foods. Numbers aside, they are absolutely tasty, and you can buy frozen unsweetened açaí puree at good health food markets. To add a flavor lift, I included pure lavender oil, often used for relaxation, but it's optional. Look for lavender oil that is food grade with no added ingredients. For best results, follow this recipe exactly.*

[ **YIELD: 2½ cups ice cream** • **EQUIPMENT NEEDED: Any style blender (a high-speed blender such as Blendtec or Vitamix will give you a smoother ice cream) and an ice-cream machine (easiest) or electric mixer** ]

1½ cups any unsweetened coconut milk

½ cup Just Like Sugar Table Top natural chicory root sweetener (not Baking). I do not recommend any other sweetener for this.

2 drops pure food-grade lavender aromatherapy oil (careful, it's strong) (optional)

Zest of ½ orange

½ cup fresh or frozen raspberries

½ cup pure 100% unsweetened açaí berry puree

1 teaspoon pure vanilla extract

2 teaspoons freshly squeezed lemon juice

⅛ teaspoon unprocessed salt

3 to 9 fresh or frozen blueberries or blackberries (for a beautiful lavender color)

¼ cup melted coconut oil (place jar in lukewarm water to melt oil)

1 tablespoon agar flakes

¼ cup thick unsweetened coconut milk, to cook agar

1. In a blender, combine the 1½ cups of coconut milk, sweetener, lavender oil, orange zest, raspberries, açaí puree, vanilla, lemon juice, and salt. Blend well until smooth and the berries are as liquefied as possible. Add a few blueberries or blackberries and blend until the color turns your favorite lavender color. Sweeten to taste.

2. Add the barely warm coconut oil, and blend again until smooth.

3. In a shallow nonstick pan over medium heat, stir the agar into the ¼ cup of coconut milk. Cook and stir gently for 2 to 3 minutes, until it is bubbling and gummy, and the flakes begin to dissolve. Add the agar mixture to the blender immediately and blend well to remove any lumps.

4. Pour the mixture in a bowl and chill for several hours in the refrigerator.

5. Next, pour the mixture into an ice-cream maker and process, or follow the instructions for using an electric mixer (see page 159).

6. Freeze in flat containers, covered with plastic wrap to prevent the formation of crystals. Remove from the refrigerator 20 minutes before serving, to soften.

**Tip:** *If you're in a hurry, just chill for at least 30 minutes and serve this as a yummy pudding.*

# Ice-Cream Sandwiches

*Homemade ice-cream sandwiches will inspire any gathering, and they're easy to prepare ahead of time. This recipe has three easy steps: blend the ice cream, mix the cookie dough, then put the sandwiches together. And let me tell you, the results are worth the effort. Make them in any size, depending on your cookie cutter. This recipe is raw and has zero-impact carbs—you won't find anything like this in a grocery store. To top it off, these look just like store-bought ice-cream sandwiches—but taste even better. The ice-cream filling is made with cashews, so it is firmer than the other ice creams. For the best flavor and texture, follow the recipe exactly.*

[ YIELD: Two dozen 2-inch sandwiches • EQUIPMENT NEEDED: Any style blender (a high-speed blender, such as Blendtec or Vitamix, will give you a smoother ice cream), a food processor, and any size cookie cutter (I use a 2-inch scalloped cutter.) ]

### FILLING

⅔ cup unsweetened coconut milk, as thick as possible. (Lite coconut milk and coconut milk beverage in a carton will not work, as they are too thin.)

1¾ cups raw cashews, soaked for 3 to 6 hours in filtered water and well drained (see page 10), measured *after* soaking

1 cup Just Like Sugar Table Top natural chicory root sweetener (not Baking). I do not recommend any other sweetener for this.

Pinch of unprocessed salt

3 tablespoons freshly squeezed lemon juice

1 tablespoon pure vanilla extract

⅓ cup melted coconut oil (place jar in lukewarm water to melt oil)

### COOKIES

2 cups raw nuts, soaked if possible (see page 10) and well drained

1½ cups medium-shredded unsweetened coconut flakes (not coconut flour)

½ teaspoon unprocessed salt

6 tablespoons pure cacao powder

2 tablespoons roasted carob powder

1 large carrot, scrubbed and unpeeled, cut into chunks (120 grams)

1 tablespoon pure vanilla extract

1¼ cups Just Like Sugar Table Top natural chicory root sweetener (not Baking)

½ teaspoon ground cinnamon

½ teaspoon maple flavoring (optional)

2 tablespoons hijiki or wakame seaweed, soaked in warm water for 10 minutes (optional, for binding)

**continues . . .**

1. For the filling: In a blender, combine the coconut milk, soaked cashews, sweetener, salt, lemon juice, and vanilla. Blend until very smooth and creamy. Sweeten to taste. Add the coconut oil last and blend well.

2. Pour the mixture into a flat pan or tray with a removable bottom or lined with parchment paper, so the mixture is no more than ½ inch thick. If it's any thicker, it is too difficult to cut when frozen. I use an 8 by 11-inch tart pan. Freeze for 2 hours or until very firm.

3. For the cookies: To a food processor, add all the cookie ingredients. Mix well until the carrot is well pureed and the dough becomes cohesive.

4. Divide the dough into two parts. Roll each piece between two pieces of parchment paper on a baking sheet. Freeze both sheets for 30 to 60 minutes until stiff.

5. To assemble: Remove the dough from the freezer. Cut with a cookie cutter, in matching pairs. Don't worry if a piece breaks; you can reroll the dough and freeze.

6. Remove the filling from the freezer. Working quickly, cut the filling with the same cutter and place on one of each cookie pair. Stack the second cookie of each pair on top. Place the sandwiches in the freezer immediately on a serving plate.

**Chocolate Ice-Cream Sandwiches:** Follow the recipe above. In step 1, add to the blender ¼ cup of Just Like Sugar Table Top natural chicory root sweetener (not Baking) and 1½ tablespoons of pure cacao powder.

*Lead me not into temptation; I can find the way myself.*

—RITA MAE BROWN

# SAUCES, FROSTINGS, AND FILLINGS

**L**ike the icing on your Paleo cake, these sweet recipes will complete any dessert and make it special. Following is a huge selection of delicious toppings, sauces, and frostings that you can mix and match for every type of treat.

Here's an easy guide to frosting quantities for your cakes:

- 24 mini cupcakes: 1 to 2 cups
- 12 regular cupcakes: 1½ to 3 cups
- 9 by 13-inch sheet cake: 1 to 2 cups
- Single-layer 8- or 9-inch round or square cake: ½ to 1 cup
- Top, sides, and filling for double-layer 8- or 9-inch round cake: 2 to 3 ½ cups
- Top, sides, and filling for triple-layer 8- or 9-inch round cake: 3 to 4 ½ cups

# 1-Minute Whipped Crème Topping

*Here's a fantastic dessert topping when you need it quick. It's made with canned coconut milk. Keep a few cans of the thickest coconut milk on hand in the refrigerator, and garnish your desserts in just a few minutes. If you need a larger quantity or you're using a slightly lighter coconut milk, then use the 5-Minute Whipped Crème Topping (page 174).*

**[ YIELD: About ²/₃ cup whipped topping • EQUIPMENT NEEDED: None ]**

1 (14-ounce) can very thick unsweetened canned coconut milk, such as Thai Kitchen

2 tablespoons Just Like Sugar Table Top natural chicory root sweetener (not Baking). I do not recommend any other sweetener for this.

1 teaspoon pure vanilla extract

1. Chill the coconut milk in the can for 4 to 8 hours, until it thickens into a lovely cream. Open the can and pour off the thin milk from the bottom to use in something else. Spoon the thickest part of the coconut cream into a small bowl.

2. Whisk in the sweetener and vanilla. Serve!

# 5-Minute Whipped Crème Topping

*This lovely crème Chantilly is the mainstay of all my recipes. It's a perfect garnish for any elegant dessert. Blend, chill, and serve on Pumpkin Pie (page 123), Strawberry Shortcake (page 42), or Awesome Fudge Brownies (page 91). Because it is thickened with agar, you can use medium to thick coconut milk, and you can make any quantity. For a simpler version, try the 1-Minute Whipped Crème Topping (page 173). For best results, follow this recipe exactly.*

**[ YIELD: 1, 2, or 3 cups topping • EQUIPMENT NEEDED: Any style blender ]**

| Desired Quantity | 1 cup | 2 cups | 3 cups |
|---|---|---|---|
| Unsweetened coconut milk, as thick as possible (see tip) | ⅔ cup | 1¼ cups | 2 cups |
| Coconut oil | 1 tablespoon | 2 tablespoons | 3 tablespoons |
| Vanilla extract | ½ teaspoon | 1 teaspoon | 1½ teaspoons |
| Just Like Sugar Table Top sweetener (not Baking) | 2 tablespoons | ¼ cup | 6 tablespoons |
| Agar flakes | ¾ tablespoon | 1½ tablespoons | 2¼ tablespoons |
| Unsweetened coconut milk, to cook the agar | ¼ cup | ½ cup | ¾ cup |

1. Have ready all the ingredients at room temperature. Choose the quantity desired and follow that column.
2. Blend the thick coconut milk, coconut oil, vanilla, and sweetener in any style blender until smooth.
3. In a shallow nonstick pan over medium heat, stir the agar into the additional coconut milk. Cook and stir gently for 2 to 3 minutes until bubbling and gummy, and the flakes begin to dissolve. Add the agar mixture to the blender immediately and blend well until it is completely liquefied and any lumps are removed.
4. Pour into a bowl and chill for 2 to 3 hours, or until thick. Then keep it out at room temperature if you're using it today. If you're making it ahead of time, this will keep in the refrigerator for 2 to 3 days, but allow 4 hours to soften at room temperature before using.

**Tips:** *Your consistency will vary a bit with different coconut milks. If it is too thick, stir with a whisk, allow it to slowly warm to room temperature, or add a bit more coconut milk of the same temperature. If it is too thin, chill longer, or allow it to slowly warm to room temperature and blend it again with more agar. Do not subject to radical temperature changes or it may develop lumps. Good thicker alternative fillings for cakes and cupcakes are Vanilla Pastry Cream with Coconut (page 186) or Vanilla Pastry Cream with Cashews (page 185).*

# Coconut Buttercream Frosting

*This is the easiest and creamiest frosting you'll ever make. Follow the variations that follow to make it in every flavor imaginable, such as banana, lemon, orange, coffee, maple, raspberry, and salted caramel. Coconut oil is very temperature sensitive, so be sure all ingredients are at room temperature, about 68° to 72°F. If it's a warm summer day and your ambient temperature is over 72°F, this frosting won't work. Follow the recipe exactly, for the perfect flavor and consistency.*

[ YIELD: 2 or 3 cups topping • EQUIPMENT NEEDED: A food processor ]

| Desired Quantity | 2 cups | 3 cups |
|---|---|---|
| Cake Size | 24 mini cupcakes, 12 regular cupcakes | 24 regular cupcakes, or one double- or triple-layer 8- to 9-inch cake |
| Thick unsweetened coconut milk | ⅔ cup | 1 cup |
| Just Like Sugar Table Top sweetener (not Baking). I do not recommend any other sweetener for this recipe. | 2 cups | 3 cups |
| Pure vanilla extract | 1 teaspoon | 2 teaspoons |
| Unprocessed salt | 2 pinches | 3 pinches |
| Solid coconut oil | 1 cup | 1½ cups |

This recipe uses coconut milk, as thick as possible (Lite coconut milk or coconut milk beverage in a carton will not work, as they are too thin.)

The secret to its creamy texture is solid coconut oil at room temperature.

1. Have ready all the ingredients at room temperature. Choose the quantity desired and follow that column.
2. In a food processor, mix the coconut milk, sweetener, vanilla, and salt until smooth and the sweetener dissolves.
3. Add the coconut oil last and mix until very smooth. Pour into a bowl.
4. Refrigerate for 1 hour until it solidifies a bit, then spread on your cake or cupcakes. This is most spreadable at room temperature. If you chill it for too long or store it in the refrigerator, it will solidify and be too hard to spread. If that happens, just set it out to warm very slowly to room temperature.

continues . . .

**variations** All are variations for 2 cups of frosting.

**Banana Buttercream Frosting:** In step 2, add 1 ripe banana.

**Espresso Latte Buttercream Frosting:** *Deliziosa!* In step 2, add 1 teaspoon of finely ground decaffeinated coffee powder.

**Lemon Buttercream Frosting:** In step 2, add the finely grated zest of one Meyer lemon. (Note: This frosting only works with Meyer lemons; other lemons are too acidic.)

**Maple Buttercream Frosting:** In step 2, add ½ teaspoon of maple flavoring and 1 additional teaspoon of vanilla.

**Orange Buttercream Frosting** (This is my favorite.): In step 2, add the zest of two oranges.

**Raspberry Buttercream Frosting:** In step 2, add nine to twelve fresh raspberries or six frozen ones, well squeezed and drained to remove any excess liquid.

**Salted Caramel Buttercream Frosting:** In step 2, add 1 tablespoon of *raw* yacón syrup, ½ teaspoon of maple flavoring, 1 more teaspoon of vanilla, and a pinch more salt.

**Vanilla Buttercream Frosting:** In step 2, add 1 scraped vanilla bean and 1 more teaspoon of vanilla.

See also Chocolate Buttercream Frosting and Chocolate Espresso Buttercream Frosting (page 178)

# Chocolate Buttercream Frosting

*You'll love this creamy chocolate frosting because it takes just a few minutes to prepare in a food processor and tastes super luscious. The secret is to add the ingredients in the exact order given, with all ingredients at room temperature. For the perfect flavor and smoothest consistency, follow this recipe exactly.*

[ YIELD: ⅓, 2⅔, or 4 cups frosting • EQUIPMENT NEEDED: A food processor ]

| Desired Quantity | 1⅓ cups | 2⅔ cups | 4 cups |
|---|---|---|---|
| Cake Size | One single-layer 8- to 9-inch cake or 24 mini muffins | One double-layer 8- to 9-inch cake or 18 cupcakes | One triple-layer 8- to 9-inch cake or 24 cupcakes |
| Unsweetened coconut milk, the thickest possible | ½ cup | 1 cup | 1½ cups |
| Just Like Sugar Table Top sweetener (not Baking) | 1½ cups | 3 cups | 4½ cups |
| Pure vanilla extract | 2 teaspoons | 1½ tablepoons | 2 tablespoons |
| Unprocessed salt | pinch | 2 pinches | ⅛ teaspoon |
| Pure cacao powder | 3 tablespoons | 6 tablespoons | ½ cup + 1 tablespoon |
| Solid coconut oil | ½ cup | 1 cup | 1½ cups |

1. Have ready all the ingredients at room temperature. Choose the quantity desired and follow that column.
2. In a food processor, place the coconut milk, sweetener, vanilla, and salt. Mix until smooth and the sweetener dissolves completely. Sift in the cacao powder to remove any lumps. Mix very well until creamy.
3. Add the solid coconut oil. Process until it is completely smooth. Pour it into a bowl.
4. Refrigerate for 1 hour, until it solidifies a bit. Remove it from the refrigerator and spread it on cake or cupcakes. This is most spreadable at room temperature. If you chill it for too long or store it in the refrigerator, it will solidify and be too hard to spread. If that happens, just set it out to warm very slowly to room temperature.

**continues . . .**

# Chocolate Buttercream Frosting (variation)

**variation** This variation is for 1⅓ cups of frosting.

**Chocolate Espresso Buttercream Frosting:**
In step 2, add 1 teaspoon of decaffeinated coffee powder. (If you're using coffee crystals, grind them to a powder first so they will dissolve.)

# Crème Cheese Frosting

You're going to fall in love with this *Crème Cheese Frosting*. It is quick to blend and tastes absolutely scrumptious. It has a sweet, tangy flavor of lemon and a consistency something like that of cream cheese but without all the calories and dairy impact. This frosting is great on *Carrot Mini Cupcakes* (page 49), *Gingerbread Cupcakes* (page 52), *Whole Apple Spice Cake* (page 45), and just about anything else you can imagine. The flavor variations below will tantalize your taste buds.

Due to the temperature sensitivity of coconut butter, this is not a good recipe for a warm summer day. If the coconut butter is cold, you may place the jar in a bowl of lukewarm water to soften it so it is easier to measure. For the best flavor and texture, have all the ingredients at room temperature, 68° to 72°F, and follow this recipe exactly.

[ YIELD: 1¼, 2½, or 3¾ cups frosting • EQUIPMENT NEEDED: Any style blender and a digital scale, for the coconut butter ]

| Desired Quantity | 1¼ cups | 2½ cups | 3¾ cups |
|---|---|---|---|
| Blender Size | Small blender, if possible | Regular blender | Regular blender |
| Cake Size | 1 layer cake or 24 mini cupcakes | One 9 by 13-inch sheet cake or 12 regular cupcakes | One double- or triple-layer 8- to 9-inch cake or 24 regular cupcakes |
| Unsweetened coconut milk | ½ cup | 1 cup | 1½ cups |
| Just Like Sugar Table Top sweetener (not Baking) | 1 cup | 2 cups | 3 cups |
| Pure vanilla extract | 1 teaspoon | 2 teaspoons | 3 teaspoons |
| Freshly squeezed lemon juice | 1 tablespoon | 2 tablespoons | 3 tablespoons |
| Unprocessed salt | Pinch | 2 pinches | 3 pinches |
| Pure coconut butter (not coconut oil), at room temperature | 110 grams (½ cup tightly packed) | 220 grams (1 cup packed) | 330 grams (1½ cups packed) |

**continues . . .**

1. Have ready all the ingredients at room temperature. Choose the quantity desired and follow that column.
2. In any style blender, place the coconut milk, sweetener, vanilla, lemon juice, and salt. Blend until smooth and the sweetener is completely dissolved.
3. Add the coconut butter last and blend until very smooth, translucent, and gummy. Pour into a bowl.
4. Refrigerate for 1 hour, until it solidifies a bit. Remove it from the refrigerator and spread it on your cake or cupcakes. The frosting is most spreadable at room temperature. If you chill it for too long or store it in the refrigerator, it will solidify and be too hard to spread. If that happens, just set it out to warm very slowly to room temperature.

---

**variations**  All variations are for 1¼ cups of frosting.

**Banana Crème Cheese Frosting:** In step 2, add ½ ripe banana.

**Cinnamon Crème Cheese Frosting:** In step 2, add ½ teaspoon of ground cinnamon.

**Coconut Crème Cheese Frosting:** At the end of step 3, add ½ cup of medium-shredded unsweetened coconut flakes (not coconut flour) and stir well.

**Lemon Crème Cheese Frosting:** In step 2, add the zest of one Meyer lemon. (Note: This frosting only works with Meyer lemons; other lemons are too acidic.)

**Maple Crème Cheese Frosting:** In step 2, add ¼ teaspoon of maple flavoring, 1 tablespoon of *raw* yacón syrup, and 2 pinches more salt.

**Orange Crème Cheese Frosting:** In step 2, add the zest of one orange.

**Raspberry Crème Cheese Frosting:** In step 2, add nine fresh or six frozen raspberries, squeezed and drained well.

**Vanilla Crème Cheese Frosting:** In step 2, add the scrapings of 1 vanilla bean and 1 more teaspoon of vanilla.

# Chocolate Crème Cheese Frosting

*Indulge in this rich and creamy frosting. The velvety chocolate consistency and tangy lemon flavor make it a world-class favorite. It can also be used as a filling or a spread. All right, just put it on everything. Irresistible on cakes, cupcakes, and even Finger Tarts (page 127), this will delight and amaze your guests (and you'll love it, too). As this frosting is quite temperature sensitive, please follow the recipe exactly.*

[ YIELD: 1, 2, or 3 cups frosting • EQUIPMENT NEEDED: Any style blender and a digital scale for the coconut butter ]

| Desired Quantity | 1 cup | 2 cups | 3 cups |
|---|---|---|---|
| Cake Size | One 9-inch cake or 24 mini muffins | 12 regular cupcakes or 4 mini loafs | One double- or triple-layer 8- to 9-inch cake or 24 cupcakes |
| Thick unsweetened coconut milk | ½ cup | 1 cup | 1½ cups |
| Just Like Sugar Table Top sweetener (not Baking) | 1½ cups | 3 cups | 4½ cups |
| Pure vanilla extract | 2 teaspoons | 1½ tablespoons | 2 tablespoons |
| Freshly squeezed lemon juice | 2 tablespoons | ¼ cup | 6 tablespoons |
| Unprocessed salt | pinch | 2 pinches | ⅛ teaspoon |
| Pure cacao powder, sifted | 3 tablespoons | 6 tablespoons | ½ cup + 1 tablespoon |
| Pure coconut butter (not coconut oil) | 50 grams (¼ cup) | 100 grams (½ cup) | 150 grams (¾ cup) |

**continues . . .**

1. Have ready all the ingredients at room temperature. Choose the quantity desired and follow that column.

2. In a blender, combine the coconut milk, sweetener, vanilla, lemon juice, and salt. Blend until very smooth and the sweetener dissolves. Sift in the cacao powder to remove any lumps, and blend until smooth.

3. Add the coconut butter last and blend very well until smooth. Pour into a bowl.

4. Refrigerate for 1 hour, until it solidifies a bit. Remove it from the refrigerator and spread it on your cake or cupcakes with a knife or a decorator tip. The frosting is most spreadable at room temperature. If you chill it for too long or store it in the refrigerator, it will solidify and be too hard to spread. If that happens, just set it out to warm very slowly to room temperature.

---

**variation  for 2 cups of frosting**

**Mocha Crème Cheese Frosting:** Add 1 teaspoon of finely ground decaffeinated coffee powder.

# Coconut Pecan Frosting

*This easy frosting is traditional on German Chocolate Cake (page 98) but I love it on brownies and nut breads, too. The secret to its magical flavor and crunchy texture is lightly toasted pecans and coconut. Because coconut oil is very temperature sensitive, it's important to have all the ingredients at room temperature. For the best flavor and consistency, follow these instructions exactly.*

**[ YIELD: 4½ cups frosting, for a double- or triple-layer 8- to 9-inch cake • EQUIPMENT NEEDED: A food processor and any style blender ]**

2 cups raw pecans, soaked if possible (see page 10)

2 cups medium-shredded unsweetened coconut flakes (not coconut flour)

2⅔ cups Just Like Sugar Table Top natural chicory root sweetener (not Baking). I do not recommend any other sweetener for this.

¾ cup thick unsweetened coconut milk (Lite coconut milk and coconut milk beverage in a carton will not work, as they are too thin.)

½ cup raw cashews, soaked in filtered water for 3 to 6 hours (see page 10)

3 tablespoons *raw* yacón syrup (for caramel flavor)

1 tablespoon pure vanilla extract

½ teaspoon unprocessed salt

½ teaspoon maple flavoring

¾ cup melted coconut oil (place jar in lukewarm water to melt oil)

1. Have ready all the ingredients at room temperature. Preheat the oven to 350°F.

2. In a food processor, chop the pecans till they are medium to small pieces but not mushy. (Or you can chop the nuts by hand.) Place the pecans and coconut in a dry, shallow baking pan and toast in the oven for 10 minutes. Set the timer, and be careful not to overbake. Remove from the oven and set aside to cool completely.

3. In a dry blender, grind the sweetener to a fine powder. Add the coconut milk, soaked cashews, yacón syrup, vanilla, salt, and maple flavoring. Blend well, stopping and stirring if necessary. The mixture should become thick and gummy.

4. Add the melted coconut oil and blend until smooth.

5. Place the mixture into a medium-size mixing bowl. Add the toasted pecans and coconut and mix well. Then chill for 30 minutes, so the frosting becomes thick and spreadable. After that, remove from the refrigerator and keep out at room temperature. If you chill it for longer than 30 minutes, it may become too hard to spread. Enjoy on cakes or cupcakes.

# Instant Mocha Buttercream Frosting

*This chocolaty frosting is velvety smooth and incredibly easy to make in a food processor. And you can spread it right on the cake without refrigerating. How's that for quick? The secret to its creamy texture is avocado. Because avocado has a mild flavor, all you taste is rich chocolate and mocha. For the best flavor and texture, follow this recipe exactly.*

**[ YIELD: 3 cups frosting • EQUIPMENT NEEDED: A food processor ]**

2½ cups Just Like Sugar Table Top natural chicory root sweetener (not Baking). I do not recommend any other sweeteners for this recipe.

2 to 3 ripe avocados, pitted and peeled (365 grams flesh)

1 tablespoon freshly squeezed lemon juice

1 tablespoon pure vanilla extract

Pinch of unprocessed salt

Zest of ½ orange

½ cup pure cacao powder

2 teaspoons instant decaffeinated coffee powder or crystals

1 tablespoon filtered water, if necessary

1. In a dry food processor fitted with the "S" blade, grind the sweetener to a very fine powder.
2. Add the avocado, lemon juice, vanilla, salt, and orange zest. Mix well until smooth and without lumps. The mixture will be creamy and bright green.
3. Sift in the cacao powder and coffee powder to remove any lumps. Mix again very well until perfectly smooth. You may need to open the processor, stir, and then mix again.
4. Check the thickness. If it's too thick, add a bit of filtered water slowly until it is a spreadable texture. If too thin, sift in 1 tablespoon of cacao powder and mix again.
5. Spread the frosting directly on your cake or use a decorator tip.

# Vanilla Pastry Cream with Cashews

*This pastry cream is made smooth and creamy by cashews, which are naturally sweet. Soaked raw cashews soften easily into a thick, velvety filling. This cream is quick to blend and has a slightly smoother consistency than the Vanilla Pastry Cream with Coconut (page 186). Both are delicious and can be used hundreds of ways, to fill cakes, cupcakes, or ice cream or garnish any dessert. For best results, follow this recipe exactly.*

**[ YIELD: 2 cups pastry cream • EQUIPMENT NEEDED: Any style blender ]**

1 cup thick unsweetened coconut milk (Lite coconut milk or coconut milk beverage in a carton will not work, as they are too thin.)

⅔ cup Just Like Sugar Table Top natural chicory root sweetener (not Baking). I do not recommend any other sweetener for this recipe.

120 grams (1¼ cups) raw cashews, soaked for 3 hours in filtered water (see page 10) and well drained

⅛ teaspoon unprocessed salt

2 teaspoons pure vanilla extract

1 to 2 lemons (for 3 tablespoons juice)

1 teaspoon agar flakes

3 tablespoons unsweetened coconut milk, to cook agar

1. In a blender, combine the 1 cup of coconut milk, sweetener, soaked cashews, salt, and vanilla. Blend well, stopping and stirring if necessary.
2. Juice the lemon(s). Add the lemon juice to the mixture in the blender and blend again until very smooth.
3. In a shallow nonstick pan over medium heat, stir the agar into the 3 tablespoons of coconut milk. Cook and stir gently for 2 to 3 minutes until it is bubbling and gummy, and the flakes begin to dissolve. Add the agar mixture to the blender immediately and blend well to remove any lumps.
4. Pour into a bowl and chill for 2 to 3 hours, or until thick.
5. That's it. Spread it on your cake, fill your cupcakes, or eat it plain.

# Vanilla Pastry Cream with Coconut

*This decadent white* crème pâtissière *(French pastry cream) is smooth and thick. It takes just minutes to blend and can be used many different ways. The delightful flavor and texture come from pure coconut butter, which is simply ground coconut pulp that gives it a thick consistency like that of cream cheese. A rich and velvety filling for cupcakes or cakes, it's perfect with Tiramisu (page 43), Strawberry Shortcake (page 42), or as a topping for any dessert. If you prefer a more soft, silky texture, try the Vanilla Pastry Cream with Cashews (see previous recipe), which is equally thick and has a nuttier flavor. For best results, follow this recipe exactly.*

**[ YIELD: 2 cups frosting • EQUIPMENT NEEDED: Any style blender and a digital scale for the coconut butter ]**

1 cup thick unsweetened coconut milk (Lite coconut milk or coconut milk beverage in a carton will not work, as these are too thin.)

½ cup Just Like Sugar Table Top natural chicory root sweetener (not Baking). I do not recommend any other sweetener for this recipe.

200 grams (about 1 cup very tightly packed) pure coconut butter (not coconut oil), at room temperature

⅛ teaspoon unprocessed salt

2 teaspoons pure vanilla extract

3 tablespoons freshly squeezed lemon juice

1. Blend all the ingredients in a blender until smooth and creamy.
2. Pour into a bowl and refrigerate to firm up—2 to 3 hours.
3. Spread on cakes, fill cupcakes, or enjoy it plain as vanilla pudding.

# Apple Butter

*This easy apple butter is so delicious and smooth, you'll want to spread it on everything. Perfect on Flax Muffins (page 56), Gingerbread Cupcakes (page 52), or Whole Apple Spice Cake (page 45), it can be blended in minutes and keeps for several days in the refrigerator. For best results, follow this recipe exactly.*

[ YIELD: 2 cups apple butter • EQUIPMENT NEEDED: Any style blender (a high-speed blender such as Blendtec or Vitamix will make it all the more smooth and creamy) ]

3 tablespoons Just Like Sugar Table Top natural chicory root sweetener (not Baking). I do not recommend any other sweetener for this recipe.

⅓ cup melted coconut oil (place jar in lukewarm water to melt oil)

2 tart apples, unpeeled, cored, and cut into ½-inch chunks

2 teaspoons freshly squeezed lemon juice

Zest of ½ lemon

Zest of ½ orange

1 tablespoon ground cinnamon

⅛ teaspoon grated nutmeg

⅛ teaspoon ground cloves

Pinch of unprocessed salt

¼ teaspoon maple flavoring

1 tablespoon *raw* yacón syrup (optional, for molasses flavor)

1. In a dry blender, grind the sweetener until it is a very fine powder.
2. Add the coconut oil, apples, lemon juice, lemon and orange zest, cinnamon, nutmeg, clove, salt, maple flavoring, and yacón syrup (if using). Blend well until it is smooth. (Note: this may take several tries, but don't give up! You may need to open the blender to stir and redistribute the apple chunks if this is the case.) Blend several times, until the apple peels are liquefied and the mixture is smooth and creamy.
3. This step is optional, but it helps dissolve the spices to make a smooth butter. Pour the mixture into a small saucepan over low heat and bring it slowly to a boil. Boil for a minute, remove from the heat, and then allow it to cool for 15 minutes.
4. Store it in a glass jar in the refrigerator for up to 4 days.

# Chocolate Hazelnut Butter

*This homemade Chocolate Hazelnut Butter is a delicious high-protein snack or a garnish for cup-cakes. It tastes something like Nutella. Use it as a filling for cakes or a topping for ice cream, or spread it on cookies. This recipe takes just minutes to whisk together. Why pay a high price for sugary nut butter when you can make it 100 percent Paleo at home? For best results, follow this recipe exactly.*

**[ YIELD: About 1 cup butter • EQUIPMENT NEEDED: None ]**

1 cup roasted, unsweetened hazelnut butter

3 tablespoons Just Like Sugar Table Top natural chicory root sweetener (not Baking). I do not recommend any other sweetener for this.

1½ tablespoons pure cacao powder

1 teaspoon pure vanilla extract

Pinch of unprocessed salt

1 teaspoon melted coconut oil (place jar in lukewarm water to melt oil) (This may or may not be needed, depending on the thickness of your hazelnut butter.)

1. Have all the ingredients except the coconut oil at room temperature.
2. Using a spoon or small whisk and a small mixing bowl, mix the hazelnut butter with the sweetener. Stir until it is smooth and the crystals dissolve.
3. Add the cacao powder, vanilla, and salt. Mix again. Sweeten to taste. If it is too thick to stir, thin it with 1 teaspoon melted coconut oil and stir slowly until smooth. Do not thin it with water.
4. Store in a glass jar in the refrigerator for several days. Use as a topping or filling. Or eat it right out of the jar. There's no shame in that!

# Chocolate Sauce

*This creamy fudge sauce is super easy to make and tastes delicious on everything from ice cream to brownies to pancakes. Serve it at room temperature, or warm it over low heat and serve as a hot fudge sauce. For best results, follow this recipe exactly.*

**[ YIELD: 1 cup sauce • EQUIPMENT NEEDED: An immersion blender (easiest) or any other style blender and a small saucepan ]**

⅔ cup filtered water

1¼ cups Just Like Sugar Table Top natural chicory root sweetener (not Baking). I do not recommend any other sweetener for this.

⅓ cup pure cacao powder, sifted in a flour sifter or fine tea strainer to remove any lumps

2 teaspoons pure vanilla extract

Pinch of unprocessed salt

¼ cup coconut oil

1. Boil the filtered water in a small saucepan over medium heat. Add the sweetener and stir with a whisk until dissolved. Add the sifted cacao powder, vanilla, and salt. Stir well until dissolved. Heat almost to boiling.
2. Blend well with an immersion blender to remove any lumps, until it is creamy and smooth. Sweeten to taste.
3. Add the coconut oil and mix until smooth.
4. Pour into a 1-cup pitcher and serve. This sauce keeps for up to a week in the refrigerator. If necessary, you can thin it with a little lukewarm water or thicken it with a bit of cacao powder.

> **variation Mayan Chocolate Sauce:** Follow the recipe above. In step 1, using a flour sifter or fine-gauge tea strainer, sift in 1 teaspoon of ground cinnamon, 1 teaspoon of chili powder, a pinch of cayenne, and 1 teaspoon of decaffeinated coffee powder.

# Cinnamon "Sugar"

*Cinnamon is a comfort food for many people. This Cinnamon "Sugar" is a quick way to add spice to your Paleo Caffè or tea. I like to sprinkle it on apple desserts, puddings, cheesecake, or ice cream. Cinnamon comes from the bark of evergreen trees and has been known since ancient times for its medicinal benefits. Cassia cinnamon is the variety most commonly sold in the United States, and is known to help balance blood sugar.*

[ YIELD: ½ cup cinnamon "sugar"  •  EQUIPMENT NEEDED: None ]

½ cup Just Like Sugar Table Top natural chicory root sweetener (not Baking). A second choice is ⅔ cup Organic Zero Erythritol.

1 tablespoon ground cinnamon

1. In a glass jar, combine the sweetener and cinnamon.
2. Put on the lid and shake well.
3. That's it! Keep it on hand (in a cool, dry place) to use anytime.

# Maple-Flavored Syrup

*This is a tasty syrup for pancakes and waffles. Pure maple sap from the tree is a true Paleo sweet-ener. However, to make 1 gallon of processed maple syrup, 55 gallons of maple sap must be boiled down into a concentrated sweetener. Modern-day maple syrup is a high-carb, refined sweetener that our Paleo ancestors never knew. You can use* raw *yacón syrup on your pancakes, which is yummilicious but quite expensive. However, this easy syrup is sweetened with chicory root and a little yacón. It is designed to give your blood sugar levels* and *your pocketbook a break. For the best flavor and texture, follow the recipe exactly.*

[ YIELD: 1½ cups syrup • EQUIPMENT NEEDED: A small saucepan ]

1⅓ cups Just Like Sugar Table Top natural chicory root sweetener (not Baking). A second choice is 1¾ cups Organic Zero Erythritol.
1½ teaspoons arrowroot powder
1 cup filtered water
1½ teaspoons pure vanilla extract
1 teaspoon maple flavoring
2 to 3 tablespoons *raw* yacón syrup
1 tablespoon coconut oil
Pinch of unprocessed salt

1. In a small saucepan, whisk together the sweetener and arrowroot powder.
2. Add the filtered water and whisk over medium heat until the crystals dissolve.
3. Add the vanilla, maple flavoring, yacón syrup, coconut oil, and salt. Heat to boiling briefly, stirring constantly. The arrowroot powder will begin to thicken into a syrupy texture.
4. When the syrup becomes almost transparent, remove from the heat and pour into a small pitcher or serving bowl. Enjoy! This syrup keeps for several days in the refrigerator.

# Raspberry "Jam"

*This Raspberry Jam is sweet and refreshing, bright red in color, perfect for Thumbprint Cookies (page 78) or Chocolate Cake (page 33). It is quick to make, using uncooked raspberries, which preserves their nutrients. Some people don't like the texture of raspberry seeds, so you may choose to strain them out. Others, however, may love the authentic "jam" experience and if so, you can keep the seeds in. For the most delicious flavor and consistency, follow this recipe exactly.*

[ YIELD: ²/₃ cup "jam" • EQUIPMENT NEEDED: Any style blender, preferably small, and a medium-gauge strainer (optional) ]

1 cup fresh or frozen raspberries
½ to ¾ cup Just Like Sugar Table Top natural chicory root sweetener (not Baking). I do not recommend any other sweetener for this recipe.
1 teaspoon pure vanilla extract
2 teaspoons freshly squeezed lemon or lime juice
1 tablespoon agar flakes
3 tablespoons filtered water, to cook agar

1. Press the raspberries to drain all the excess liquid. Especially if the raspberries are frozen, it is important to drain out as much liquid as possible.
2. Place the raspberries, sweetener, vanilla, and lemon juice in any style blender. Liquefy completely.
3. If you choose to strain out the raspberry seeds, pour the mixture into a medium-gauge strainer over a mixing bowl. Stir with a rubber spatula, tapping the strainer until all pulp passes through. Pour the strained raspberries back into the blender. Sweeten to taste.
4. In a small pan over medium heat, stir the agar into the water. Cook and stir gently for 2 to 3 minutes until it is bubbly and gummy and the flakes begin to dissolve. Add the agar mixture to the blender immediately and blend well to remove any lumps.
5. Pour the mixture into a small bowl and chill for 1 hour to thicken. Spread it on cakes, cookies . . . all right— it tastes great on everything!

*He who loves the world as his body may
be entrusted with the empire.*
—LAO-TZU, 600 BCE

# 5-MINUTE MILK SHAKES, SMOOTHIES, AND OTHER BEVERAGES

**W**hat better and quicker way is there for concentrating nutrition than a blended drink? In this chapter you'll find a huge variety of easy beverages, from Paleo Caffè to smoothies high in flavor and nutrition.

## MILK SHAKES

Life without milk shakes would hardly be worth living! Here's a Paleo collection of classic milk shake flavors, such as vanilla, chocolate, and strawberry. They're all dairy-free—of course—and made with any unsweetened coconut milk. Enjoy.

# Vanilla Milk Shake

*This has a classic flavor, and a thick, creamy texture with coconut milk and vanilla bean.*

**[ YIELD: 2 servings • EQUIPMENT NEEDED: Any style blender ]**

1½ teaspoons pure vanilla extract, or 1 vanilla bean (optional)

1¾ cups unsweetened coconut milk

3 tablespoons Just Like Sugar Table Top natural chicory root sweetener (not Baking). I do not recommend any other sweetener for this.

2 tablespoons coconut oil

Pinch of unprocessed salt

1 cup ice (optional)

1. If you're using a vanilla bean, split the bean lengthwise with a sharp knife and scrape the vanilla seeds out of the pod. In a blender, combine the coconut milk, sweetener, coconut oil, vanilla, vanilla bean (if using), and salt. Blend until smooth and creamy. Add the ice last (if using) and blend briefly.

# Banana Milk Shake

*This is a tasty shake, refreshing and nutritious. It is easy to make with blended banana and coconut milk.*

**[ YIELD: 2 servings • EQUIPMENT NEEDED: Any style blender ]**

1¾ cups unsweetened coconut milk

3 tablespoons Just Like Sugar Table Top natural chicory root sweetener (not Baking). I do not recommend any other sweetener for this.

2 tablespoons coconut oil

1 teaspoon pure vanilla extract

2 teaspoons freshly squeezed lemon juice

Pinch of unprocessed salt

1 banana

¼ teaspoon spices of your choice: ground cinnamon, ground cardamom, and/or grated nutmeg

½ cup ice (optional)

1. In a blender, combine the coconut milk, sweetener, coconut oil, vanilla, lemon juice, salt, banana, and spices. Blend until smooth and creamy. Add the ice last (if using) and blend briefly.

# Chocolate Milk Shake

*You really can't beat the taste and texture of a good chocolate milk shake. This one is thick and sweet with pure cacao and coconut milk.*

**[ YIELD: 2 servings • EQUIPMENT NEEDED: Any style blender ]**

1¾ cups unsweetened coconut milk

¼ cup Just Like Sugar Table Top natural chicory root sweetener (not Baking). I do not recommend any other sweetener for this.

2 tablespoons coconut oil

1 teaspoon pure vanilla extract

2 tablespoons pure cacao powder

¼ cup smooth hazelnut butter or almond butter (optional)

Pinch of unprocessed salt

½ cup ice (optional)

Unsweetened cocoa nibs, for garnish

1. In a blender, combine the coconut milk, sweetener, coconut oil, vanilla, cacao powder, nut butter (if using), and salt. Blend until smooth and creamy. Add the ice last (if using) and blend briefly. Garnish with unsweetened cacao nibs.

> **variation Chocolate Banana Milk Shake:**
> Add ½ banana and blend.

# Mocha Mudd Milk Shake

*This milk shake is thick and divine. It has the rich, deep flavor of pure cacao with coffee that will satisfy any sweet cravings.*

**[ YIELD: 2 servings • EQUIPMENT NEEDED: Any style blender ]**

1¾ cups unsweetened coconut milk

¼ cup Just Like Sugar Table Top natural chicory root sweetener (not Baking). I do not recommend any other sweetener for this.

2 tablespoons coconut oil

1 teaspoon pure vanilla extract

2 tablespoons pure cacao powder

1 teaspoon instant decaffeinated coffee powder or crystals

½ teaspoon ground cinnamon

Pinch of unprocessed salt

1 tablespoon *raw* yacón syrup (optional)

½ cup ice (optional)

1. In a blender, combine the coconut milk, sweetener, coconut oil, vanilla, cacao powder, coffee powder, cinnamon, salt, and yacón syrup (if using). Blend until smooth and creamy. Add ice last (if using) and blend briefly.

# Strawberry Milk Shake

*There's something about the super smoothness of a thick strawberry milk shake. This one is luscious and alive with strawberries and creamy coconut milk.*

**[ YIELD: 2 servings • EQUIPMENT NEEDED: Any style blender ]**

1¾ cups unsweetened coconut milk

3 tablespoons Just Like Sugar Table Top natural chicory root sweetener (not Baking). I do not recommend any other sweetener for this.

2 tablespoons coconut oil

1 teaspoon pure vanilla extract

2 teaspoons freshly squeezed lemon juice

Pinch of unprocessed salt

9 to 12 fresh or frozen strawberries (about 1½ cups)

Zest of ½ orange

½ cup ice (optional)

1. In a blender, combine the coconut milk, sweetener, coconut oil, vanilla, lemon juice, salt, strawberries, and orange zest. Blend until smooth and creamy. Add the ice last (if using) and blend briefly.

> **variation Raspberry Milk Shake:** Follow the recipe for the Strawberry Milk Shake, adding 1 cup of fresh or frozen raspberries instead of strawberries.

# Strawberry Banana Milk Shake

*Rich banana with refreshing strawberry is a classic creamy milk shake you just can't beat.*

**[ YIELD: 2 servings • EQUIPMENT NEEDED: Any style blender ]**

1¾ cups unsweetened coconut milk

3 tablespoons Just Like Sugar Table Top natural chicory root sweetener (not Baking). I do not recommend any other sweetener for this.

2 tablespoons coconut oil

1 teaspoon pure vanilla extract

2 teaspoons freshly squeezed lemon juice

Pinch of unprocessed salt

9 fresh or frozen strawberries (about 1⅓ cups)

1 banana

Zest of ½ orange

½ cup ice (optional)

1. In a blender, combine the coconut milk, sweetener, coconut oil, vanilla, lemon juice, salt, strawberries, banana, and orange zest. Blend until smooth and creamy. Add the ice last (if using) and blend briefly.

## HIGH-ANTIOXIDANT SMOOTHIES

These smoothies have been carefully designed to be both out of this world delicious *and* nutritious, too. They optimize and balance the body as a breakfast, pick-me up, or dessert any time of day. I use whole fresh fruits and vegetables and avoid using high-carb sweet fruits or fruit juices. Instead, I sweeten these with naturally low-carb Just Like Sugar Table Top sweetener. These recipes can be made in any style blender, but they will be much smoother and creamier in a high-speed blender such as a Blendtec or Vitamix.

# Blueberry Harmony Smoothie

*A heavenly blend of coconut milk with blueberries and high antioxidant açaí berries. It's refreshing, nutritious, and a beautiful bright purple. It doesn't get much better than this, folks!*

[ YIELD: 2 servings • EQUIPMENT NEEDED: Any style blender ]

1½ cups unsweetened coconut milk
⅔ cup blueberries
½ cup pure unsweetened 100% açaí berry puree (see tip)
6 strawberries
1 teaspoon pure vanilla extract
2 teaspoons freshly squeezed lemon juice
1 tablespoon coconut oil
Suggested sweetener: 2 tablespoons Just Like Sugar Table Top natural chicory root sweetener (not Baking), or to taste

1. In a blender, combine all the ingredients and blend well. Enjoy immediately.

> **Tip:** *If you can't find pure unsweetened 100 percent açaí berry puree, try unsweetened elderberries, black currants, or chokeberries, which all have a high antioxidant content a deep red color, and delicious flavor. See Resources (page 217).*

# Cacao Power Smoothie

*This rich blend of 100% cacao chocolate powder with nuts, cinnamon, and orange will nourish and balance your body, mind, and spirit. Who knew a smoothie could do so much good?*

**[ YIELD: 2 servings • EQUIPMENT NEEDED: Any style blender ]**

1 cup unsweetened coconut milk or filtered water

1½ tablespoons pure cacao powder

1 orange, peeled, sliced, and seeded

¼ cup pecans or your choice of nuts, soaked if possible (see page 10)

Suggested sweetener: 4 tablespoons Just Like Sugar Table Top natural chicory root sweetener (not Baking), or to taste

1 tablespoon *raw* yacón syrup

1 teaspoon pure vanilla extract

¼ teaspoon ground cinnamon

⅛ teaspoon anise powder (optional)

Handful of mint leaves (optional)

1 teaspoon maca powder (optional)

1. In a blender, combine all the ingredients and blend well. Enjoy immediately.

# Cinnamon Blood Sugar Normalizer Smoothie

*This subtle blend of creamy coconut milk, comforting cinnamon, mild carob, and strawberries makes me feel mellow, strong, and relaxed. It will do the same for you.*

**[ YIELD: 2 servings • EQUIPMENT NEEDED: Any style blender ]**

1½ cups unsweetened coconut milk
2 teaspoons ground cinnamon
3 tablespoons hemp seeds
1 tablespoon carob powder
6 fresh or frozen strawberries
Suggested sweetener: 1 tablespoon Just
   Like Sugar Table Top natural chicory root
   sweetener (not Baking), or to taste
1 tablespoon *raw* yacón syrup
2 teaspoons pure vanilla extract

1. In a blender, combine all the ingredients and blend well. Enjoy immediately.

# Deep Green Cleanse Smoothie

*This high-antioxidant green drink is loaded with phytonutrients and nutrient-dense foods that leave me feeling balanced and alive. Want to feel the same? Try this smoothie!*

**[ YIELD: 2 servings • EQUIPMENT NEEDED: Any style blender ]**

1 cup filtered water
1 tart apple, unpeeled, cored,
   and cut into chunks
½ lemon or lime, peeled and
   seeded
4 leaves kale or chard, or fennel tops
1 inch fresh ginger, chopped
   or grated
Handful of fresh parsley
1 tablespoon Just Like Sugar
   Table Top natural chicory
   root sweetener (not Baking)
   (optional)

1. In a blender, combine all the ingredients and blend well. Enjoy immediately.

# Food of the Gods Chocolate Smoothie

*A rich and velvety smooth drink for serious chocolate lovers, this is a sensuous blend of 100% cacao, strawberries, and creamy avocado.*

**[ YIELD: 2 servings • EQUIPMENT NEEDED: Any style blender ]**

1 cup unsweetened coconut milk or filtered water
2 tablespoons pure cacao powder
Suggested sweetener: 2 tablespoons Just Like Sugar Table Top natural chicory root sweetener (not Baking), or to taste
½ avocado, pitted and peeled
6 fresh or frozen strawberries
1 teaspoon pure vanilla extract
1 tablespoon *raw* yacón syrup
¼ teaspoon maple flavoring

1. In a blender, combine all the ingredients and blend well. Enjoy immediately.

# Minty Green Uplift and Clarity Smoothie

*This is a smooth and creamy blend of mint, kiwi, cucumber, and avocado that is both delicious and refreshing.*

**[ YIELD: 2 servings • EQUIPMENT NEEDED: Any style blender ]**

1 cup filtered water or unsweetened coconut milk
1 handful mint leaves
1 green apple, unpeeled, cored, and cut into chunks
Handful of kale, chard, or spinach leaves
2 kiwis
½ cucumber, cut into chunks
½ avocado, pitted and peeled
1 tablespoon freshly squeezed lime juice
Suggested Sweetener: 1 tablespoon Just Like Sugar Table Top natural chicory root sweetener (not Baking), or to taste

1. In a blender, combine all the ingredients and blend well. Enjoy immediately.

# Orang-a-tang Smoothie

*A tangy, creamy blend of coconut milk, orange, and strawberry, with a hint of banana. If I were an orangutan, I'd be so happy to drink this, I'd be swinging in the trees.*

**[ YIELD: 2 servings • EQUIPMENT NEEDED: Any style blender ]**

1 cup unsweetened coconut milk
Zest of ½ orange
1 orange, peeled, sliced, and seeded
6 fresh or frozen strawberries
½ banana
Suggested sweetener: 3 tablespoons Just Like Sugar Table Top natural chicory root sweetener (not Baking), or to taste
1 tablespoon coconut oil
4 teaspoons freshly squeezed lemon juice

1. In a blender, combine all the ingredients and blend well. Enjoy immediately.

# Red Heart and Digestive Healing Smoothie

*This heartwarming drink combines tart raspberries, sweet orange, and strawberries, with a hint of ginger. Fresh beet adds a deep red color and powerful nutrition. Yummy and joyful—you can't beat that.*

**[ YIELD: 2 servings • EQUIPMENT NEEDED: Any style blender ]**

1 cup filtered water
½ cup fresh raspberries
¼ fresh beet (choose a small beet, which is usually less bitter)
Zest of ½ orange
1 orange, peeled, sliced, and seeded
6 fresh or frozen strawberries
1 inch fresh ginger, chopped or grated
Suggested sweetener: 2 tablespoons Just Like Sugar Table Top natural chicory root sweetener (not Baking), or to taste
2 plums, seeded, or 4 additional strawberries
1 tablespoon hemp seeds
1 teaspoon freshly squeezed lemon juice
Pinch of grated nutmeg or ground cardamom
2 tablespoons dried goji berries (optional)

1. In a blender, combine all the ingredients and blend well. Enjoy immediately.

# Superfood Energy Revitalize Smoothie

*Liven up your day with this powerhouse of vitality. Strawberries, tangerine, and beet are flavored with cinnamon and ginger. Delish!*

**[ YIELD: 2 servings • EQUIPMENT NEEDED: Any style blender ]**

1 cup filtered water or coconut milk
8 fresh or frozen strawberries (about 1 cup)
1 tangerine, peeled, sliced, and seeded
¼ fresh beet (choose a small beet, which is usually less bitter)
½ inch fresh ginger, chopped or grated, or ¼ teaspoon ground
Suggested sweetener: 2 tablespoons Just Like Sugar Table Top natural chicory root sweetener (not Baking), or to taste
4 tablespoons raw hemp seeds
2 teaspoons freshly squeezed lemon juice
¼ teaspoon ground cinnamon

1. In a blender, combine all the ingredients and blend well. Enjoy immediately.

# Watermelon Buzz Smoothie

*This is a refreshing and energizing blend of fresh watermelon, strawberries, beet, carrot, apple, and açaí berries, with a bright red color. Perfect for a summertime drink.*

**[ YIELD: 2 servings • EQUIPMENT NEEDED: Any style blender ]**

½ cup filtered water
1 slice watermelon, seeded (about 1½ cups)
4 fresh or frozen strawberries
1 slice beet (choose a small beet, which is usually less bitter)
1 carrot, scrubbed, cut into chunks
½ tart apple, unpeeled, cut into chunks
½ cup unsweetened fresh berries, such as raspberries, elderberries, chokeberries, black currants, or pure unsweetened 100% açaí berry puree; or ¼ cup dried berries
Suggested sweetener: 1 tablespoon Just Like Sugar Table Top natural chicory root sweetener (not Baking), or to taste
1 teaspoon freshly squeezed lemon juice
1 (0.2-ounce) packet Emergen-C Lite Vitamin-C Booster (use the low-carb lite version)

1. In a blender, combine all the ingredients and blend well. Enjoy immediately.

# 6-Step Design-Your-Own Smoothie

*Here's where we get creative. What are you craving right now? What flavor combination will enhance your day? What's in season? What do you have on hand? Make yourself a special treat every day as a quick pick-me-up, an appetizer, or a dessert.*

**[ YIELD: 2 servings • EQUIPMENT NEEDED: Any style blender ]**

### STEP 1: LIQUID
1 cup filtered water, coconut milk, cultured coconut milk, or coconut water

### STEP 2: FRUIT
1 cup real fruit, not juice; stick with low-carb tart fruits, such as blueberries, tart apple, açai berries, lemon, raspberries, kiwi, plum, pomegranate, green apple, orange, grapefruit, and/or watermelon. (Use sweet fruits such as papaya, peach, banana, cherries, mango, grapes, strawberries, and pineapple, in small quantities, if at all, as these are high in sugars.)

### STEP 3: FLAVORING OR EXTRA NUTRITION
Pure vanilla extract, pure cacao powder, carob powder, fresh ginger, freshly squeezed lemon juice, orange zest, fresh mint leaves, grated nutmeg, ground cinnamon, ground cloves, ground cardamom, dried oregano, dried thyme, spirulina, green powder, Emergen-C Lite Vitamin-C Booster, bee pollen, royal jelly, rose hips, chlorella, blue green algae, mesquite powder, and maca powder are all possible options.

### STEP 4: SWEETENER
1 to 2 tablespoons Just Like Sugar Table Top natural chicory root sweetener (not Baking). A second choice is 1 to 2 tablespoons *raw* yacón syrup.

### STEP 5: THICKENER
2 to 4 tablespoons: raw hemp seeds; any raw nuts, soaked if possible (see page 10); avocado; coconut oil; almond butter; mesquite or suma powder; cocoa butter; and/or steamed sweet potato

### STEP 6: VEGETABLE (OPTIONAL)
0 to ½ cup: Raw kale, spinach, chard, carrot, cilantro, basil, fennel tops, parsley, beet, collards, bok choy, cucumber, celery, sweet pepper, and so on

Place all the ingredients in any style blender in the order given, starting with the liquid in Step 1, then the fruit, then the solid and powdered ingredients. Blend on high speed for 30 to 60 seconds, or until smooth. Serve and enjoy.

# Paleo Caffè

*If you miss your daily java boost from a Starbucks Caffè Latte or Caramel Macchiato with whipped cream, this Paleo brew could change your life. Coffee and caffeine are not Paleo. While some coffee substitutes are made with barley, I use chicory and dandelion root. Roasted chicory root tastes similar to coffee, and is often used in Cajun blends. Dandelion root is rich in vitamins and minerals. Just brew it like coffee and add the flavorings of your choice. Now you can enjoy your favorite coffee in true Paleo form.*

[ YIELD: Two 16-ounce servings • EQUIPMENT NEEDED: A French press coffeemaker, or a fine-mesh tea strainer ]

2 tablespoons roasted chicory root granules (see Resources, page 217)

4 cups boiling filtered water

1. Place the granules in a French press and fill it with the boiling water. Let steep for 5 minutes.
2. Then press the plunger, pour into two large coffee mugs, and enjoy!

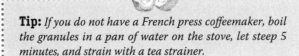

**Tip:** *If you do not have a French press coffeemaker, boil the granules in a pan of water on the stove, let steep 5 minutes, and strain with a tea strainer.*

continues . . .

## Paleo Caffè (variations)

### variations

**Iced Paleo Caffè:** Make your caffè double strength and serve over ice.

**Paleo Caffè Frappé:** Make your caffè double strength. Blend in a blender with 1 cup of ice, or with your own Homemade Coffee Creamer (page 20) frozen into cubes. Sweeten to taste and add your favorite flavorings (see below):

### Optional Additions and Flavorings

**Cream:** Add ¼ to ½ cup of any unsweetened coconut milk to your cup. (Add it cold or warm.)

**Chocolate:** Add 1 to 3 teaspoons of pure cacao powder to your cup.

**Cinnamon:** Add ¼ teaspoon of ground cinnamon to your cup.

**Nutmeg:** Add ⅛ teaspoon of grated nutmeg to your cup.

**Vanilla:** Add ½ teaspoon of pure vanilla extract to your cup.

**Salted Caramel:** Add 1 tablespoon of *raw* yacón syrup and 2 pinches of unprocessed salt to your cup.

**Hazelnut or Maple:** Add ¼ teaspoon of hazelnut or maple flavoring to your cup.

# Paleo Chai Latte

*Maybe you crave the warm spices and caffeine hit of Starbucks Chai Tea Latte. Maybe you miss the authentic flavor of old-fashioned Himalayan tea. Whatever you desire, this delectable brew will warm your body and soul. Instead of black tea, I use Tulsi tea, also called Holy Basil, which tastes like black tea and is naturally caffeine-free.*

**[ YIELD: Two 16-ounce servings • EQUIPMENT NEEDED: A small saucepan and a fine-mesh tea strainer ]**

2 cups filtered water
2 to 4 tea bags Tulsi tea, or your favorite caffeine-free tea
2 cups any unsweetened coconut milk
3 to 4 tablespoons Just Like Sugar Table Top natural chicory root sweetener (not Baking). A second choice is ⅓ cup Organic Zero Erythritol.
1 tablespoon *raw* yacón syrup (optional, for caramel taste)
1 teaspoon pure vanilla extract
Pinch of freshly ground black pepper
2 teaspoons ground cardamom or whole seeds
2 teaspoons ground cinnamon, or 2 sticks
¼ teaspoon ground cloves, or 3 whole
¼ teaspoon ground ginger, or ¼ inch fresh ginger, sliced thinly
2 star anise pods, or ¼ teaspoon ground or whole aniseed (optional)

1. In a small saucepan, boil the filtered water.
2. Stir the tea into the boiling water and let steep for 3 minutes.
3. Add the coconut milk, sweetener, yacón syrup (if using), vanilla, pepper, cardamom, cinnamon, cloves, ginger, and anise (if using). Stir and bring to boiling. Remove from the heat, cover, and let steep for 3 minutes. Strain and enjoy!

### variations

**Chocolate Chai:** Add 1 tablespoon of pure cacao powder and 1 tablespoon more granulated sweetener.

**Iced Chai Latte:** Serve over ice cubes.

**Chai Frappé:** Blend in any style blender with ice.

# Paleo Hot Chocolate

*Hot Chocolate is a comforting pick-me-up. You can enjoy this delicious treat year-round and still be 100 percent Paleo. It's easy to make, low in carbs, and absolutely yummy. All you have to do is put the ingredients in your mug and fill it with hot filtered water.*

**[ YIELD: One 16-ounce serving • EQUIPMENT NEEDED: A saucepan or kettle, to boil the water ]**

2 tablespoons pure cacao powder
¼ cup Just Like Sugar Table Top natural chicory root sweetener (not Baking). I do not recommend any other sweetener for this.
1 teaspoon pure vanilla extract
¼ cup any unsweetened coconut milk
Boiling filtered water

1. In a large mug or portable coffee tumbler, combine the cacao powder, sweetener, vanilla, and coconut milk.
2. Add boiling filtered water to fill the cup. That's it! Stir well and enjoy.

---

### variations

**Mocha:** Add 1 teaspoon of decaffeinated coffee crystals.

**Cinnamon:** Add ½ teaspoon of ground cinnamon.

**Maple:** Add ¼ teaspoon of maple flavoring.

**Mayan:** Add a pinch of cayenne.

**Valencia Orange:** Add grated orange zest.

**Salted Caramel** (my personal favorite): Add 1 tablespoon of *raw* yacón syrup and two pinches of unprocessed salt.

# Holiday Eggnog

*This Eggnog is easy to make, dairy-free, and delicious. Warm and rich with a hint of nutmeg, it was a favorite at my holiday party. My guests say it tastes even better than the traditional version.*

**[ YIELD: 8 to 10 servings • EQUIPMENT NEEDED: Any style blender and a large pot ]**

About 54 ounces any unsweetened coconut milk (I use four [13.5-ounce] cans medium-thick.)

1 cup Just Like Sugar Table Top natural chicory root sweetener (not Baking). I do not recommend any other sweeteners for this.

2 teaspoons pure vanilla extract

1½ teaspoons grated nutmeg, plus extra to serve

2 tablespoons *raw* yacón syrup (optional, for a brown sugar taste)

12 egg yolks

Ground cinnamon, to serve

1. In a blender, combine half of the coconut milk with all of the sweetener, vanilla, 1½ teaspoons of nutmeg, yacón syrup (if using), and egg yolks. Blend well until creamy and smooth.

2. If you wish to serve it hot: Pour the mixture into a large pot on the stove over low heat. Add the remaining coconut milk. Sweeten to taste. Warm it slowly, and do not boil.

3. If serving the eggnog lukewarm, pour it into a serving pitcher and add the remaining coconut milk. Sweeten to taste. To keep the pitcher warm, place it in a larger pot filled with 3 inches of hot water over minimum heat.

4. Serve in cups, garnished with grated nutmeg and ground cinnamon.

# Holiday Spiced Punch

*One of the most festive items at any holiday party is a spicy punch. This version combines low-carb cranberry tea, star anise, and orange peel to create delightful nonalcoholic drink everyone can enjoy.*

**[ YIELD: 12 to 15 servings • EQUIPMENT NEEDED: A large soup pot ]**

3 quarts filtered water
½ to 1 cup Just Like Sugar Table Top natural chicory root sweetener (not Baking). A second choice is ⅔ to ⅓ cup Organic Zero Erythritol.
16 tea bags cranberry or hibiscus tea
2 inches fresh ginger, sliced thinly
½ cup crushed fresh cranberries
Handful star anise
3 cinnamon sticks
1 tablespoon whole cloves
½ teaspoon ground cardamom
1 teaspoon grated nutmeg
½ teaspoon whole black peppercorns
½ teaspoon whole allspice
½ vanilla bean, or 2 teaspoons pure vanilla extract
1 whole orange, unpeeled and sliced thinly
1 pomegranate or apple, sliced (no need to peel or core)

1. Pour the filtered water into a large soup pot. As it heats, add all the remaining ingredients.
2. Do not boil, but bring just to boiling and then simmer over very low heat for 30 minutes. Sweeten and spice to taste.
3. Strain and serve warm, ladling into punch cups.

> **variation Summertime Iced Punch:** You can make this ahead of time, chill it, and serve it cold over ice. Sweeten with Just Like Sugar Table Top sweetener (not Baking), not Organic Zero Erythritol, the latter may develop crystals when chilled.

# METRIC CONVERSIONS

The recipes in this book have not been tested with metric measurements, so some variations might occur.

Remember that the weight of dry ingredients varies according to the volume or density factor: 1 cup of flour weighs far less than 1 cup of sugar, and 1 tablespoon doesn't necessarily hold 3 teaspoons.

### General Formula for Metric Conversion

| | |
|---|---|
| Ounces to grams | Multiply ounces by 28.35 |
| Grams to ounces | Multiply grams by 0.035 |
| Pounds to grams | Multiply pounds by 453.5 |
| Pounds to kilograms | Multiply pounds by 0.45 |
| Cups to liters | Multiply cups by 0.24 |
| Fahrenheit to Celsius | Subtract 32 from Fahrenheit temperature, multiply by 5, divide by 9 |
| Celsius to Fahrenheit | Multiply Celsius temperature by 9, divide by 5, add 32 |

### Volume (Liquid) Measurements

1 teaspoon = ⅙ fluid ounce = 5 milliliters
1 tablespoon = ½ fluid ounce = 15 milliliters
2 tablespoons = 1 fluid ounce = 30 milliliters
¼ cup = 2 fluid ounces = 60 milliliters
⅓ cup = 2⅔ fluid ounces = 79 milliliters
½ cup = 4 fluid ounces = 118 milliliters
1 cup or ½ pint = 8 fluid ounces = 250 milliliters
2 cups or 1 pint = 16 fluid ounces = 500 milliliters
4 cups or 1 quart = 32 fluid ounces = 1,000 milliliters
1 gallon = 4 liters

### Volume (Dry) Measurements

| | |
|---|---|
| ¼ teaspoon = 1 milliliter | ½ cup = 118 milliliters |
| ½ teaspoon = 2 milliliters | ⅔ cup = 158 milliliters |
| ¾ teaspoon = 4 milliliters | ¾ cup = 177 milliliters |
| 1 teaspoon = 5 milliliters | 1 cup = 225 milliliters |
| 1 tablespoon = 15 milliliters | 4 cups or 1 quart = 1 liter |
| ¼ cup = 59 milliliters | ½ gallon = 2 liters |
| ⅓ cup = 79 milliliters | 1 gallon = 4 liters |

### Weight (Mass) Measurements

1 ounce = 30 grams
2 ounces = 55 grams
3 ounces = 85 grams
4 ounces = ¼ pound = 125 grams
8 ounces = ½ pound = 240 grams
12 ounces = ¾ pound = 375 grams
16 ounces = 1 pound = 454 grams

### Linear Measurements

½ inch = 1⅓ cm
1 inch = 2½ cm
6 inches = 15 cm
8 inches = 20 cm
10 inches = 25 cm
12 inches = 30 cm
20 inches = 50 cm

### Oven Temperature Equivalents Fahrenheit (F) and Celsius (C)

100°F = 38°C
200°F = 95°C
250°F = 120°C
300°F = 150°C
350°F = 180°C
400°F = 205°C
450°F = 230° C

# RESOURCES

## INGREDIENT SOURCES

**Agar flakes,** also called kanten flakes—A good whole foods market, Asian markets, Edenfoods.com, or Amazon.com

**Arrowroot powder**—A good whole foods market, Bobsredmill.com, or Amazon.com

**Berries** (frozen açaí berry puree; fresh, frozen, or dried elderberries, black currants, chokeberries)—A good whole foods market when in season or online at Frontiercoop.com, Nuts.com, Americanspice.com, Starwest-botanicals.com, or Amazon.com

**Buckwheat, raw** (also called buckwheat groats)—A good whole foods market or Bobsredmill.com

**Cacao nibs,** pure and unsweetened—A good whole foods market Navitasnaturals.com, Sunfood.com, or Livesuperfoods.com

**Cacao powder, pure**—A good whole foods market, Navitasnaturals.com, Livesuperfoods.com, Wholelifesuperfoods.com, or Amazon.com

**Chicory root granules, roasted**—(Coffee substitute) A good whole foods market or Frontiercoop.com

**Chlorella powder**—A good whole foods market, Frontiercoop.com, Sunfood.com, or Chlorella Manna from Livesuperfoods.com

**Chocolate bar,** 100% cacao (Le 100% Criollo Dark Chocolate Bar by Pralus)—Atthemeadow.com or Chocosphere.com

**Chocolate paste** (also called cacao liquor)—Navitasnaturals.com, Livesuperfoods.com, or Sunfood.com

**Coconut butter** (also called creamed coconut or coconut creamed concentrate)—A good whole foods market, Artisanafoods .com, Tropicaltraditions.com, or Edward andsons.com, or homemade (page 21)

**Coconut milk,** thick (Shake the can and listen to check for thickness.)—A good whole foods market or Thaikitchen.com

**Coconut oil,** unprocessed—A good whole foods market, Hummingbirdwholesale .com, Nutiva.com, Auntpattys.glorybee .com, or Tropicaltraditions.com

**Coconut, young**—Young coconuts are sold in good whole foods markets, food co-ops, or Asian markets.

**Dandelion root roasted granules**—Buy from Frontiercoop.com, mountainroseherbs .com, or pacificbotanicals.com. You can also find them raw at local food co-ops and roast them yourself. To roast them, bake at 300°F, stirring every 5 minutes, for 20 minutes, or until they turn a slightly golden color.

**Decaffeinated coffee crystals**—A good whole foods market or Amazon.com

**Flaxseeds** (both dark and golden)—A good whole foods market, Bobsredmill.com, or Therawfoodworld.com

**Hemp seeds**—A good whole foods market, Navitasnaturals.com, or Livesuperfoods .com

**Just Like Sugar Table Top** natural chicory root sweetener (1-pound green bag) (not Baking)—Some whole foods markets, JustLikeSugarInc.com, Vitacost.com, Net rition.com, or Amazon.com

**Lavender oil,** rose oil (100% pure oil, undiluted, food-grade quality)—A good whole foods market, Edenbotanicals .com, Anandaapothecary.com, or Taos herb.com

**Maca powder**—A good whole foods market, Navitasnaturals.com, or Livesuperfoods .com

**Nut milk bag** (for straining coconut milk)—A good whole foods market or Amazon.com

**Nutritional yeast**—A good whole foods market or Frontiercoop.com

**Nuts**—Hummingbirdwholesale.com or Sun organicfarm.com

**Organic Zero Erythritol**—A good whole foods market, Wholesomesweeteners.com, or Amazon.com

**Poppy seeds** (in bulk)—Frontiercoop.com, Herbalcom.com, or Amazon.com

**Rose oil** (100% pure oil, undiluted, food-grade quality)—A good whole foods market, Edenbotanicals.com, Ananda apothecary.com or Taosherb.com.

**Salt** (Himalayan or Celtic Salt or any unprocessed sea salt)—A good whole foods market, Livesuperfoods.com, Sunfood .com, or Amazon.com

**Seaweed vegetables** (hijiki, wakame)—Any good whole foods market

**Tulsi tea**, also called Holy Basil tea—Available in tea bags in whole foods markets. For the best quality, I suggest economical bulk teas, such as a 1-pound package from Frontiercoop.com.

**Vinegar** (Bragg Raw Organic Apple Cider Vinegar or any live apple cider vinegar)— A good whole foods market or Bragg.com

**Yacón syrup,** *raw*—Some whole foods markets, Navitasnaturals.com, Wholelifesuperfoods.com, Sunfood.com, or Amazon.com

## PALEO DIET ONLINE RESOURCES

Paleodiet.com

whole9life.com

## BOOKS

Cordain, Loren. *The Paleo Diet: Lose Weight and Get Healthy by Eating the Foods You Were Designed to Eat.* Wiley, 2010.

Fallon, Sally. *Nourishing Traditions: The Cookbook That Challenges Politically Correct Nutrition and the Diet Dictocrats.* Newtrends Publishing, Inc., revised 1999.

Fragoso, Sarah. *Everyday Paleo.* Victory Belt Publishing, 2011.

Joulwan, Melissa. *Well Fed: Paleo Recipes for People Who Love to Eat.* Smudge Publishing, 2011.

Mayfield, Julie Sullivan. *Paleo Comfort Foods: Homestyle Cooking for a Gluten-Free Kitchen.* Victory Belt Publishing, 2011.

Price, Dr. Weston. *Nutrition and Physical Degeneration*, 8th ed. Pottenger Nutrition Publishing, 2008.

Sisson, Mark. *The Primal Blueprint 21-Day Total Body Transformation.* Primal Nutrition, 2009.

Wolf, Robb. *The Paleo Solution: The Original Human Diet.* Victory Belt Publishing, 2010.

# PALEO DESSERTS ARE COMPATIBLE WITH MANY ALTERNATIVE DIETS

If you're on a special diet and feel deprived, this book can be a true companion. Paleo Desserts are compatible with many alternative diets. Besides being Paleo and gluten-free /celiac-friendly, all these recipes are vegetarian, meaning they contain no meat. All recipes in this book are free of the common allergens: dairy, corn, potatoes, peanuts, and soy. They are also diabetic-friendly. In this book you will find 73 vegan recipes, such as Key Lime Pie. There are 67 tree nut-free recipes, and 35 desserts that are raw, such as Easy Chocolate Mousse. And the good news is they're all made with fresh, whole-food ingredients, which I find even more delicious than their refined counterparts.

Note: In this chart "tree nuts" are almonds, walnuts, pecans, cashews, macadamias, hazelnuts, Brazil nuts, pistachios, and other similar nuts. Coconut is not considered a tree nut. Seeds, such as flaxseeds and hemp seeds, are not considered nuts for the purposes of this chart.

# Recipes by Diet

## Cakes and Cupcakes

| Cakes and Cupcakes | GLUTEN-FREE, CELIAC FRIENDLY | DAIRY-FREE | EGG-FREE | VEGAN | DIABETIC FRIENDLY | PEANUT-FREE | SOY-FREE | RAW | TREE NUT–FREE |
|---|:---:|:---:|:---:|:---:|:---:|:---:|:---:|:---:|:---:|
| Applesauce Cupcakes | ◆ | ◆ | | | ◆ | ◆ | ◆ | | |
| Carrot Mini Cupcakes | ◆ | ◆ | | | ◆ | ◆ | ◆ | | |
| Chocolate Cake, Raspberry Filling | ◆ | ◆ | | | ◆ | ◆ | ◆ | | ◆ |
| Chocolate Cupcakes | ◆ | ◆ | | | ◆ | ◆ | ◆ | | ◆ |
| Fluffy Lemon Cupcakes | ◆ | ◆ | | | ◆ | ◆ | ◆ | | ◆ |
| Gingerbread Cupcakes | ◆ | ◆ | | | ◆ | ◆ | ◆ | | |
| Honey Cake | ◆ | ◆ | | | ◆ | ◆ | ◆ | | |
| Luscious Lemon Layer Cake | ◆ | ◆ | | | ◆ | ◆ | ◆ | | |
| Poppy-Seed Hot Fudge Sundae Cake | ◆ | ◆ | | | ◆ | ◆ | ◆ | | ◆ |
| Red Velvet Cake or Cupcakes | ◆ | ◆ | | | ◆ | ◆ | ◆ | | ◆ |
| Spicy Carrot Ginger Cake | ◆ | ◆ | | | ◆ | ◆ | ◆ | | |
| Strawberry Shortcake | ◆ | ◆ | | | ◆ | ◆ | ◆ | | ◆ |
| Tiramisu | ◆ | ◆ | | | ◆ | ◆ | ◆ | | ◆ |
| Tres Leches Cake | ◆ | ◆ | | | ◆ | ◆ | ◆ | | ◆ |
| White Coconut Sponge Cake | ◆ | ◆ | | | ◆ | ◆ | ◆ | | ◆ |
| Whole Apple Spice Cake | ◆ | ◆ | | | ◆ | ◆ | ◆ | | |
| Yellow Birthday Cake | ◆ | ◆ | | | ◆ | ◆ | ◆ | | ◆ |

## Muffins and Breads

| Muffins and Breads | GLUTEN-FREE, CELIAC FRIENDLY | DAIRY-FREE | EGG-FREE | VEGAN | DIABETIC FRIENDLY | PEANUT-FREE | SOY-FREE | RAW | TREE NUT–FREE |
|---|:---:|:---:|:---:|:---:|:---:|:---:|:---:|:---:|:---:|
| Banana Bread | ◆ | ◆ | | | ◆ | ◆ | ◆ | | |
| Blueberry Muffins | ◆ | ◆ | | | ◆ | ◆ | ◆ | | |
| Cranberry Nut Bread | ◆ | ◆ | | | ◆ | ◆ | ◆ | | |
| Flax Muffins | ◆ | ◆ | | | ◆ | ◆ | ◆ | | |
| Pumpkin Bread | ◆ | ◆ | | | ◆ | ◆ | ◆ | | |
| Zucchini Muffins | ◆ | ◆ | | | ◆ | ◆ | ◆ | | |

## Cookies and Bars

| Cookies and Bars | GLUTEN-FREE, CELIAC FRIENDLY | DAIRY-FREE | EGG-FREE | VEGAN | DIABETIC FRIENDLY | PEANUT-FREE | SOY-FREE | RAW | TREE NUT–FREE |
|---|:---:|:---:|:---:|:---:|:---:|:---:|:---:|:---:|:---:|
| Biscotti | ◆ | ◆ | | | ◆ | ◆ | ◆ | | |
| Blueberry Lemon Cheesecake Bars | ◆ | ◆ | | | ◆ | ◆ | ◆ | | |
| Chocolate Chip Cookies | ◆ | ◆ | | | ◆ | ◆ | ◆ | | |
| Chocolate Haystack Cookies | ◆ | ◆ | ◆ | ◆ | ◆ | ◆ | ◆ | ◆ | |
| Coconut Macaroons | ◆ | ◆ | | | ◆ | ◆ | ◆ | | ◆ |
| Double Chocolate Chip Espresso Cookies | ◆ | ◆ | | | ◆ | ◆ | ◆ | | |
| Granola Bars | ◆ | ◆ | | | ◆ | ◆ | ◆ | | |
| Hazelnut Butter Cookies | ◆ | ◆ | | | ◆ | ◆ | ◆ | | |
| Lemon Bars | ◆ | ◆ | ◆ | ◆ | ◆ | ◆ | ◆ | | ◆ |
| Mexican Wedding Cookies | ◆ | ◆ | | | ◆ | ◆ | ◆ | | |

## Cookies and Bars

| Cookies and Bars | GLUTEN-FREE, CELIAC FRIENDLY | DAIRY-FREE | EGG-FREE | VEGAN | DIABETIC FRIENDLY | PEANUT-FREE | SOY-FREE | RAW | TREE NUT-FREE |
|---|---|---|---|---|---|---|---|---|---|
| No-Oatmeal No-Raisin Cookies | ◆ | ◆ | | | ◆ | ◆ | ◆ | | |
| Raspberry Crumble Bars | ◆ | ◆ | | | ◆ | ◆ | ◆ | | |
| Rugelach | ◆ | ◆ | | | ◆ | ◆ | ◆ | | |
| Thumbprint Cookies | ◆ | ◆ | | | ◆ | ◆ | ◆ | | |
| Trail Mix Cookies | ◆ | ◆ | | | ◆ | ◆ | ◆ | | |

## Chocolate Desserts

| Chocolate Desserts | GLUTEN-FREE, CELIAC FRIENDLY | DAIRY-FREE | EGG-FREE | VEGAN | DIABETIC FRIENDLY | PEANUT-FREE | SOY-FREE | RAW | TREE NUT-FREE |
|---|---|---|---|---|---|---|---|---|---|
| Awesome Fudge Brownies | ◆ | ◆ | | | ◆ | ◆ | ◆ | | |
| Black Forest Cake | ◆ | ◆ | | | ◆ | ◆ | ◆ | | ◆ |
| Chocolate Bavarian Cream Filling | ◆ | ◆ | | | ◆ | ◆ | ◆ | | ◆ |
| Chocolate Cream Pie | ◆ | ◆ | ◆ | ◆ | ◆ | ◆ | ◆ | | |
| Chocolate Fudge | ◆ | ◆ | ◆ | ◆ | ◆ | ◆ | ◆ | ◆ | |
| Chocolate Lava Cake | ◆ | ◆ | | | ◆ | ◆ | ◆ | | ◆ |
| Chocolate-Covered Strawberries | ◆ | ◆ | ◆ | ◆ | ◆ | ◆ | ◆ | | |
| Coffee Toffee Pie | ◆ | ◆ | ◆ | ◆ | ◆ | ◆ | | | |
| Dark Chocolate Cheesecake | ◆ | ◆ | ◆ | ◆ | ◆ | ◆ | ◆ | | |
| Dark Chocolate Truffles | ◆ | ◆ | ◆ | ◆ | ◆ | ◆ | ◆ | ◆ | |
| Devil's Food Double Chocolate Cake | ◆ | ◆ | | | ◆ | ◆ | ◆ | | ◆ |
| German Chocolate Cake | ◆ | ◆ | | | ◆ | ◆ | ◆ | | |
| Homemade Chocolate Chips | ◆ | ◆ | ◆ | ◆ | ◆ | ◆ | ◆ | | ◆ |
| Superfood Black Fudge | ◆ | ◆ | ◆ | ◆ | ◆ | ◆ | ◆ | ◆ | |

## Pies and Tarts

| Pies and Tarts | GLUTEN-FREE, CELIAC FRIENDLY | DAIRY-FREE | EGG-FREE | VEGAN | DIABETIC FRIENDLY | PEANUT-FREE | SOY-FREE | RAW | TREE NUT-FREE |
|---|---|---|---|---|---|---|---|---|---|
| Apple Tart | ◆ | ◆ | | | ◆ | ◆ | ◆ | | ◆ |
| Banana Cream Pie | ◆ | ◆ | ◆ | ◆ | ◆ | ◆ | ◆ | | |
| Berry Tart | ◆ | ◆ | ◆ | ◆ | ◆ | ◆ | ◆ | | |
| Cheesecake | ◆ | ◆ | ◆ | ◆ | ◆ | ◆ | ◆ | | |
| Cherry Pie | ◆ | ◆ | | | ◆ | ◆ | ◆ | | ◆ |
| Coconut Cream Pie | ◆ | ◆ | ◆ | ◆ | ◆ | ◆ | ◆ | | ◆ |
| Dutch Apple Pie | ◆ | ◆ | | | ◆ | ◆ | ◆ | | |
| Finger Tarts | ◆ | ◆ | | | ◆ | ◆ | ◆ | | |
| Flaky Baked Piecrust | ◆ | ◆ | | | ◆ | ◆ | ◆ | | ◆ |
| Key Lime Pie | ◆ | ◆ | ◆ | ◆ | ◆ | ◆ | ◆ | | |
| Lemon Cheesecake with Berries | ◆ | ◆ | ◆ | ◆ | ◆ | ◆ | ◆ | | |
| Minute Piecrust | ◆ | ◆ | ◆ | ◆ | ◆ | ◆ | ◆ | ◆ | |
| Pecan Pie | ◆ | ◆ | | | ◆ | ◆ | ◆ | | |
| Pumpkin Cheesecake | ◆ | ◆ | ◆ | ◆ | ◆ | ◆ | ◆ | | |
| Pumpkin Pie | ◆ | ◆ | | | ◆ | ◆ | ◆ | | ◆ |

## Crisps, Crumbles, and Other Treats

| | GLUTEN-FREE, CELIAC FRIENDLY | DAIRY-FREE | EGG-FREE | VEGAN | DIABETIC FRIENDLY | PEANUT-FREE | SOY-FREE | RAW | TREE NUT-FREE |
|---|---|---|---|---|---|---|---|---|---|
| Apple Cranberry Crisp | ◆ | ◆ | ◆ | ◆ | ◆ | ◆ | ◆ | | |
| Belgian Waffles | ◆ | | | | ◆ | ◆ | ◆ | | ◆ |
| Berry Cobbler | ◆ | | | | ◆ | ◆ | ◆ | | ◆ |
| Chocolate Hazelnut Butter Cups | ◆ | ◆ | ◆ | ◆ | ◆ | ◆ | ◆ | ◆ | |
| Crêpes Suzettes | ◆ | | | | ◆ | ◆ | ◆ | | ◆ |
| Paleo Pancakes | ◆ | | | | ◆ | ◆ | ◆ | | ◆ |
| Pear Ginger Crumble | ◆ | ◆ | ◆ | ◆ | ◆ | ◆ | ◆ | | ◆ |
| Trail Mix | ◆ | ◆ | ◆ | ◆ | ◆ | ◆ | ◆ | | ◆ |

## Puddings and Mousses

| | GLUTEN-FREE, CELIAC FRIENDLY | DAIRY-FREE | EGG-FREE | VEGAN | DIABETIC FRIENDLY | PEANUT-FREE | SOY-FREE | RAW | TREE NUT-FREE |
|---|---|---|---|---|---|---|---|---|---|
| Easy Chocolate Mousse | ◆ | ◆ | ◆ | ◆ | ◆ | ◆ | ◆ | ◆ | ◆ |
| Flan with Dulce de Leche | ◆ | ◆ | ◆ | ◆ | ◆ | ◆ | ◆ | | ◆ |
| Gell-o with Fruit and Whipped Crème | ◆ | ◆ | ◆ | ◆ | ◆ | ◆ | ◆ | | ◆ |
| Instant Mocha Mousse | ◆ | ◆ | ◆ | ◆ | ◆ | ◆ | ◆ | ◆ | ◆ |
| Lemon-Berry Parfait | ◆ | ◆ | ◆ | ◆ | ◆ | ◆ | ◆ | | ◆ |
| Raspberry Rose Delight Mousse | ◆ | ◆ | ◆ | ◆ | ◆ | ◆ | ◆ | | ◆ |

## Frozen Desserts

| | GLUTEN-FREE, CELIAC FRIENDLY | DAIRY-FREE | EGG-FREE | VEGAN | DIABETIC FRIENDLY | PEANUT-FREE | SOY-FREE | RAW | TREE NUT-FREE |
|---|---|---|---|---|---|---|---|---|---|
| Açaí Berry Lavender Ice Cream | ◆ | ◆ | ◆ | ◆ | ◆ | ◆ | ◆ | | ◆ |
| Cappuccino Ice Cream | ◆ | ◆ | ◆ | ◆ | ◆ | ◆ | ◆ | | ◆ |
| Chocolate Chip Ice Cream | ◆ | ◆ | ◆ | ◆ | ◆ | ◆ | ◆ | | ◆ |
| Chocolate Ice Cream | ◆ | ◆ | ◆ | ◆ | ◆ | ◆ | ◆ | | ◆ |
| Ice-Cream Sandwiches | ◆ | ◆ | ◆ | ◆ | ◆ | ◆ | ◆ | ◆ | ◆ |
| Mint Grasshopper Ice Cream | ◆ | ◆ | ◆ | ◆ | ◆ | ◆ | ◆ | | ◆ |
| Strawberry Rose Ice Cream | ◆ | ◆ | ◆ | ◆ | ◆ | ◆ | ◆ | | ◆ |
| Vanilla Ice Cream | ◆ | ◆ | ◆ | ◆ | ◆ | ◆ | ◆ | | ◆ |

## Sauces, Frostings, and Fillings

| | GLUTEN-FREE, CELIAC FRIENDLY | DAIRY-FREE | EGG-FREE | VEGAN | DIABETIC FRIENDLY | PEANUT-FREE | SOY-FREE | RAW | TREE NUT-FREE |
|---|---|---|---|---|---|---|---|---|---|
| 1-Minute Whipped Crème Topping | ◆ | ◆ | ◆ | ◆ | ◆ | ◆ | ◆ | ◆ | ◆ |
| 5-Minute Whipped Crème Topping | ◆ | | | | ◆ | ◆ | ◆ | | ◆ |
| Apple Butter | ◆ | ◆ | ◆ | ◆ | ◆ | ◆ | ◆ | ◆ | ◆ |
| Chocolate Buttercream Frosting | ◆ | ◆ | ◆ | ◆ | ◆ | ◆ | ◆ | ◆ | ◆ |
| Chocolate Crème Cheese Frosting | ◆ | ◆ | ◆ | ◆ | ◆ | ◆ | ◆ | ◆ | ◆ |
| Chocolate Hazelnut Butter | ◆ | ◆ | ◆ | ◆ | ◆ | ◆ | ◆ | ◆ | |
| Chocolate Sauce | ◆ | ◆ | ◆ | ◆ | ◆ | ◆ | ◆ | ◆ | ◆ |
| Cinnamon "Sugar" | ◆ | ◆ | ◆ | ◆ | ◆ | ◆ | ◆ | ◆ | ◆ |
| Coconut Buttercream Frosting | ◆ | ◆ | ◆ | ◆ | ◆ | ◆ | ◆ | ◆ | ◆ |

## Sauces, Frostings, and Fillings

| | Gluten-Free, Celiac Friendly | Dairy-Free | Egg-Free | Vegan | Diabetic Friendly | Peanut-Free | Soy-Free | Raw | Tree Nut-Free |
|---|---|---|---|---|---|---|---|---|---|
| Coconut Pecan Frosting | ◆ | ◆ | ◆ | ◆ | ◆ | ◆ | ◆ | | |
| Crème Cheese Frosting | ◆ | ◆ | ◆ | ◆ | ◆ | ◆ | ◆ | ◆ | ◆ |
| Instant Mocha Buttercream Frosting | ◆ | ◆ | ◆ | ◆ | ◆ | ◆ | ◆ | ◆ | ◆ |
| Maple Flavored Syrup | ◆ | ◆ | ◆ | ◆ | ◆ | ◆ | ◆ | | ◆ |
| Raspberry "Jam" | ◆ | ◆ | ◆ | ◆ | ◆ | ◆ | ◆ | | ◆ |
| Vanilla Pastry Cream with Cashews | ◆ | ◆ | ◆ | ◆ | ◆ | ◆ | ◆ | | |
| Vanilla Pastry Cream with Coconut | ◆ | ◆ | ◆ | ◆ | ◆ | ◆ | ◆ | | ◆ |

## 5-Minute Milk Shakes, Smoothies, and Other

| | Gluten-Free, Celiac Friendly | Dairy-Free | Egg-Free | Vegan | Diabetic Friendly | Peanut-Free | Soy-Free | Raw | Tree Nut-Free |
|---|---|---|---|---|---|---|---|---|---|
| **Milk Shakes** | | | | | | | | | |
| Vanilla Milk Shake | ◆ | ◆ | ◆ | ◆ | ◆ | ◆ | ◆ | ◆ | ◆ |
| Banana Milk Shake | ◆ | ◆ | ◆ | ◆ | ◆ | ◆ | ◆ | ◆ | ◆ |
| Chocolate Milk Shake | ◆ | ◆ | ◆ | ◆ | ◆ | ◆ | ◆ | ◆ | ◆ |
| Mocha Mudd Milk Shake | ◆ | ◆ | ◆ | ◆ | ◆ | ◆ | ◆ | ◆ | ◆ |
| Strawberry Milk Shake | ◆ | ◆ | ◆ | ◆ | ◆ | ◆ | ◆ | ◆ | ◆ |
| Strawberry Banana Milk Shake | ◆ | ◆ | ◆ | ◆ | ◆ | ◆ | ◆ | | ◆ |
| **High-Antioxidant Smoothies** | | | | | | | | | |
| Blueberry Harmony Smoothie | ◆ | ◆ | ◆ | ◆ | ◆ | ◆ | ◆ | ◆ | ◆ |
| Cacao Power Smoothie | ◆ | ◆ | ◆ | ◆ | ◆ | ◆ | ◆ | ◆ | |
| Cinnamon Blood Sugar Normalizer Smoothie | ◆ | ◆ | ◆ | ◆ | ◆ | ◆ | ◆ | ◆ | ◆ |
| Deep Green Cleanse Smoothie | ◆ | ◆ | ◆ | ◆ | ◆ | ◆ | ◆ | ◆ | ◆ |
| Food of the Gods Chocolate Smoothie | ◆ | ◆ | ◆ | ◆ | ◆ | ◆ | ◆ | ◆ | |
| Minty Green Uplift and Clarity Smoothie | ◆ | ◆ | ◆ | ◆ | ◆ | ◆ | ◆ | ◆ | ◆ |
| Orang-a-tang Smoothie | ◆ | ◆ | ◆ | ◆ | ◆ | ◆ | ◆ | ◆ | ◆ |
| Red Heart and Digestive Healing Smoothie | ◆ | ◆ | ◆ | ◆ | ◆ | ◆ | ◆ | ◆ | ◆ |
| Superfood Energy Revitalize Smoothie | ◆ | ◆ | ◆ | ◆ | ◆ | ◆ | ◆ | ◆ | ◆ |
| Watermelon Buzz Smoothie | ◆ | ◆ | ◆ | ◆ | ◆ | ◆ | ◆ | ◆ | ◆ |
| 6-Step Design-Your-Own-Smoothie | ◆ | ◆ | ◆ | ◆ | ◆ | ◆ | ◆ | ◆ | ◆ |
| **Hot Drinks** | | | | | | | | | |
| Paleo Caffè | ◆ | ◆ | ◆ | ◆ | ◆ | ◆ | ◆ | | ◆ |
| Paleo Chai Latte | ◆ | ◆ | ◆ | ◆ | ◆ | ◆ | ◆ | | ◆ |
| Paleo Hot Chocolate | ◆ | ◆ | ◆ | ◆ | ◆ | ◆ | ◆ | | ◆ |
| Holiday Eggnog | ◆ | ◆ | | | ◆ | ◆ | ◆ | | ◆ |
| Holiday Spiced Punch | ◆ | ◆ | ◆ | ◆ | ◆ | ◆ | ◆ | | ◆ |
| **TOTAL BY DIET** | 125 | 125 | 125 | 73 | 125 | 125 | 125 | 35 | 67 |

# ACKNOWLEDGMENTS

This book could never have come to pass without the following people. I owe you all a debt of gratitude for your generosity of spirit to help make this book the best it can be.

Kathleen Spike, my life coach, deserves recognition for her steadfast enthusiasm, for challenging me to excellence at every step, and for testing recipes.

Fred Brown, deserves a deep bow of gratitude for his encouragement, and for sending me into the deep uncharted waters of Paleo Desserts with only coconut and chicory root.

I am grateful to Sifu Daniel Villasenor, qigong and yoga master who unwittingly seeded this book with his departure in 2004. Thanks Daniel, for sharing the ancient Taoistic principles of food and life. It is our challenge to bring the wisdom of these chiseled guidelines into our modern lives.

A warm thank you to Dr. Chiaoli Lu, ND, DAOM, LAc, Director of the Mercy and Wisdom Healing, for her knowledgeable advice, inspiration, and for sponsoring my talk series.

I offer appreciation to Dr. Kamto Lee ND, DAOM, LAc of Serene Care Clinic for helping integrate Western naturopathic medicine with ancient Chinese herbal medicine and diet.

Thanks to Dr. Robert B. Kellum, N.D., Ph.D., of HealthBridge, Inc., for assisting me in my research on sweeteners, and the benefits of chicory root.

I appreciate the contribution of Will Meysing, my weight lifting friend, who introduced me to the Paleo Diet, and shared many amazing Paleo meals.

Thank you to my photographer Lloyd Lemmermann for his patience and trained eye.

An enormous debt of gratitude goes to Isabelle Bleeker of Da Capo Press for guiding the book toward excellence with patience and wit. To the fabulous editors at Da Capo Press, Renée Sedliar, Annie Lenth, and Iris Bass, thank you for making my writing better than it is. To Alex Camlin, Creative Director at Da Capo Press, appreciation for a mouthwateringly beautiful book cover and design.

To Barbara Hampson, thank you for making comments on my book as an experienced chef. And to Heather Strang for adding zest to the recipes in her inimitable way.

Thanks to the doctors whose works inspired the recipes: Dr. Weston A. Price, Dr. Francis M. Pottenger, Dr. Loren Cordain, Dr. Robert Lustig, Dr. Joel Fuhrman, Dr. Caldwell B. Esselstyn, Dr. Nancy Appleton, Dr. Bessie Jo Tillman, Dr. Coda Martin, Dr. Otto Heinrich Warburg, Dr. Dietrich Klinghardt, and Dr. John Veltheim.

I offer thundering applause for my hundreds of taste testers. They evolved into a volunteer corps of Portland dessert tasters. (Could there be a better volunteer gig than this?!) Tasters reserved their desserts via e-mail and promptly came to my home to pick up their items to taste. In return they gave me an honest critique. A special debt of gratitude goes to my toughest critics: Rochelle (Rocky) Stilwell, Claude Cruz, and Kathleen Spike.

Finally, to all my friends, professional colleagues, and clients, thank you for your contribution to this book and for all you have taught me along the way.

# INDEX

Cashew nuts
about, 9, 10–11
in Berry Tart, 126
Coconut Pecan Frosting, 183
in Flan with Dulce de Leche, 155–156
in Ice-Cream Sandwiches with variation, 168–169
in Lemon-Berry Parfait, 154
in Raspberry Rose Delight Mousse, 153
Vanilla Pastry Cream with Cashews, 185
Celiac-friendly recipes list, 221–225
Chai Latte with variations, Paleo, 212
Chard
in Deep Green Cleanse Smoothie, 203
in Minty Green Uplift and Clarity Smoothie, 204
Cheesecake
Blueberry Cheesecake (var.), 129
Blueberry Lemon Cheesecake Bars, 83
Cheesecake with variations, 128–129
Cherry Cheesecake (var.), 129
Chocolate Caramel Pecan Cheesecake (var.), 129
Chocolate Chip Cheesecake (var.), 129
Chocolate Marble Cheesecake (var.), 130
Chocolate Raspberry Cheesecake (var.), 96
Dark Chocolate Cheesecake, 95–96
German Chocolate Cheesecake (var.), 96
Lemon Cheesecake with Berries, 131–132
Marble Berry Cheesecake (var.), 130
Pumpkin Cheesecake, 133–134
Raspberry Cheesecake (var.), 130
Strawberry Cheesecake (var.), 130
Cherries
Black Forest Cake, 93
Black Forest Cherry Pie (var.), 119
pitting, 118
Cherry Cheesecake (var.), 129
Cherry Pie with variations, 118–119

Chicory root granules, for Paleo Caffè with variations, 210–211
Chinese medicine, 5
Chlorella powder
about, 105
in Superfood Black Fudge, 105–106
Chocolate
about, 7–8, 89
Black Forest Cake, 93
Coffee Toffee Pie, 102–103
Dark Chocolate Cheesecake with variations, 95–96
Dark Chocolate Truffles and variations, 109–110
Devil's Food Double Chocolate Cake, 97
Fudge Brownies, 91–92
German Chocolate Cake, 98–99
German Chocolate Cheesecake (var.), 96
German Chocolate Cream Pie (var.), 101
Superfood Black Fudge, 105–106
See also Cacao chocolate; Cacao nibs; Cacao powder; Truffles
Chocolate Banana Milk Shake (var.), 197
Chocolate Bavarian Cream Filling or Mousse, 100
in Tiramisu, 43
Chocolate Belgian Waffles (var.), 142
Chocolate beverages
Chocolate Banana Milk Shake (var.), 197
Chocolate Chai (var.), 212
Chocolate Milk Shake, 197
Cinnamon Paleo Hot Chocolate (var.), 213
Maple Paleo Hot Chocolate (var.), 213
Mayan Paleo Hot Chocolate (var.), 213
Mocha Paleo Hot Chocolate (var.), 213
Paleo Hot Chocolate, 213
Salted Caramel Paleo Hot Chocolate (var.), 213
Valencia Orange Paleo Hot Chocolate (var.), 213

Chocolate Buttercream Frosting with variation, 177–178
  on Devil's Food Double Chocolate Cake, 97
Chocolate Cake with Raspberry Filling, 33
Chocolate Caramel Pecan Cheesecake (var.), 129
Chocolate Chai (var.), 212
Chocolate Chai Truffles (var.), 110
Chocolate Chips, Homemade, 108
  Chocolate Chip Cappuccino Ice Cream (var.), 164
  Chocolate Chip Cheesecake (var.), 129
  Chocolate Chip Cookies, 65
  Chocolate Chip Ice Cream, 162
  Double Chocolate Chip Espresso Cookies, 69
  Double Chocolate Chip Ice Cream (var.), 163
  in Granola Bars, 84–85
  Mint Chocolate Chip Ice Cream (var.), 165
  No-Oatmeal Chocolate Chip Cookies (var.), 75
  in Trail Mix Cookies, 80
  in Trail Mix with variations, 146–147
Chocolate Coconut Cream Pie (var.), 120
Chocolate-Covered Strawberries, 107
Chocolate Cream Pie, 101
Chocolate Crème Cheese Frosting with variation, 181–182
  on Devil's Food Double Chocolate Cake, 97
  for Finger Tarts with variation, 127
  for Poppy-Seed Hot Fudge Sundae Cake, 37–38
  on White Coconut Sponge Cake, 47
Chocolate Cupcakes, 50–51
Chocolate-Dipped Macaroons (var.), 68
Chocolate Espresso Buttercream Frosting (var.), 178

Chocolate fillings and spreads
  Chocolate Bavarian Cream Filling or Mousse, 100
  Chocolate Buttercream Frosting, 177–178
  Chocolate Crème Cheese Frosting, 181–182
  Chocolate Espresso Buttercream Frosting (var.), 178
  Chocolate Hazelnut Butter, 188
  Mocha Crème Cheese Frosting (var.), 182
  in Poppy-Seed Hot Fudge Sundae Cake, 37–38
Chocolate Fudge, 104
Chocolate Hawaiian Truffles (var.), 110
Chocolate Haystack Cookies, 66
Chocolate Hazelnut Butter, 188
Chocolate Hazelnut Butter Cookies (var.), 72
Chocolate Hazelnut Butter Cups, 145
Chocolate Hazelnut Fudge (var.), 104
Chocolate Hazelnut Piecrust (var.), 113
Chocolate Hazelnut Truffles (var.), 110
Chocolate Ice-Cream Sandwiches (var.), 169
Chocolate Ice Cream with variation, 163
Chocolate Lava Cake, 94
Chocolate Marble Cheesecake (var.), 130
Chocolate Marble Pumpkin Pie (var.), 124
Chocolate Milk Shake with variation, 197
Chocolate Mousse with variations, 151
Chocolate Orange Truffles (var.), 110
Chocolate Paleo Caffè (var.), 211
Chocolate Pecan Pie (var.), 122
Chocolate Piecrust (var.), 113
  for Chocolate Chip Cheesecake (var.), 129
  for Chocolate Marble Cheesecake (var.), 130
Chocolate Raspberry Cheesecake (var.), 96
Chocolate Rose Truffles (var.), 110
Chocolate Sauce with variation, 189
  on Belgian Waffles, 142
  in Chocolate Coconut Cream Pie (var.), 120

3 1901 05376 8661